WOLVERINE FIRST CLASS

WOLVERINE-BY-NIGHT

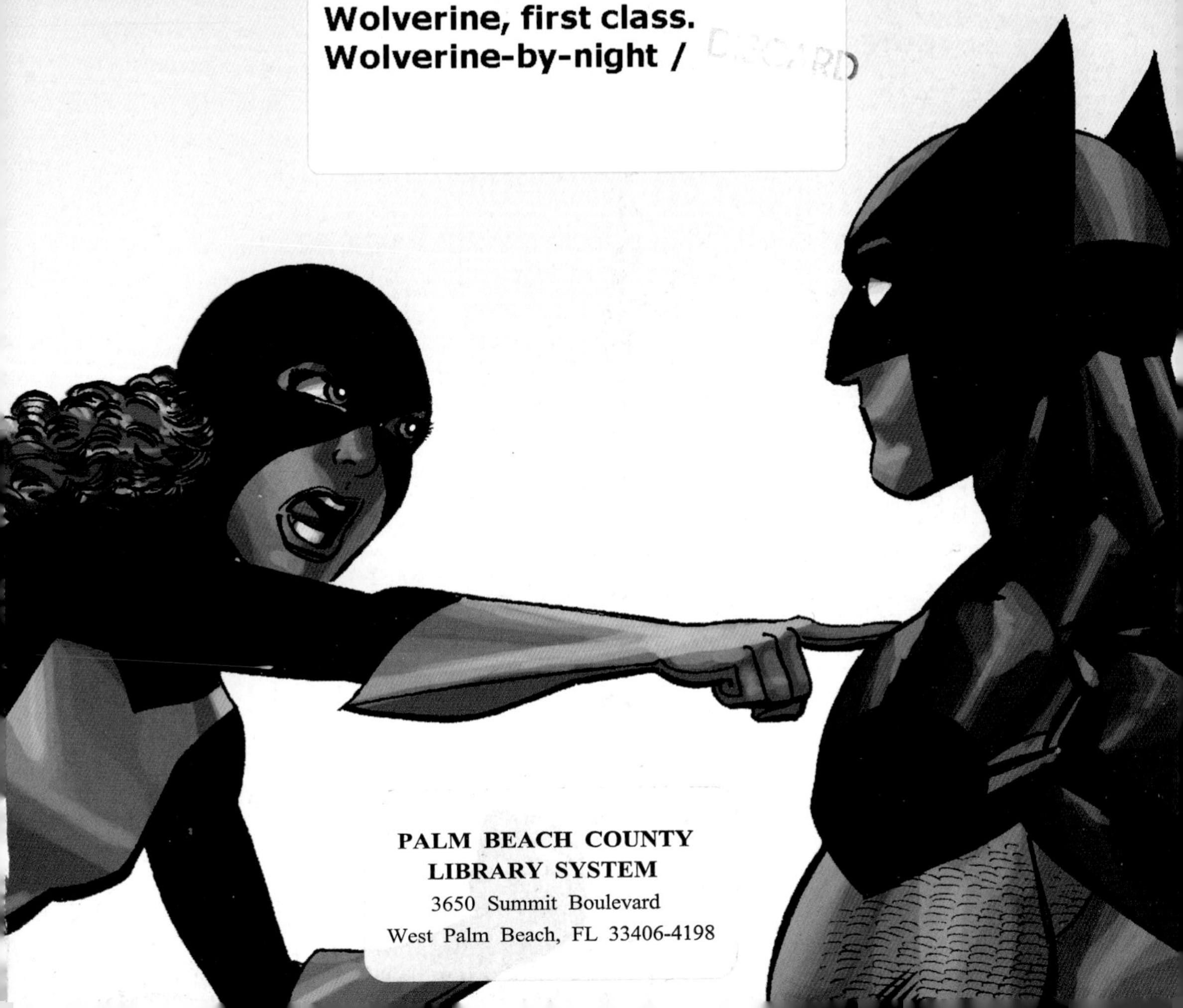

WOLVERINE-BY-NIGHT

WRITER: *Fred Van Lente*
ART: *Francis Portela, Hugo Petrus & Scott Koblish*
COLORIST: *Ulises Arreola*
LETTERER: *Virtual Calligraphy's Joe Caramagna*
COVER ARTISTS: *Salva Espin, Karl Kesel & Wilfredo Quintana;*
and David Williams & Ulises Arreola
CONSULTING EDITOR: *Ralph Macchio*
EDITORS: *Nathan Cosby & Mark Paniccia*
ASSISTANT EDITOR: *Jordan D. White*

WOLVERINE AND POWER PACK #2
WRITER: *Marc Sumerak*
ART: *Scott Koblish*
COLORISTS: *GuriHiru*
LETTERER: *Dave Sharpe*
EDITOR: *Nathan Cosby*

COLLECTION EDITOR: *Alex Starbuck*
ASSISTANT EDITORS: *Cory Levine & John Denning*
EDITORS, SPECIAL PROJECTS: *Jennifer Grünwald & Mark D. Beazley*
SENIOR EDITOR, SPECIAL PROJECTS: *Jeff Youngquist*
PRODUCTION: *Jerron Quality Color*
SENIOR VICE PRESIDENT OF SALES: *David Gabriel*

EDITOR IN CHIEF: *Joe Quesada*
PUBLISHER: *Dan Buckley*
EXECUTIVE PRODUCER: *Alan Fine*

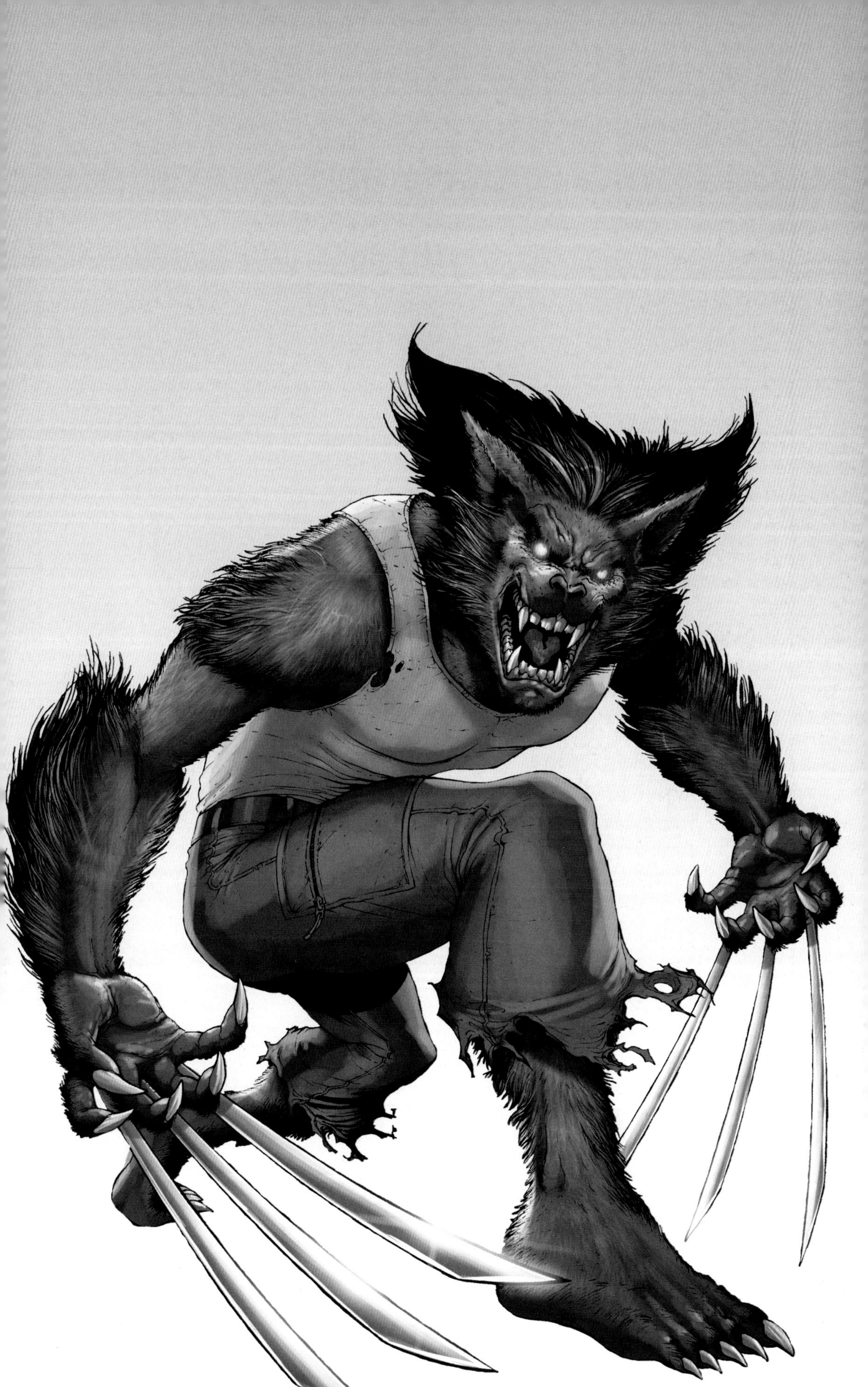

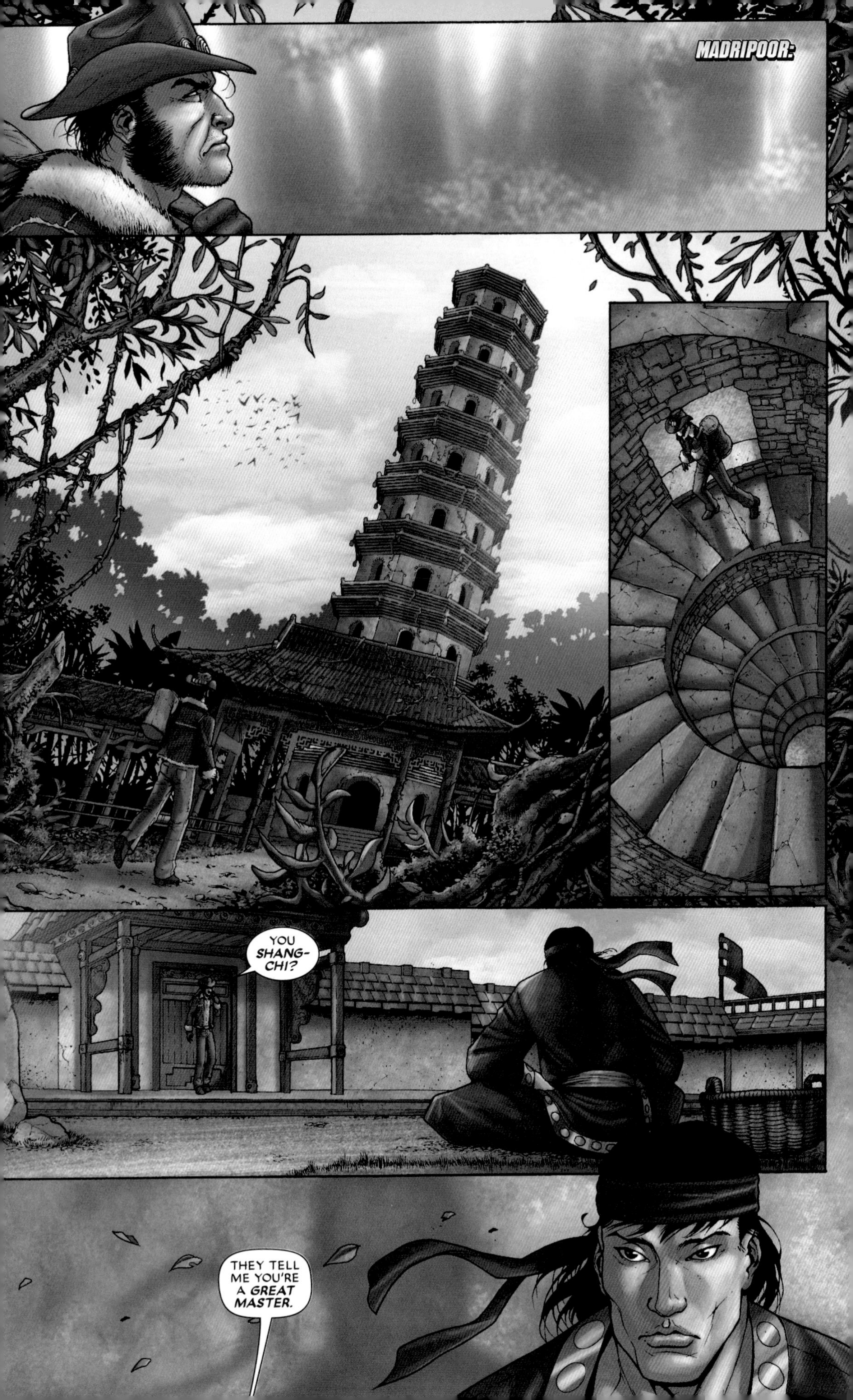
MADRIPOOR:
YOU SHANG-CHI?
THEY TELL ME YOU'RE A GREAT MASTER.

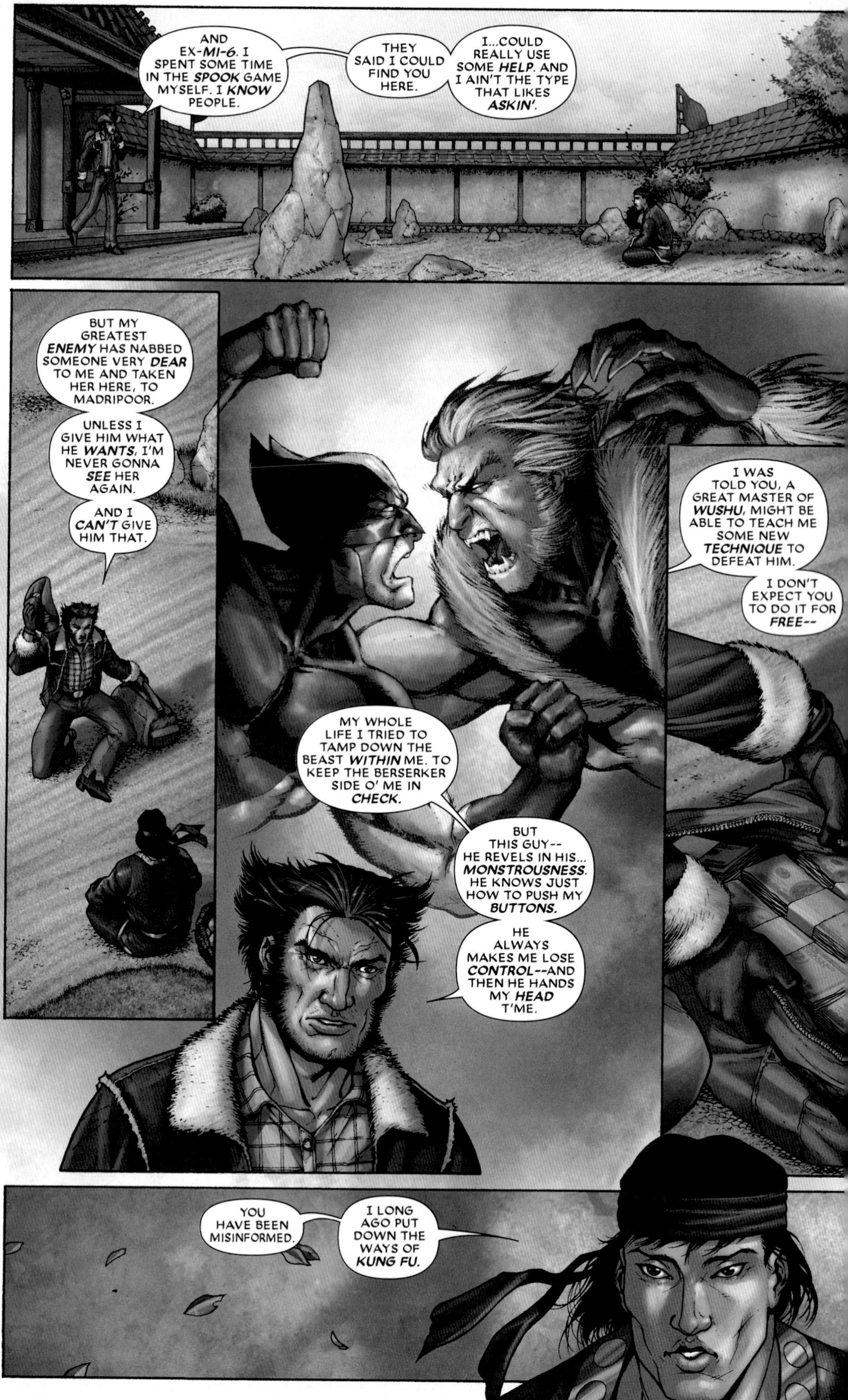
AND EX-MI-6. I SPENT SOME TIME IN THE SPOOK GAME MYSELF. I KNOW PEOPLE.
THEY SAID I COULD FIND YOU HERE.
I...COULD REALLY USE SOME HELP. AND I AIN'T THE TYPE THAT LIKES ASKIN'.
BUT MY GREATEST ENEMY HAS NABBED SOMEONE VERY DEAR TO ME AND TAKEN HER HERE, TO MADRIPOOR.
UNLESS I GIVE HIM WHAT HE WANTS, I'M NEVER GONNA SEE HER AGAIN.
AND I CAN'T GIVE HIM THAT.
I WAS TOLD YOU, A GREAT MASTER OF WUSHU, MIGHT BE ABLE TO TEACH ME SOME NEW TECHNIQUE TO DEFEAT HIM.
I DON'T EXPECT YOU TO DO IT FOR FREE--
MY WHOLE LIFE I TRIED TO TAMP DOWN THE BEAST WITHIN ME. TO KEEP THE BERSERKER SIDE O' ME IN CHECK.
BUT THIS GUY-- HE REVELS IN HIS... MONSTROUSNESS. HE KNOWS JUST HOW TO PUSH MY BUTTONS.
HE ALWAYS MAKES ME LOSE CONTROL--AND THEN HE HANDS MY HEAD T'ME.
YOU HAVE BEEN MISINFORMED.
I LONG AGO PUT DOWN THE WAYS OF KUNG FU.

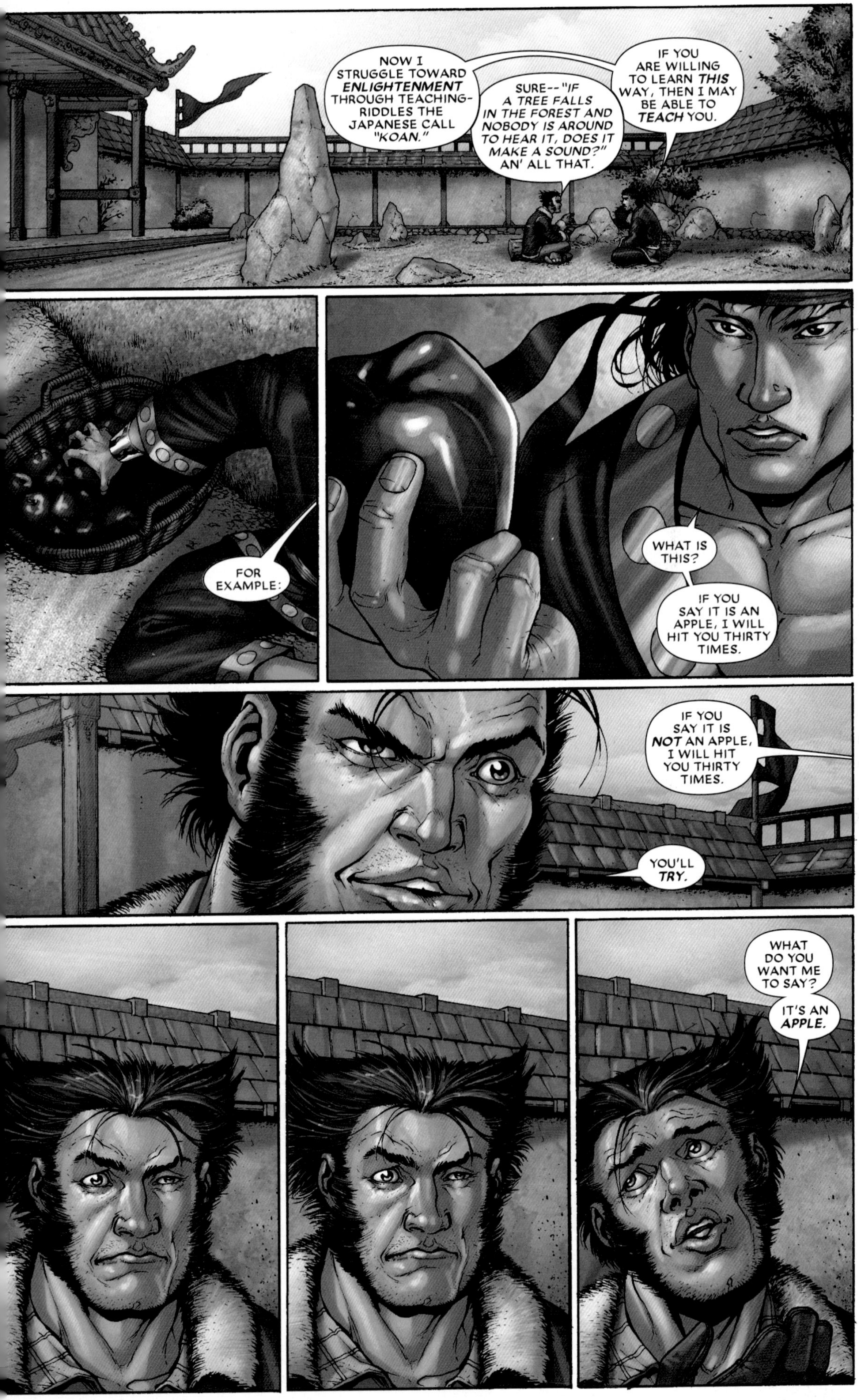
NOW I STRUGGLE TOWARD ENLIGHTENMENT THROUGH TEACHING-RIDDLES THE JAPANESE CALL "KOAN."
SURE--"IF A TREE FALLS IN THE FOREST AND NOBODY IS AROUND TO HEAR IT, DOES IT MAKE A SOUND?" AN' ALL THAT.
IF YOU ARE WILLING TO LEARN THIS WAY, THEN I MAY BE ABLE TO TEACH YOU.
FOR EXAMPLE:
WHAT IS THIS?
IF YOU SAY IT IS AN APPLE, I WILL HIT YOU THIRTY TIMES.
IF YOU SAY IT IS NOT AN APPLE, I WILL HIT YOU THIRTY TIMES.
YOU'LL TRY.
WHAT DO YOU WANT ME TO SAY?
IT'S AN APPLE.

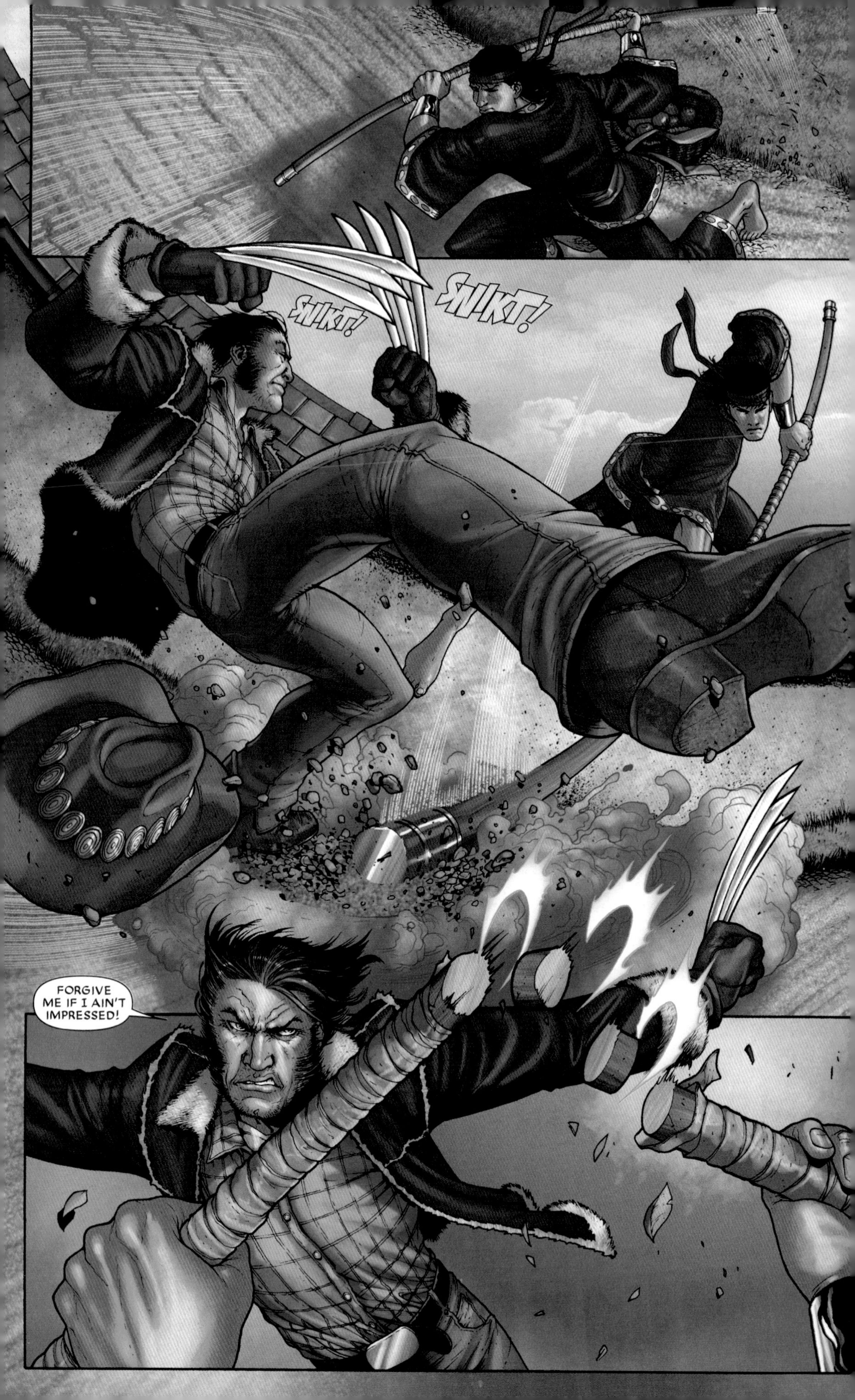
SNIKT!
SNIKT!
FORGIVE ME IF I AIN'T IMPRESSED!

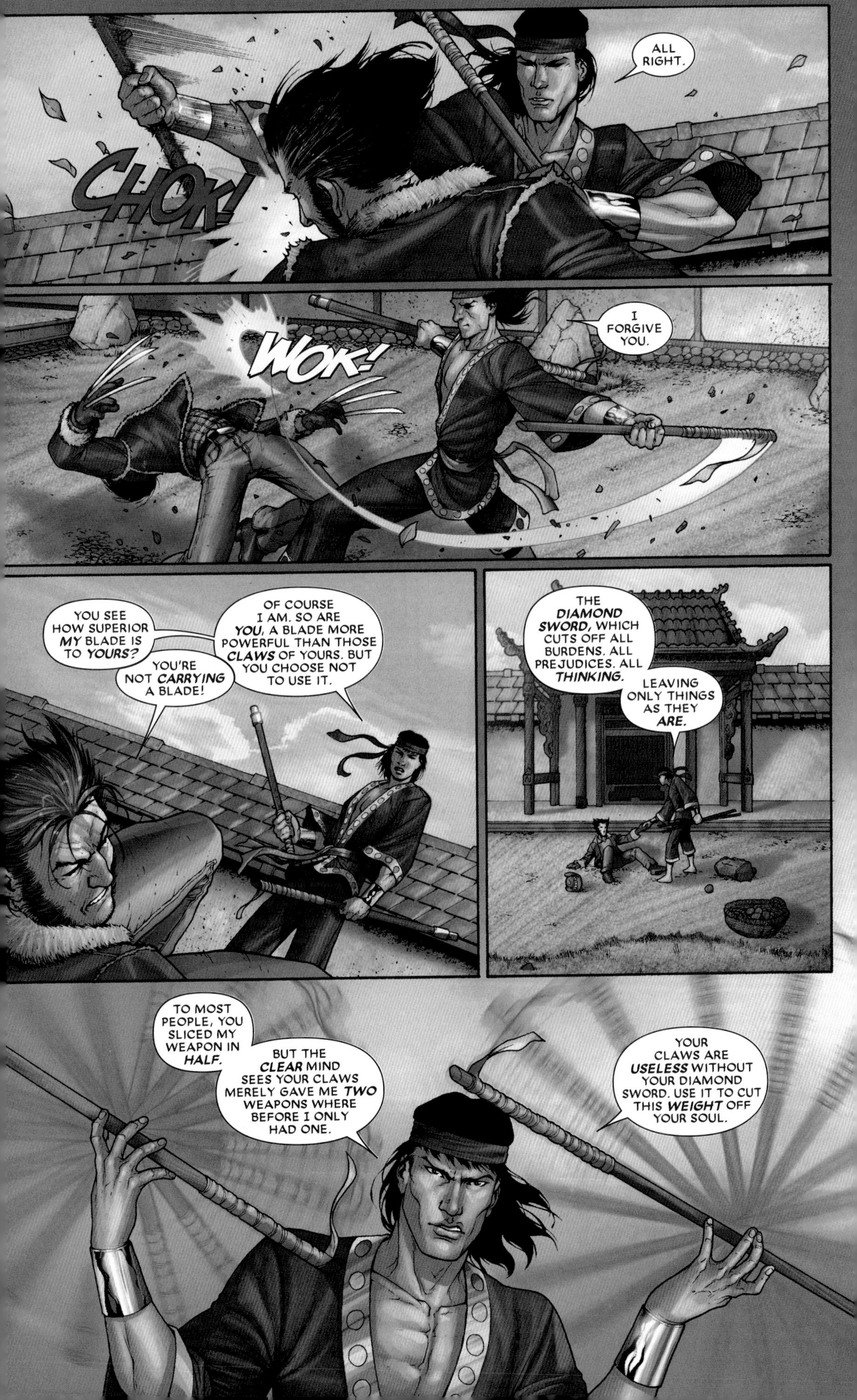
ALL RIGHT.
CHOK!
WOK!
I FORGIVE YOU.
YOU SEE HOW SUPERIOR MY BLADE IS TO YOURS?
YOU'RE NOT CARRYING A BLADE!
OF COURSE I AM. SO ARE YOU, A BLADE MORE POWERFUL THAN THOSE CLAWS OF YOURS. BUT YOU CHOOSE NOT TO USE IT.
THE DIAMOND SWORD, WHICH CUTS OFF ALL BURDENS. ALL PREJUDICES. ALL THINKING.
LEAVING ONLY THINGS AS THEY ARE.
TO MOST PEOPLE, YOU SLICED MY WEAPON IN HALF.
BUT THE CLEAR MIND SEES YOUR CLAWS MERELY GAVE ME TWO WEAPONS WHERE BEFORE I ONLY HAD ONE.
YOUR CLAWS ARE USELESS WITHOUT YOUR DIAMOND SWORD. USE IT TO CUT THIS WEIGHT OFF YOUR SOUL.

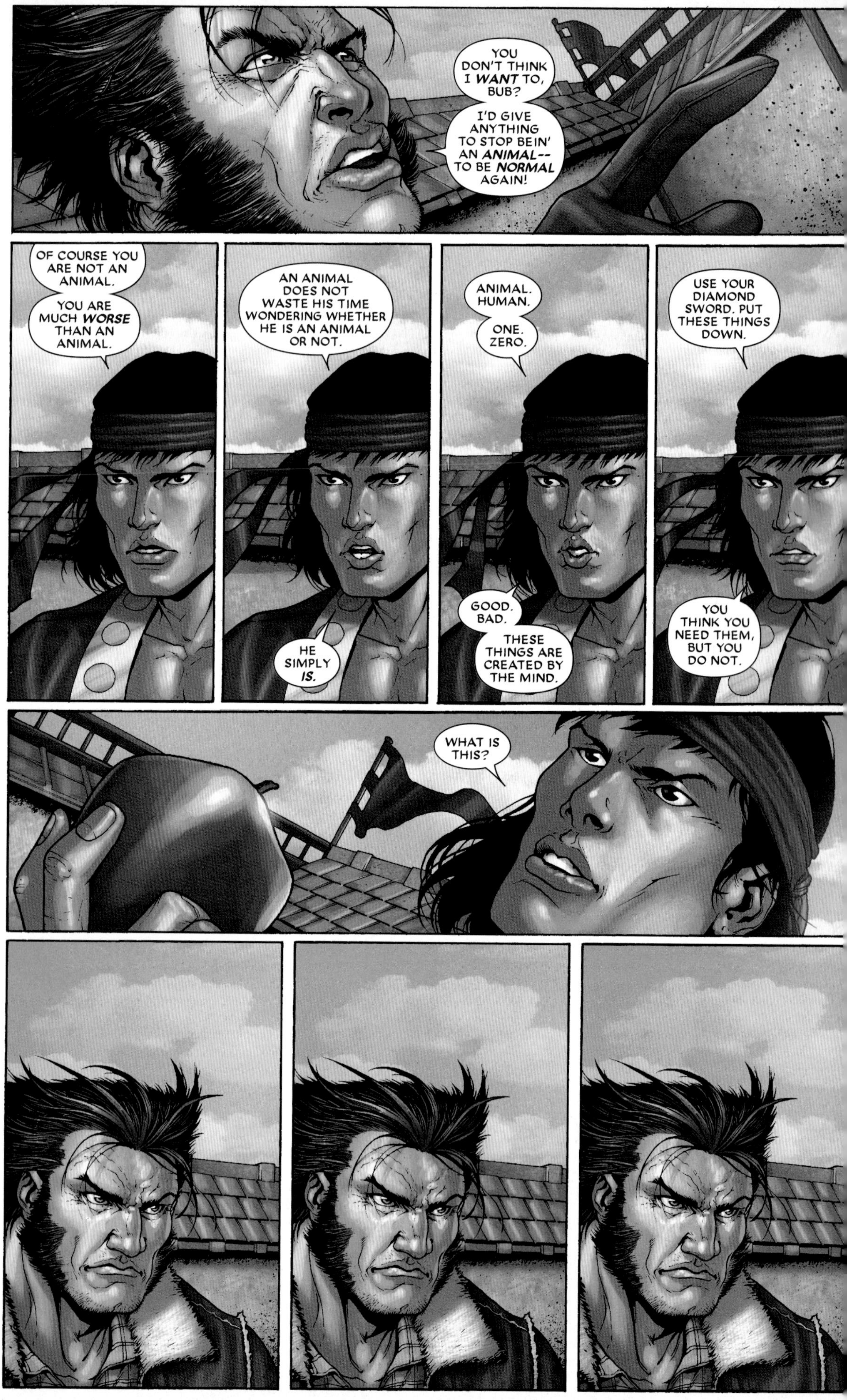
YOU DON'T THINK I *WANT* TO, BUB?
I'D GIVE ANYTHING TO STOP BEIN' AN *ANIMAL*-- TO BE *NORMAL* AGAIN!
OF COURSE YOU ARE NOT AN ANIMAL.
YOU ARE MUCH *WORSE* THAN AN ANIMAL.
AN ANIMAL DOES NOT WASTE HIS TIME WONDERING WHETHER HE IS AN ANIMAL OR NOT.
HE SIMPLY *IS.*
ANIMAL. HUMAN.
ONE. ZERO.
GOOD. BAD.
THESE THINGS ARE CREATED BY THE MIND.
USE YOUR DIAMOND SWORD. PUT THESE THINGS DOWN.
YOU THINK YOU NEED THEM, BUT YOU DO NOT.
WHAT IS THIS?

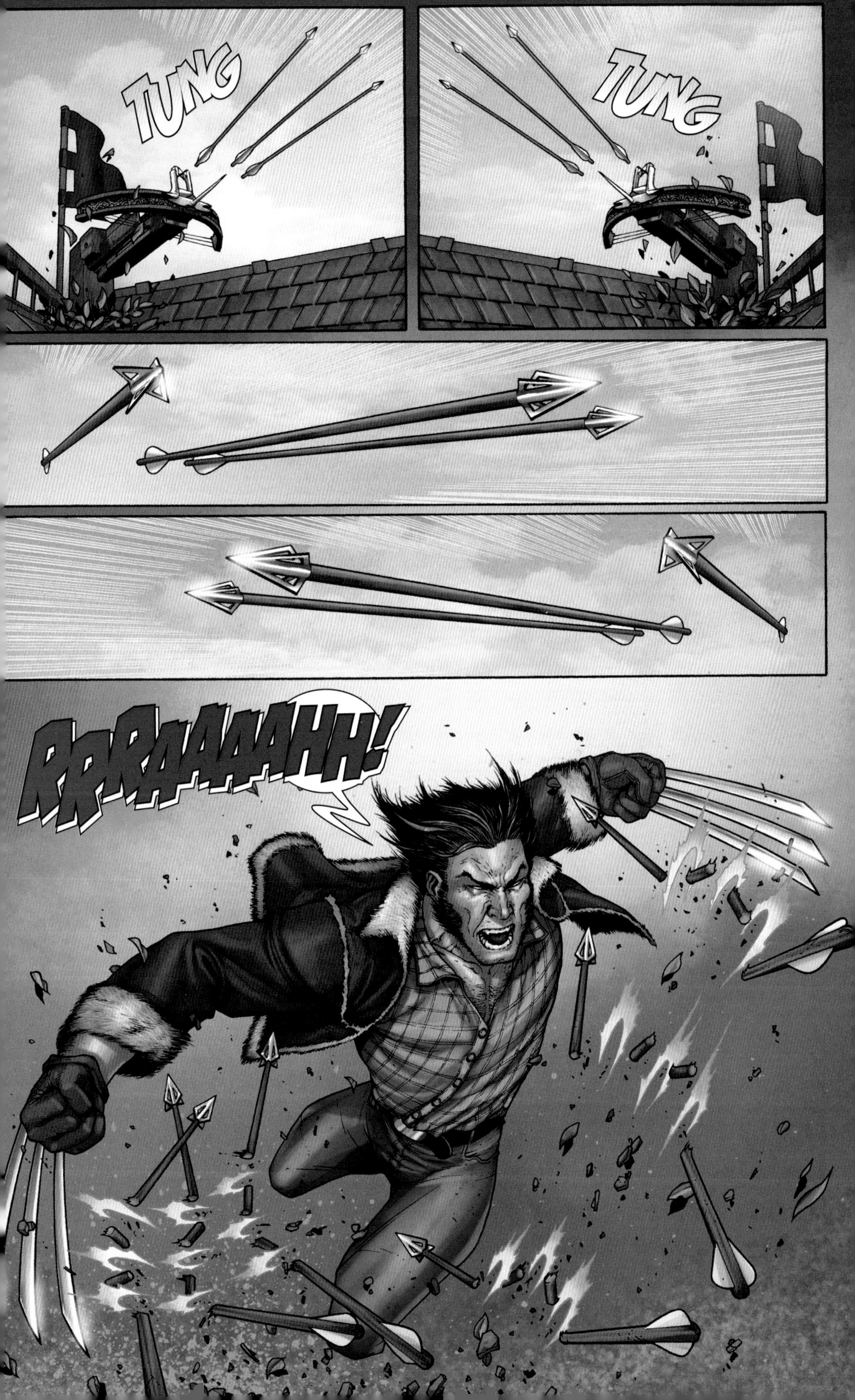
TUNG
TUNG
RRRAAAAAHH!

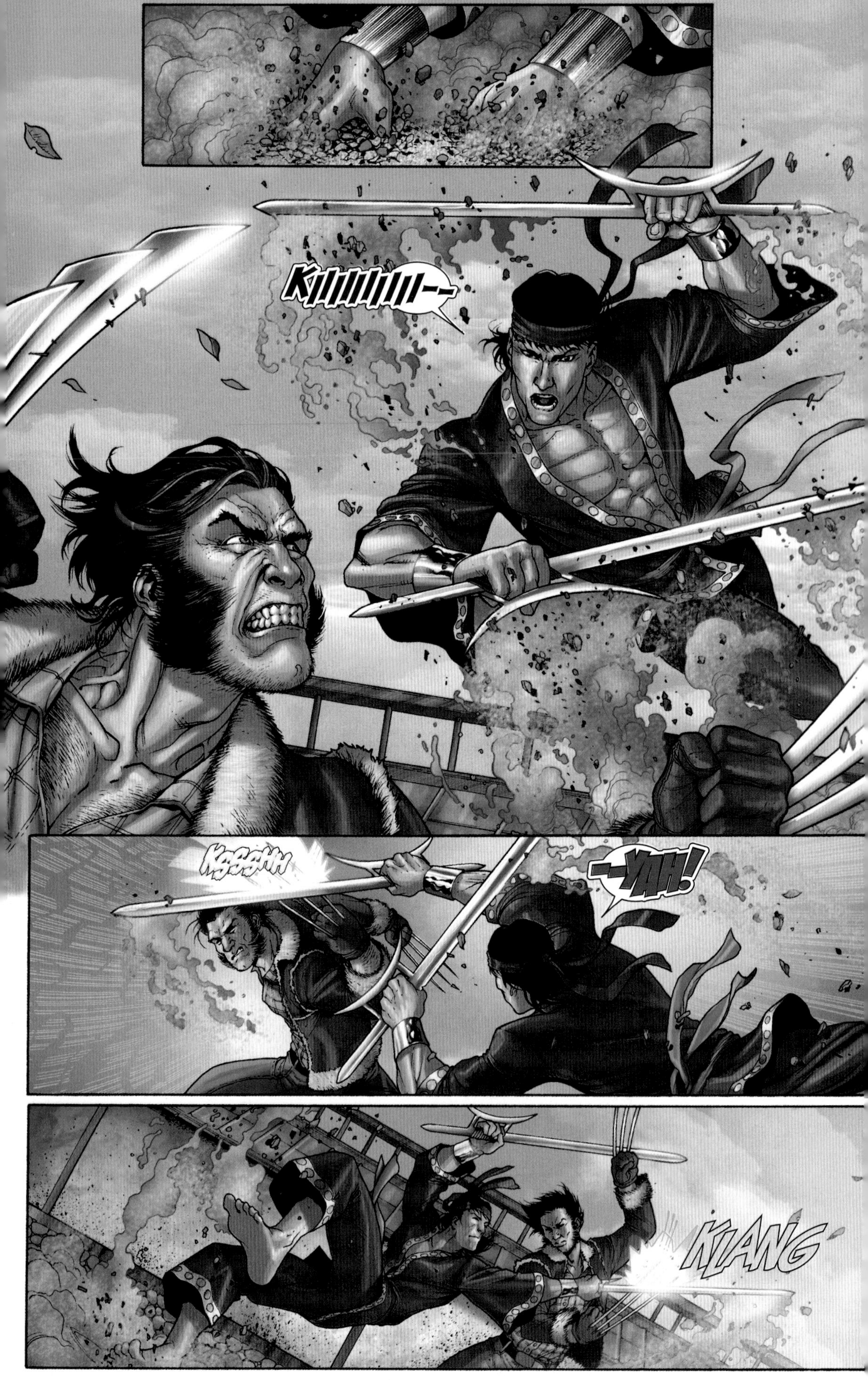
KIIIIIIIIII--
KSSSHH
--YAH!
KLANG

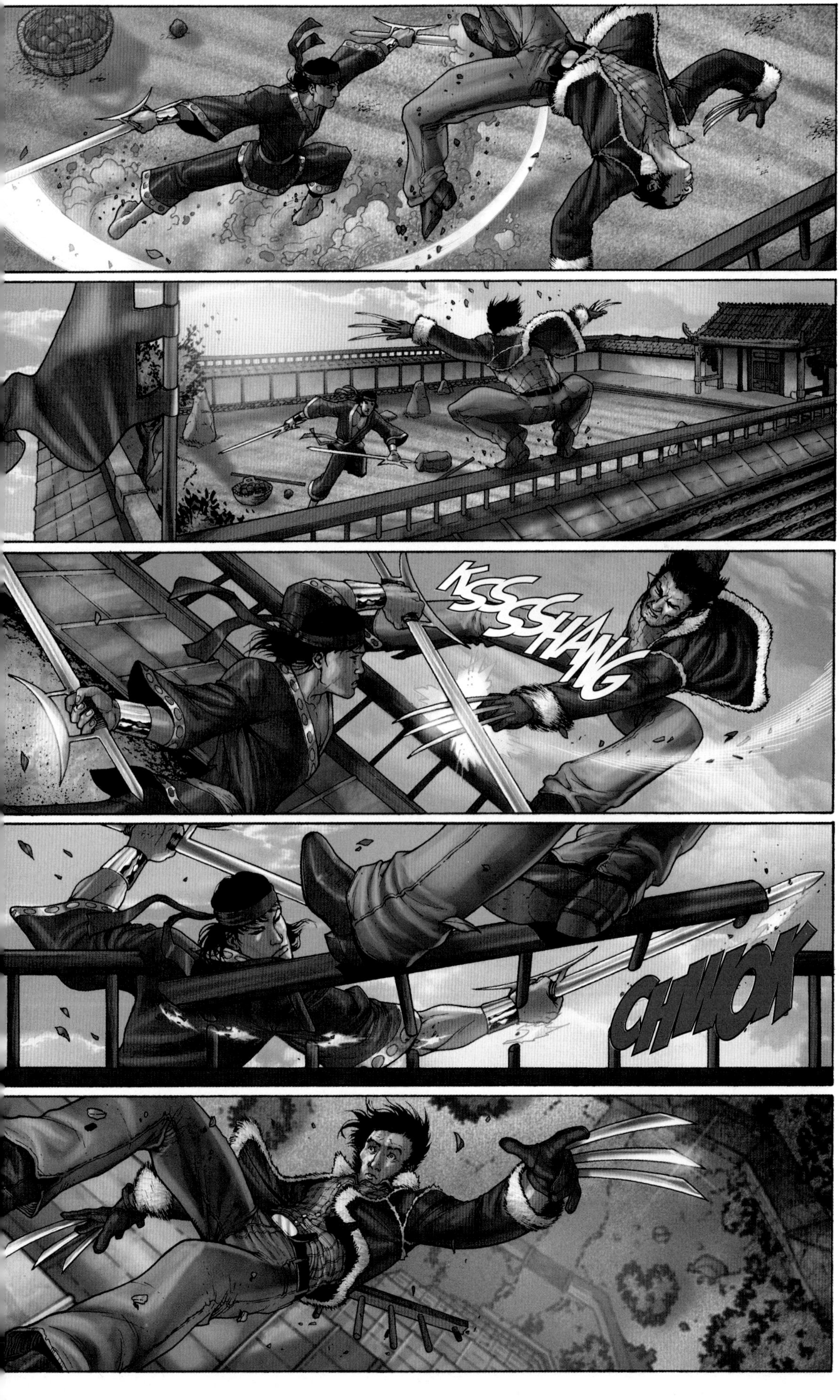
KSSSSHANG
CHUNK

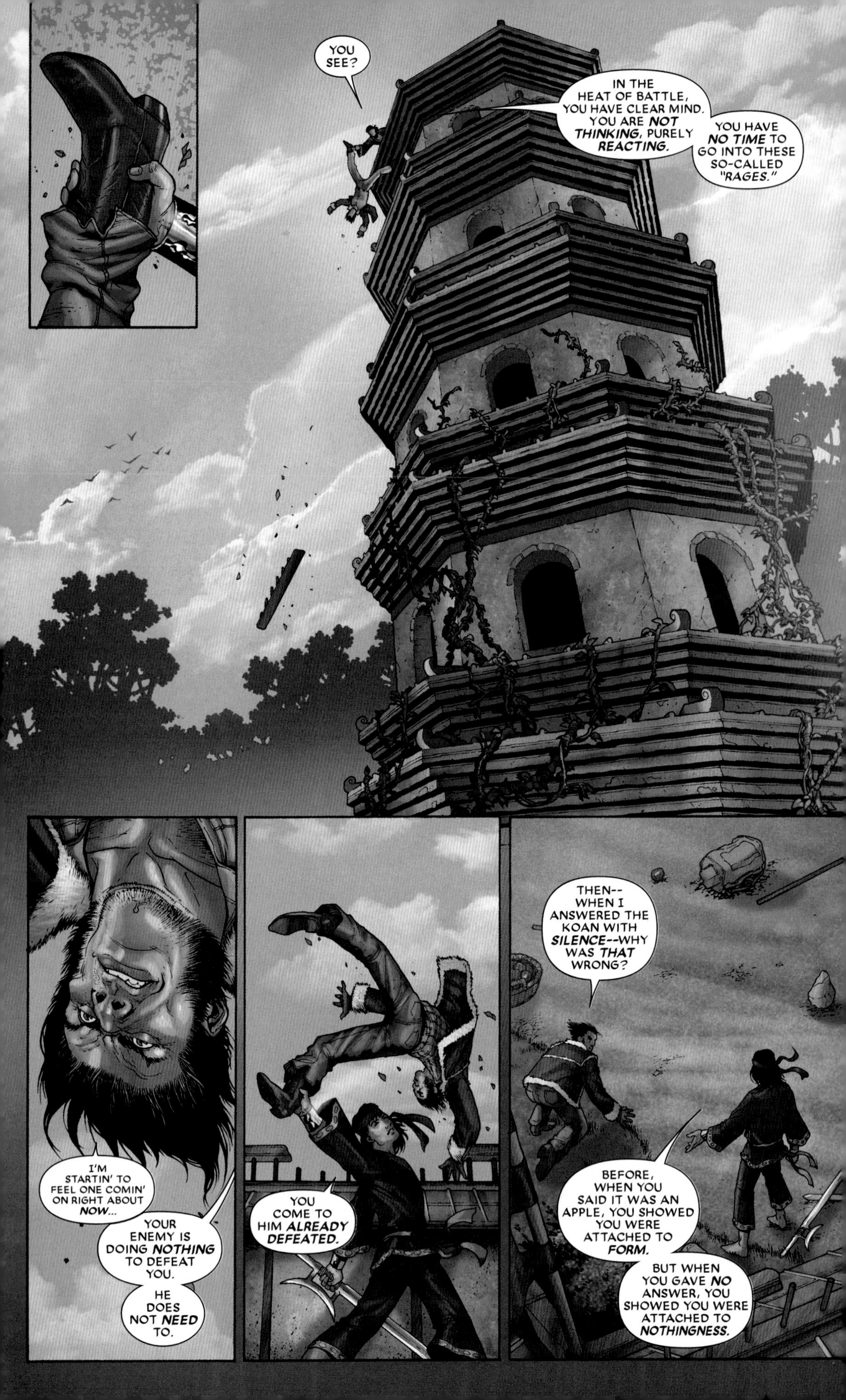
YOU SEE?
IN THE HEAT OF BATTLE, YOU HAVE CLEAR MIND. YOU ARE NOT THINKING, PURELY REACTING.
YOU HAVE NO TIME TO GO INTO THESE SO-CALLED "RAGES."
I'M STARTIN' TO FEEL ONE COMIN' ON RIGHT ABOUT NOW...
YOUR ENEMY IS DOING NOTHING TO DEFEAT YOU.
HE DOES NOT NEED TO.
YOU COME TO HIM ALREADY DEFEATED.
THEN--WHEN I ANSWERED THE KOAN WITH SILENCE--WHY WAS THAT WRONG?
BEFORE, WHEN YOU SAID IT WAS AN APPLE, YOU SHOWED YOU WERE ATTACHED TO FORM.
BUT WHEN YOU GAVE NO ANSWER, YOU SHOWED YOU WERE ATTACHED TO NOTHINGNESS.

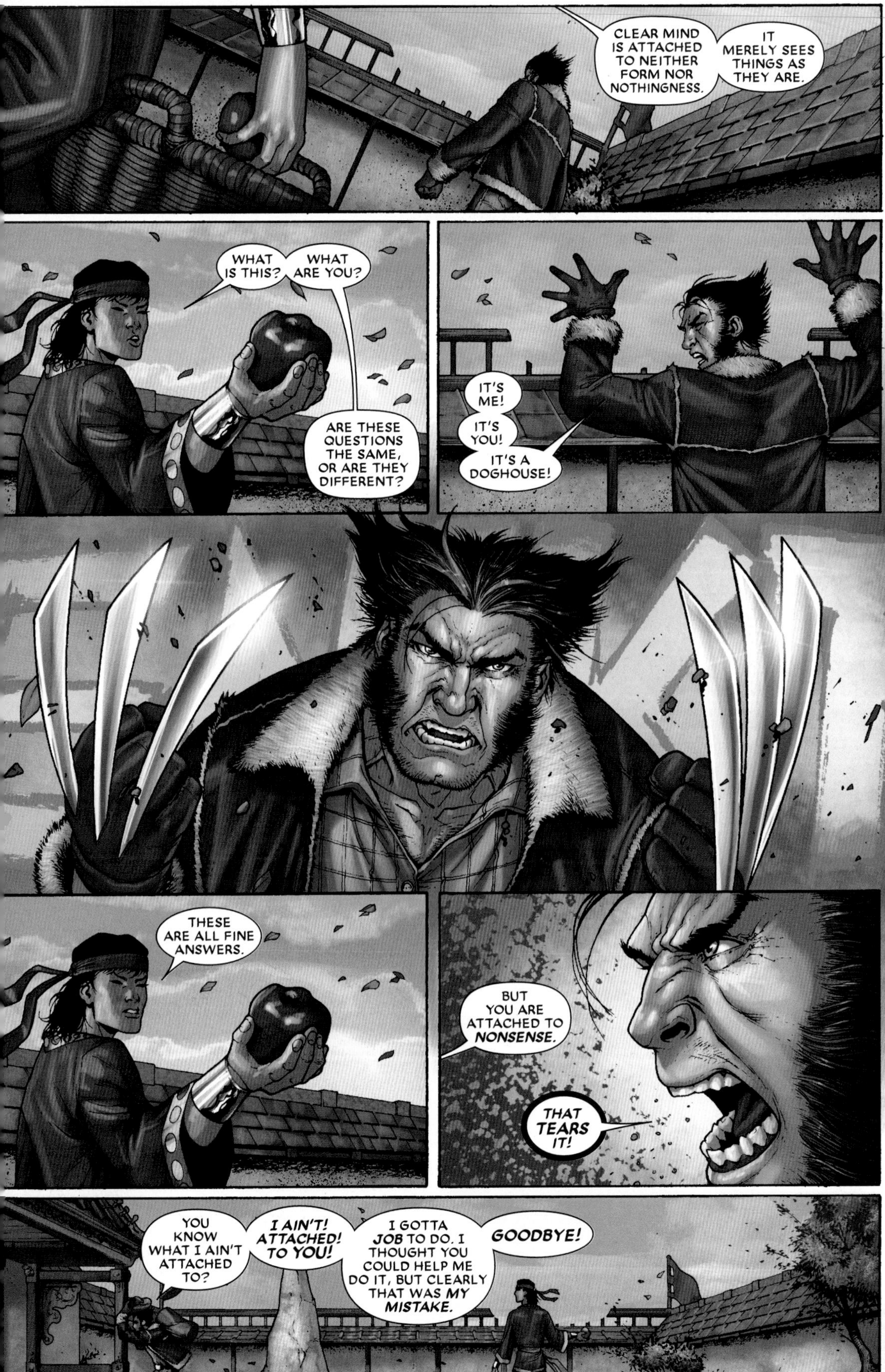
CLEAR MIND IS ATTACHED TO NEITHER FORM NOR NOTHINGNESS.
IT MERELY SEES THINGS AS THEY ARE.
WHAT IS THIS?
WHAT ARE YOU?
ARE THESE QUESTIONS THE SAME, OR ARE THEY DIFFERENT?
IT'S ME!
IT'S YOU!
IT'S A DOGHOUSE!
THESE ARE ALL FINE ANSWERS.
BUT YOU ARE ATTACHED TO NONSENSE.
THAT TEARS IT!
YOU KNOW WHAT I AIN'T ATTACHED TO?
I AIN'T! ATTACHED! TO YOU!
I GOTTA JOB TO DO. I THOUGHT YOU COULD HELP ME DO IT, BUT CLEARLY THAT WAS MY MISTAKE.
GOODBYE!

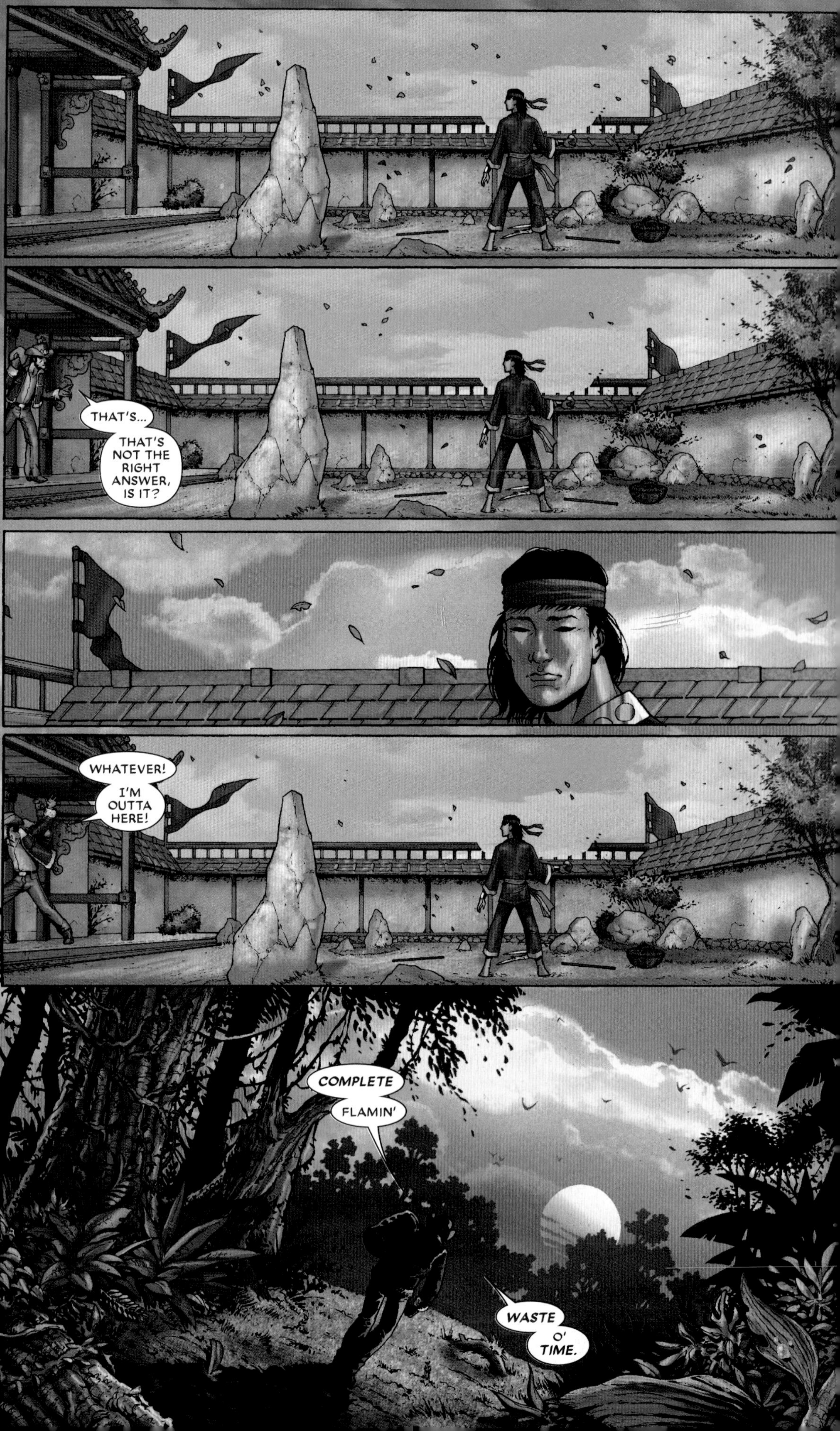
THAT'S...
THAT'S NOT THE RIGHT ANSWER, IS IT?
WHATEVER!
I'M OUTTA HERE!
COMPLETE
FLAMIN'
WASTE
O' TIME.

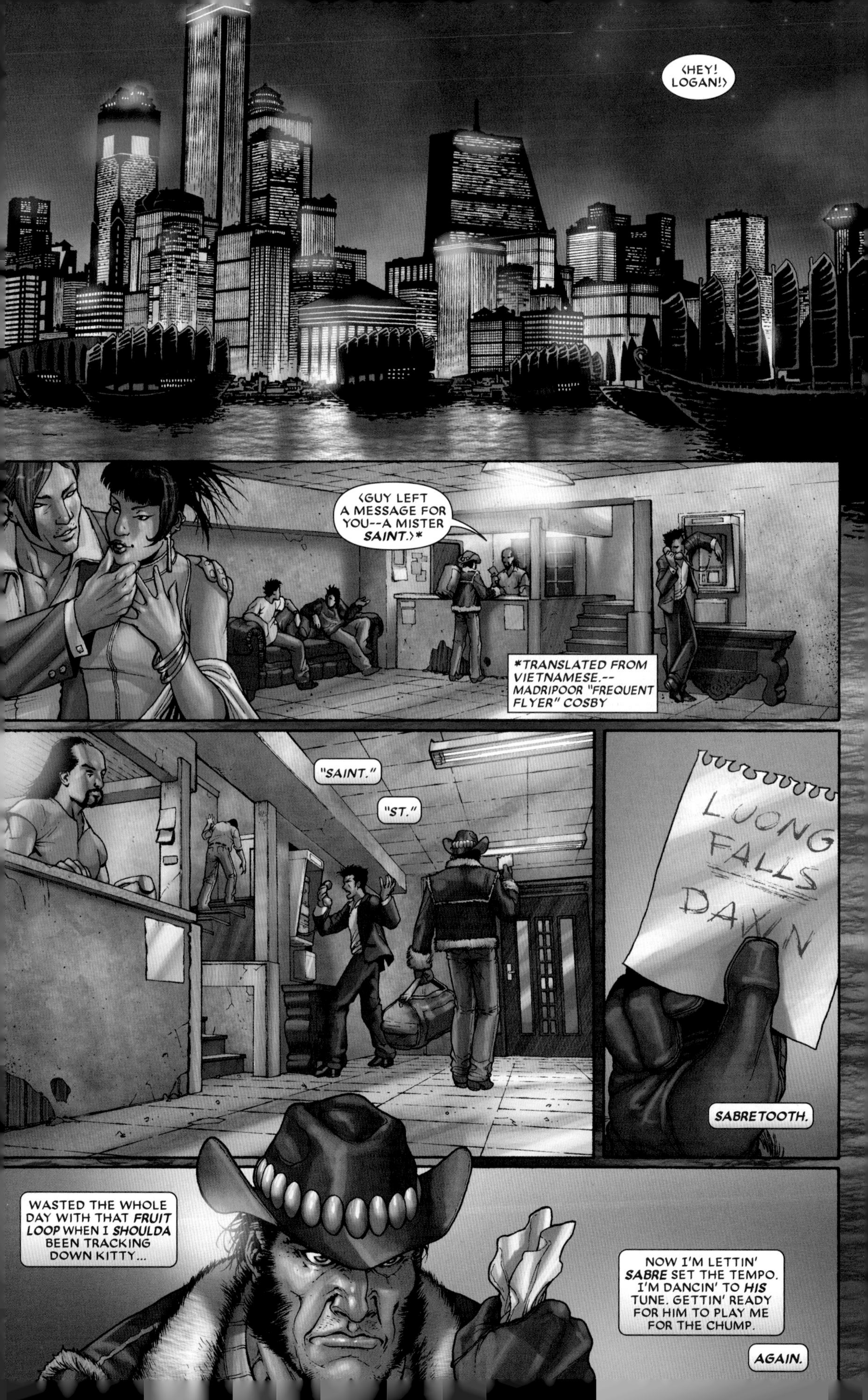

‹HEY! LOGAN!›
‹GUY LEFT A MESSAGE FOR YOU--A MISTER SAINT.›*
*TRANSLATED FROM VIETNAMESE.-- MADRIPOOR "FREQUENT FLYER" COSBY
"SAINT."
"ST."
LUONG FALLS DAWN
SABRETOOTH.
WASTED THE WHOLE DAY WITH THAT FRUIT LOOP WHEN I SHOULDA BEEN TRACKING DOWN KITTY...
NOW I'M LETTIN' SABRE SET THE TEMPO. I'M DANCIN' TO HIS TUNE. GETTIN' READY FOR HIM TO PLAY ME FOR THE CHUMP.
AGAIN.

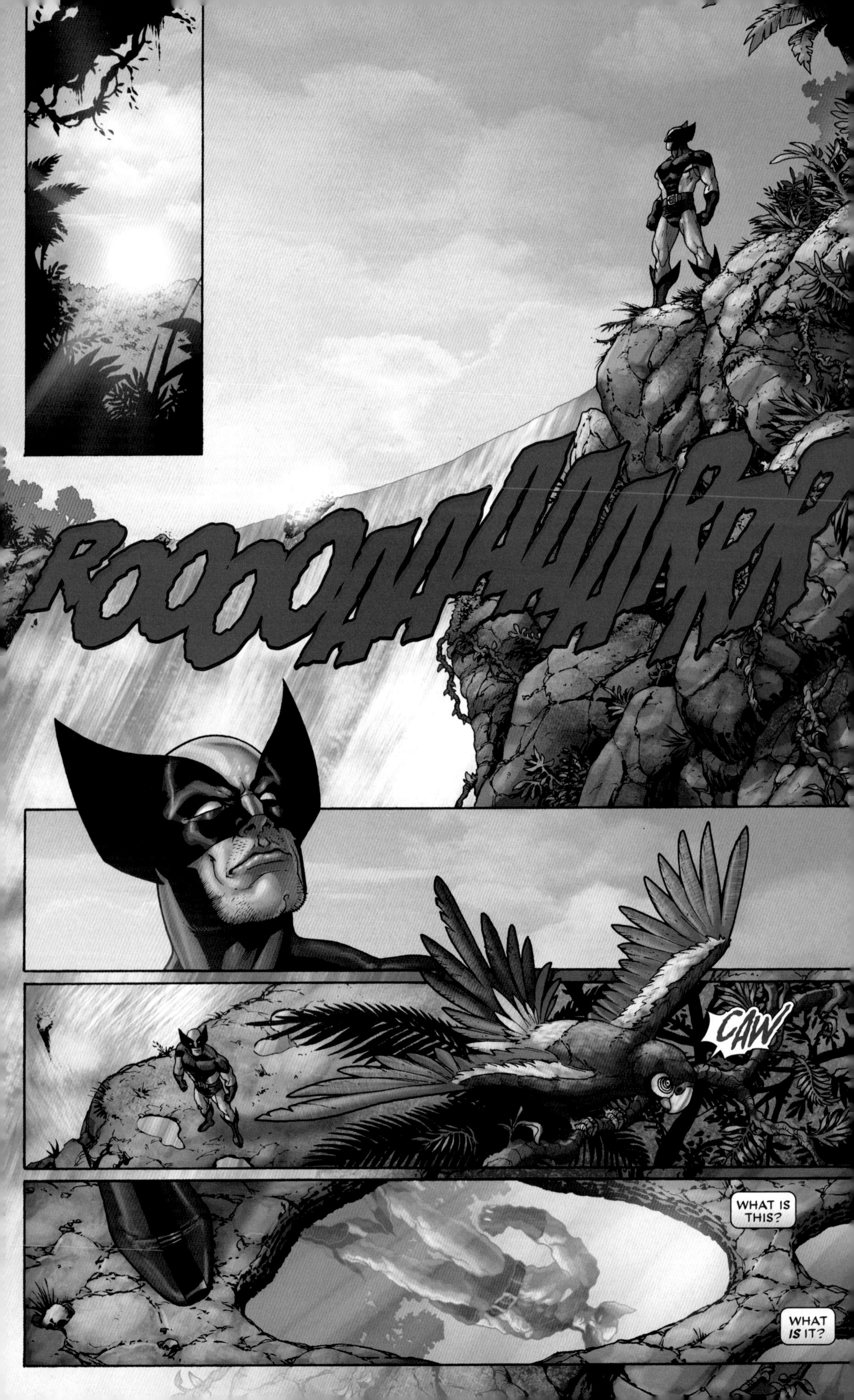
ROOOOAAAARRR
CAW
WHAT IS THIS?
WHAT IS IT?

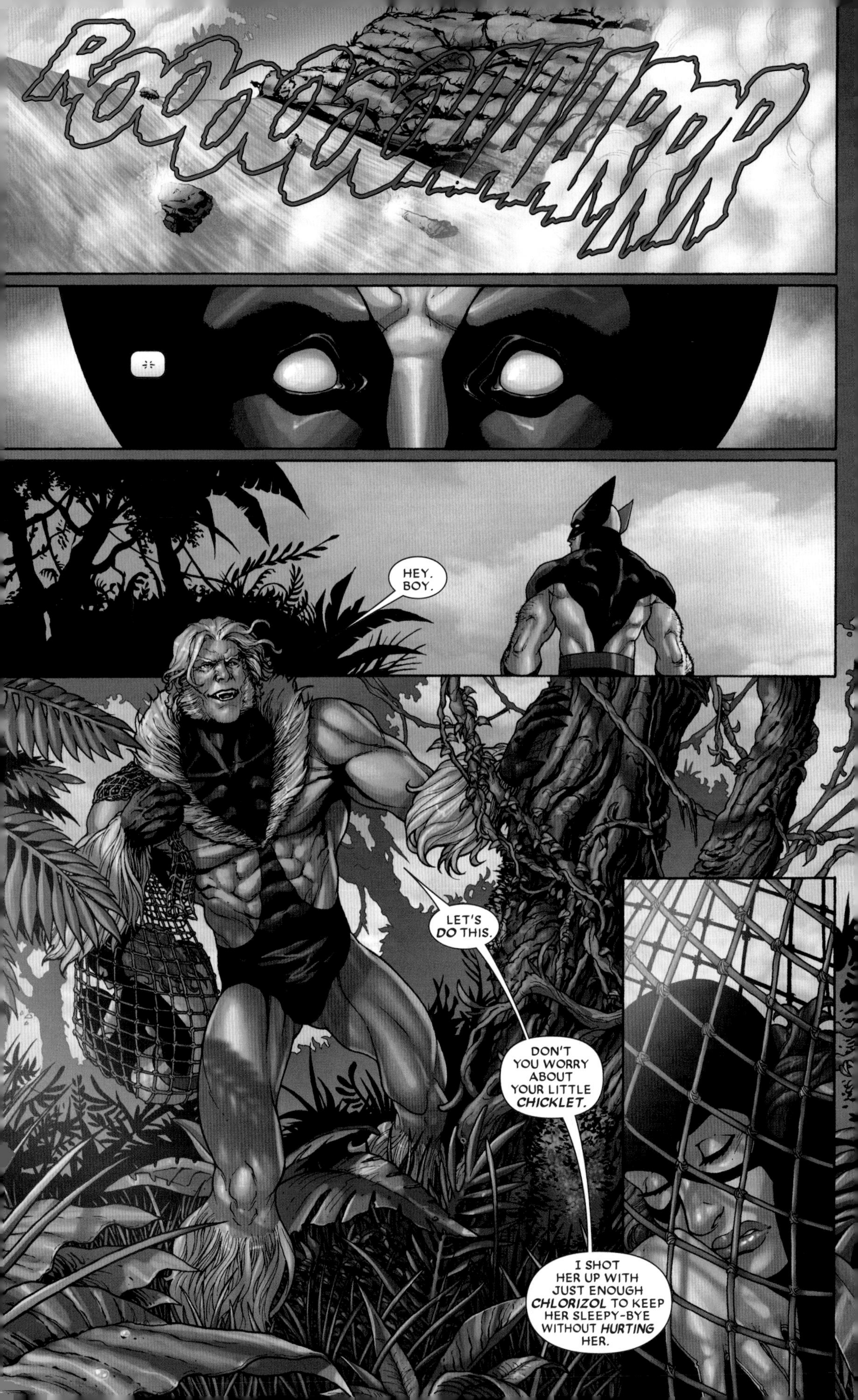
HEY. BOY.
LET'S *DO* THIS.
DON'T YOU WORRY ABOUT YOUR LITTLE *CHICKLET.*
I SHOT HER UP WITH JUST ENOUGH *CHLORIZOL* TO KEEP HER SLEEPY-BYE WITHOUT *HURTING* HER.

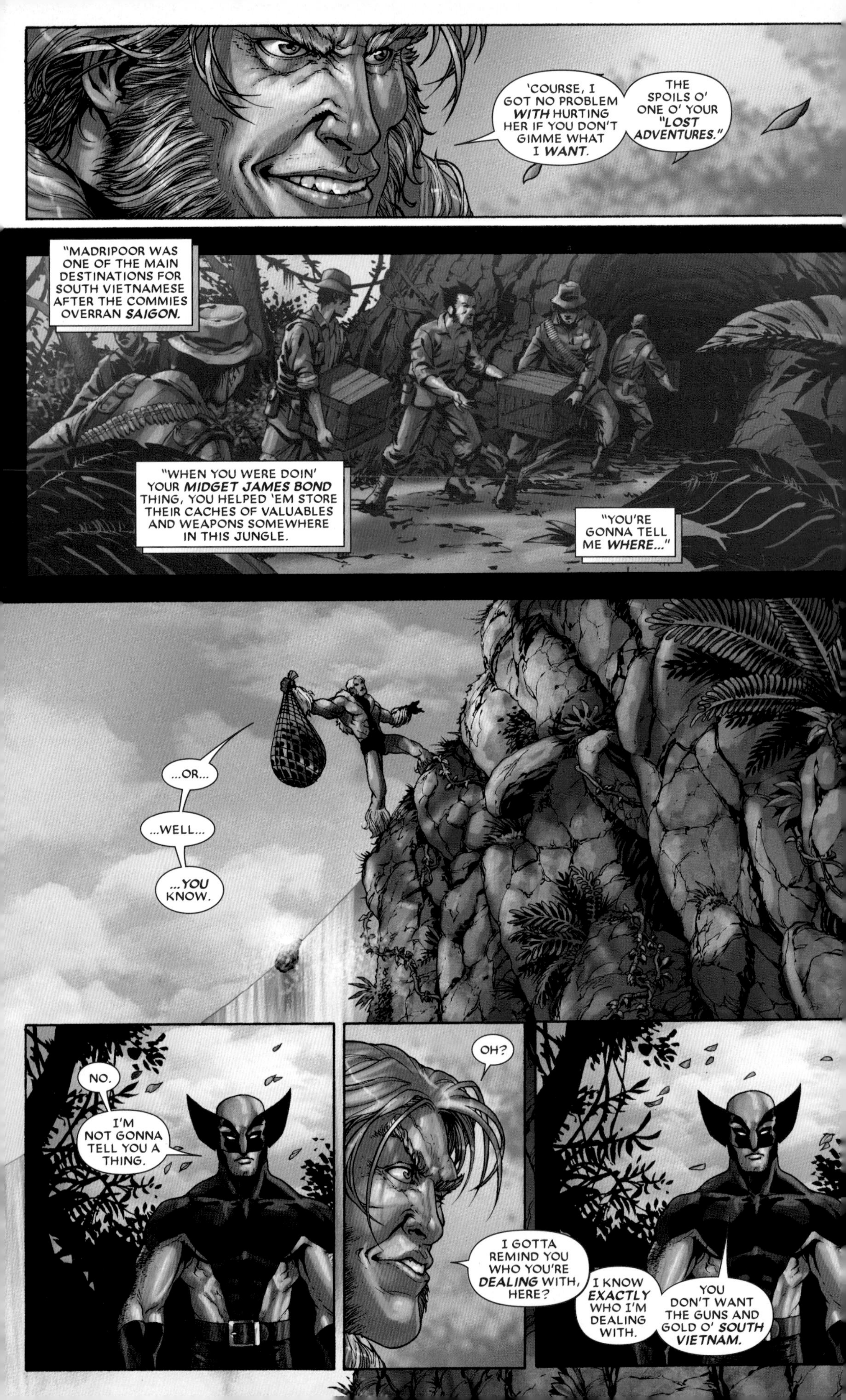
'COURSE, I GOT NO PROBLEM WITH HURTING HER IF YOU DON'T GIMME WHAT I WANT.
THE SPOILS O' ONE O' YOUR "LOST ADVENTURES."
"MADRIPOOR WAS ONE OF THE MAIN DESTINATIONS FOR SOUTH VIETNAMESE AFTER THE COMMIES OVERRAN SAIGON.
"WHEN YOU WERE DOIN' YOUR MIDGET JAMES BOND THING, YOU HELPED 'EM STORE THEIR CACHES OF VALUABLES AND WEAPONS SOMEWHERE IN THIS JUNGLE.
"YOU'RE GONNA TELL ME WHERE..."
...OR...
...WELL...
...YOU KNOW.
NO.
I'M NOT GONNA TELL YOU A THING.
OH?
I GOTTA REMIND YOU WHO YOU'RE DEALING WITH, HERE?
I KNOW EXACTLY WHO I'M DEALING WITH.
YOU DON'T WANT THE GUNS AND GOLD O' SOUTH VIETNAM.

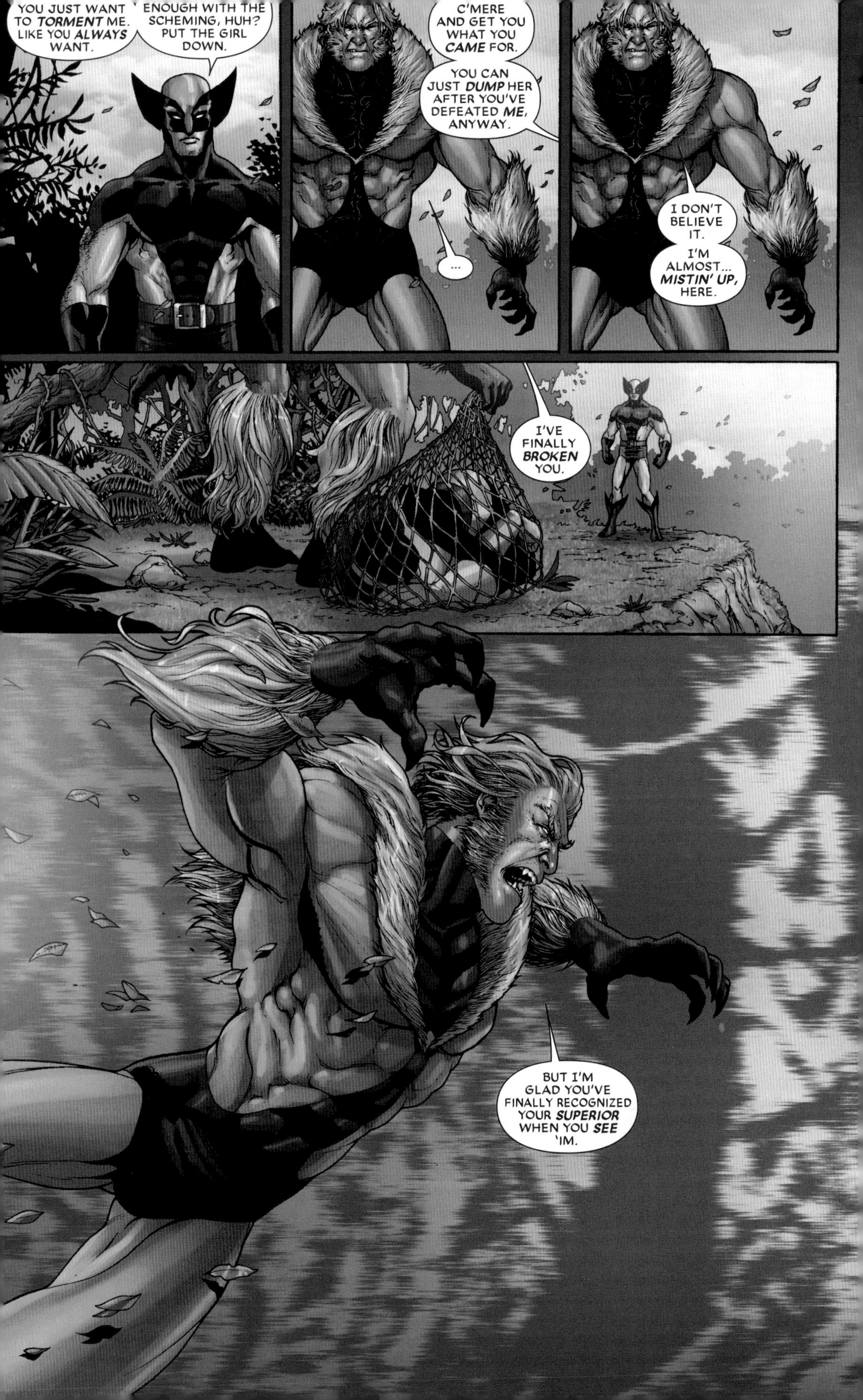
YOU JUST WANT TO TORMENT ME. LIKE YOU ALWAYS WANT.
ENOUGH WITH THE SCHEMING, HUH? PUT THE GIRL DOWN.
C'MERE AND GET YOU WHAT YOU CAME FOR.
YOU CAN JUST DUMP HER AFTER YOU'VE DEFEATED ME, ANYWAY.
...
I DON'T BELIEVE IT.
I'M ALMOST... MISTIN' UP, HERE.
I'VE FINALLY BROKEN YOU.
BUT I'M GLAD YOU'VE FINALLY RECOGNIZED YOUR SUPERIOR WHEN YOU SEE 'IM.

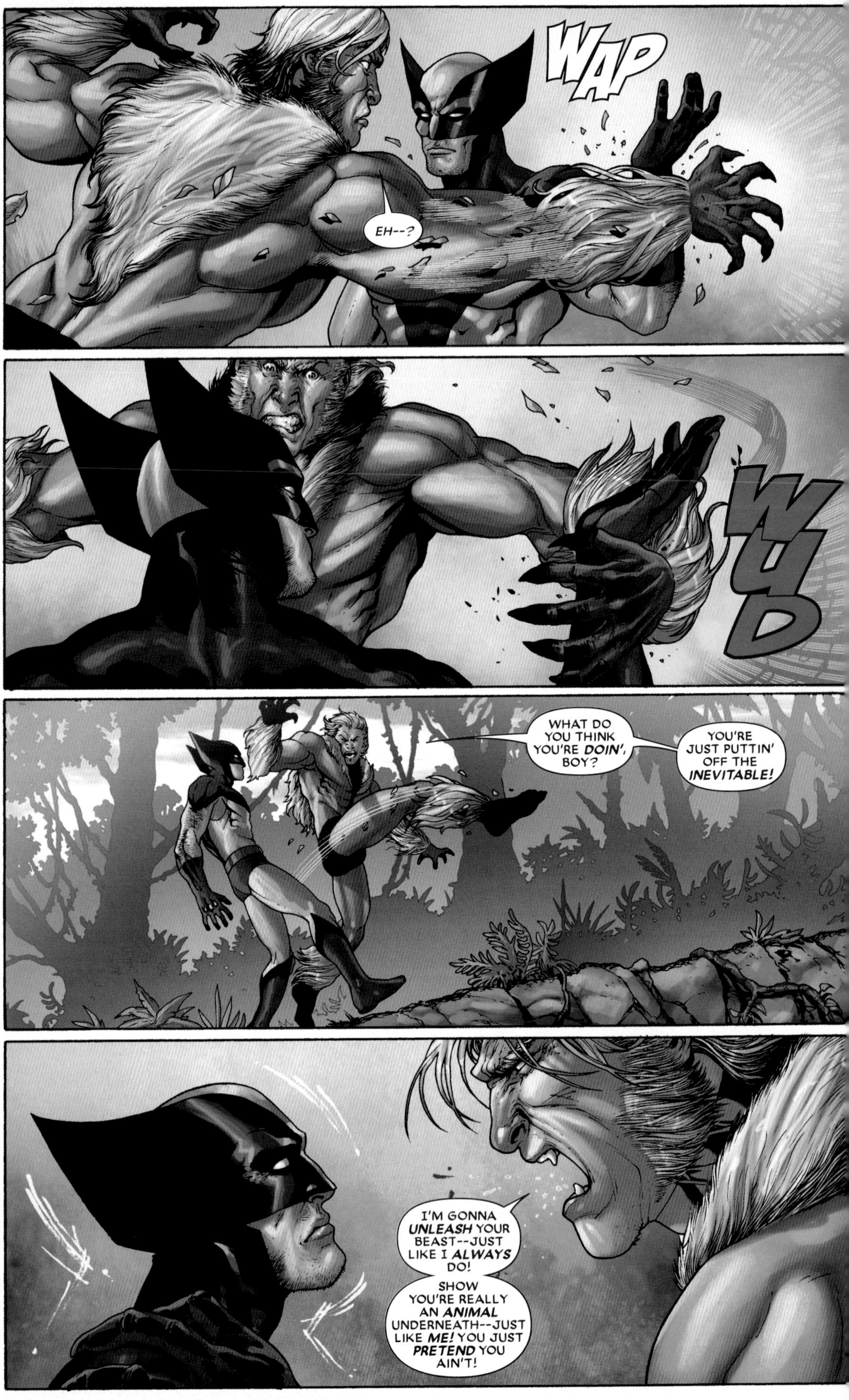

WAP
EH--?
WUD
WHAT DO YOU THINK YOU'RE DOIN', BOY?
YOU'RE JUST PUTTIN' OFF THE INEVITABLE!
I'M GONNA UNLEASH YOUR BEAST--JUST LIKE I ALWAYS DO!
SHOW YOU'RE REALLY AN ANIMAL UNDERNEATH--JUST LIKE ME! YOU JUST PRETEND YOU AIN'T!

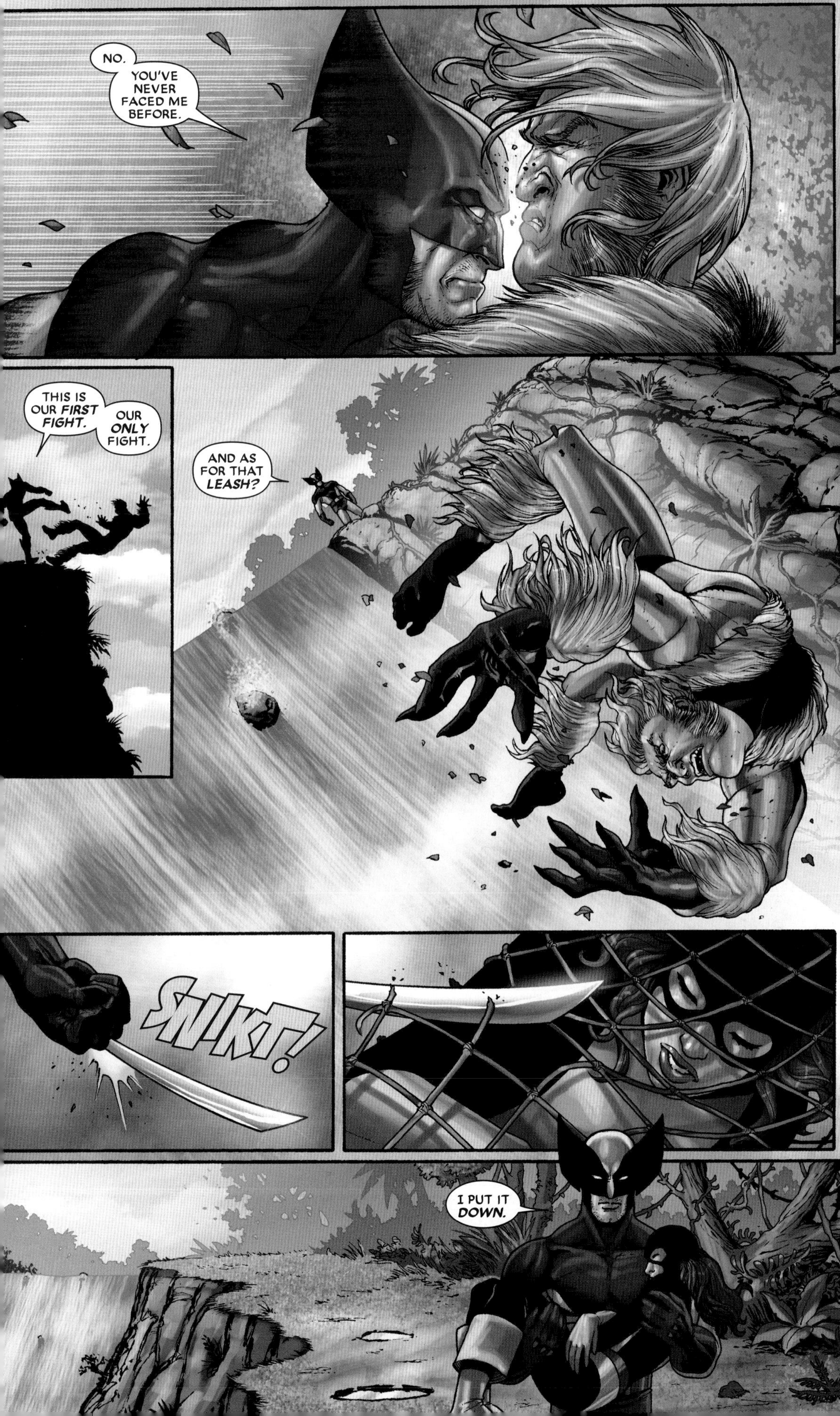
NO.
YOU'VE NEVER FACED ME BEFORE.
THIS IS OUR *FIRST* *FIGHT.*
OUR *ONLY* FIGHT.
AND AS FOR THAT *LEASH?*
SNIKT!
I PUT IT *DOWN.*

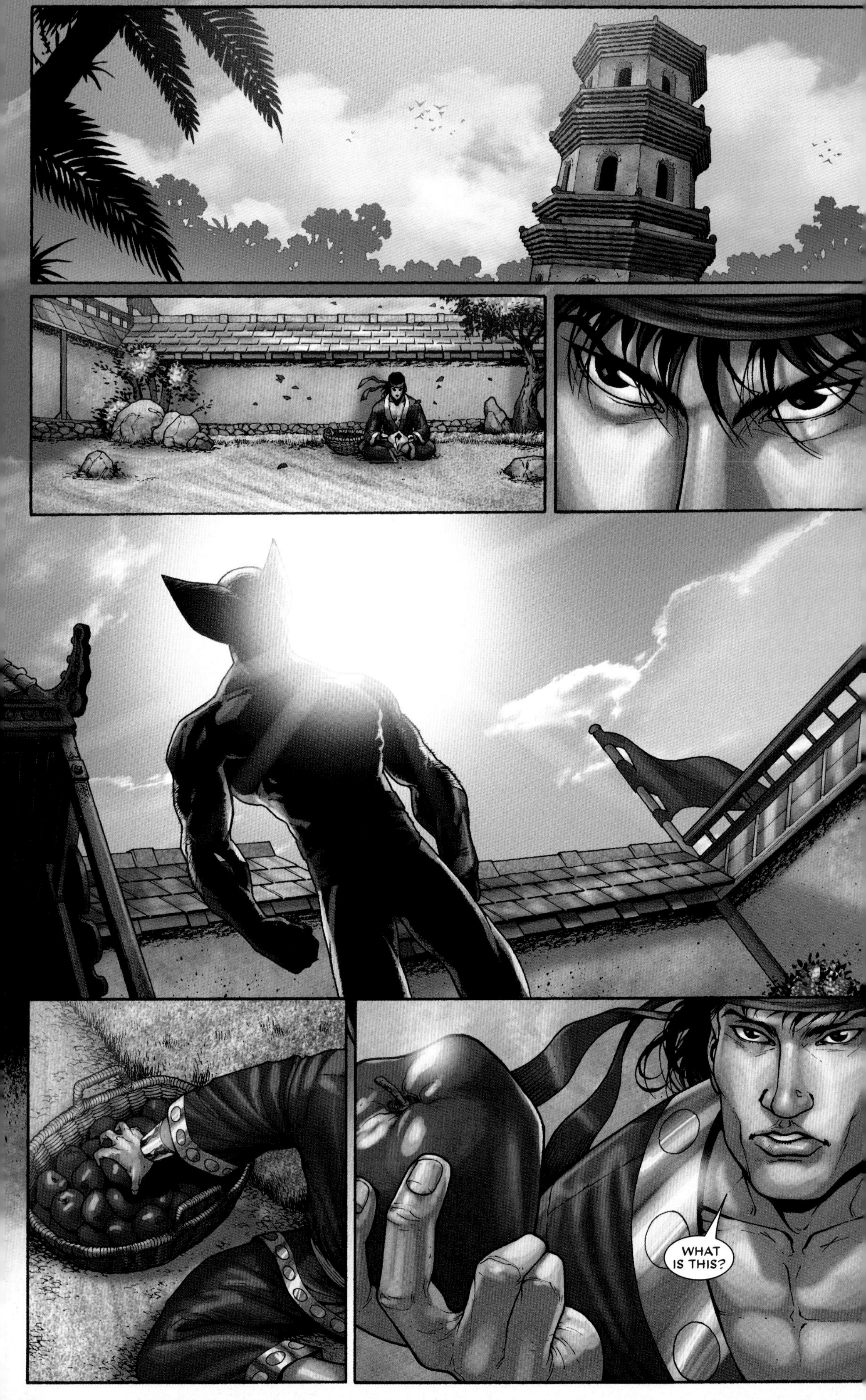
WHAT IS THIS?

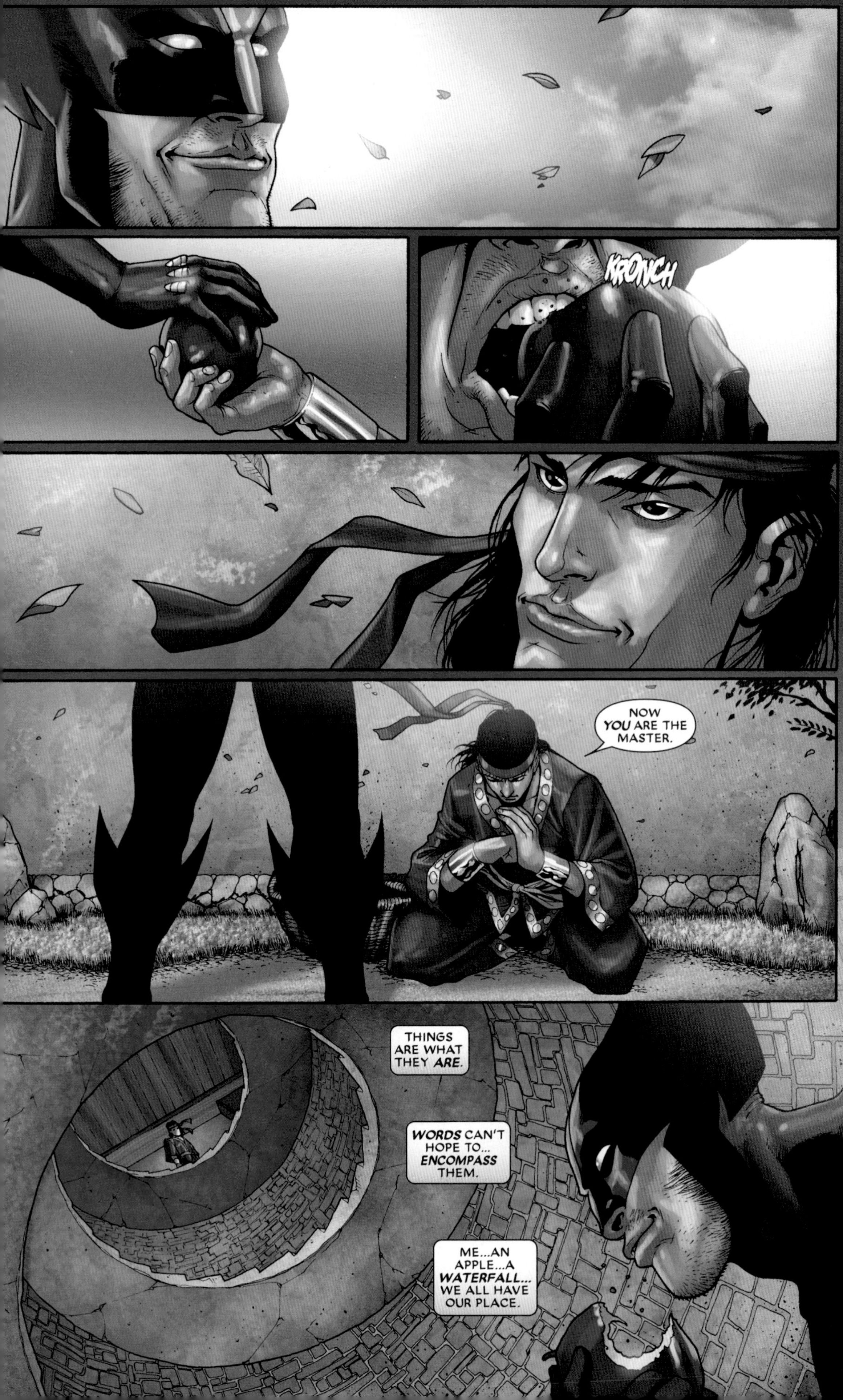
KRONCH
NOW YOU ARE THE MASTER.
THINGS ARE WHAT THEY ARE.
WORDS CAN'T HOPE TO... ENCOMPASS THEM.
ME...AN APPLE...A WATERFALL... WE ALL HAVE OUR PLACE.

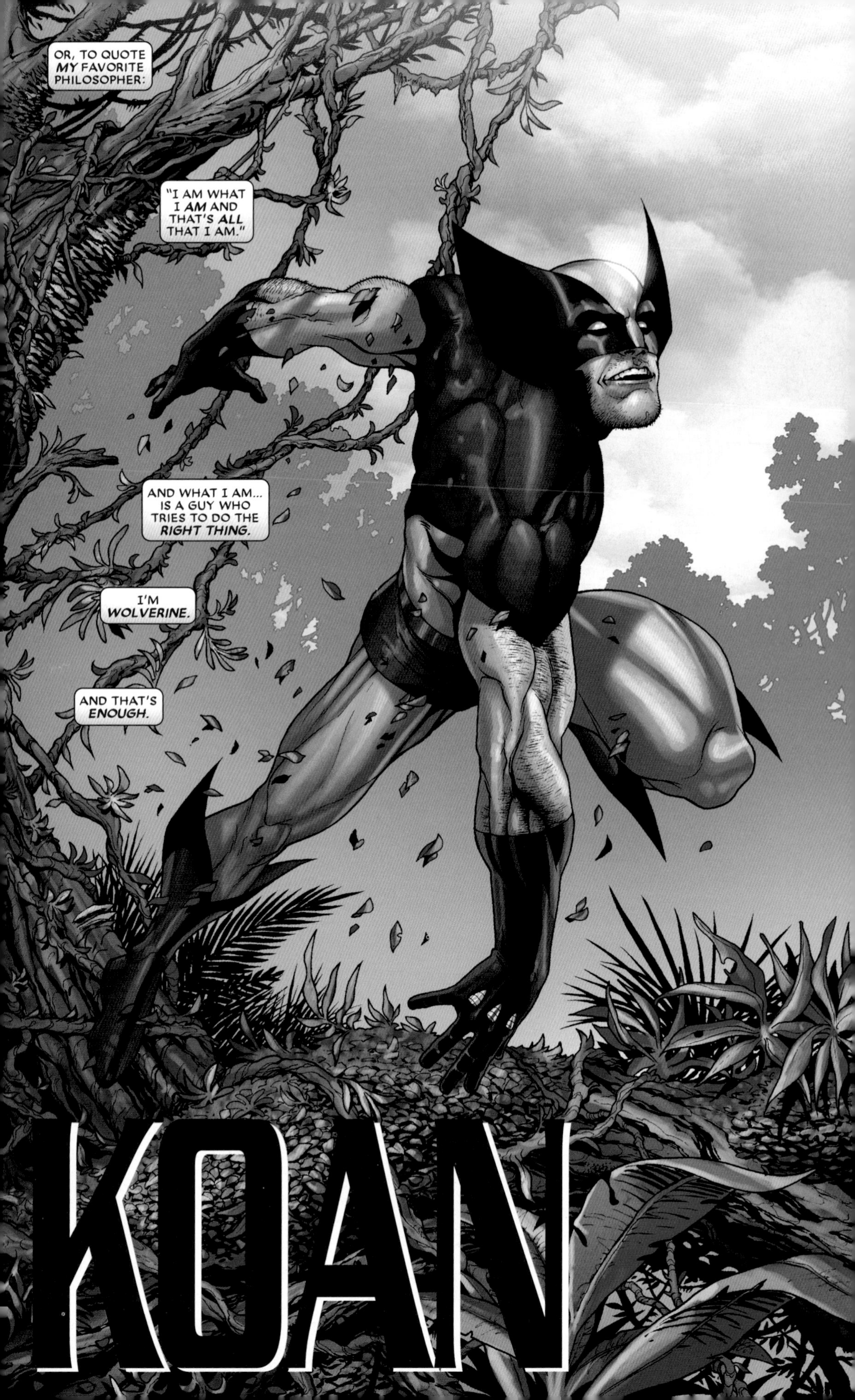
OR, TO QUOTE MY FAVORITE PHILOSOPHER:
"I AM WHAT I AM AND THAT'S ALL THAT I AM."
AND WHAT I AM... IS A GUY WHO TRIES TO DO THE RIGHT THING.
I'M WOLVERINE.
AND THAT'S ENOUGH.
KOAN

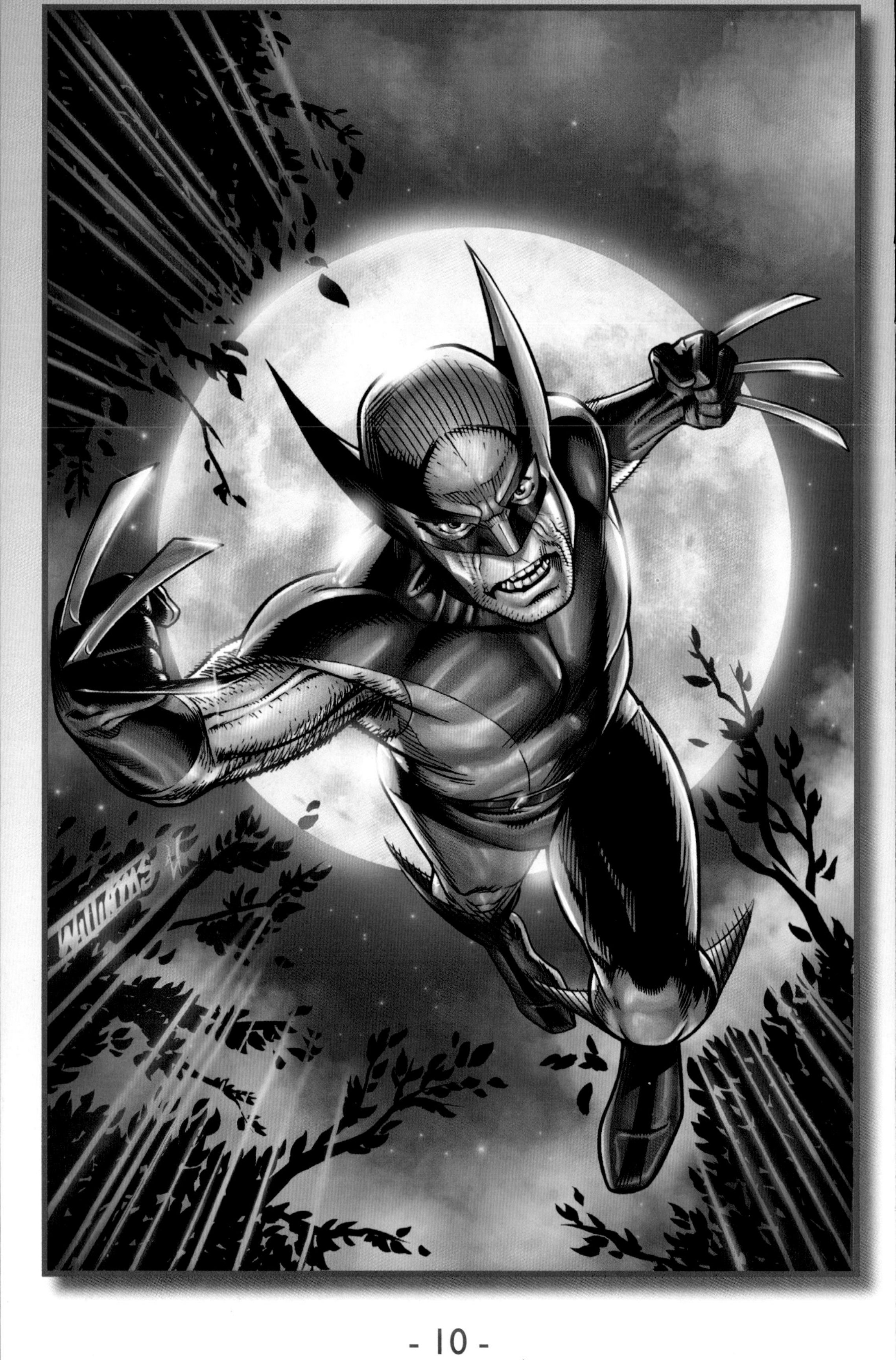

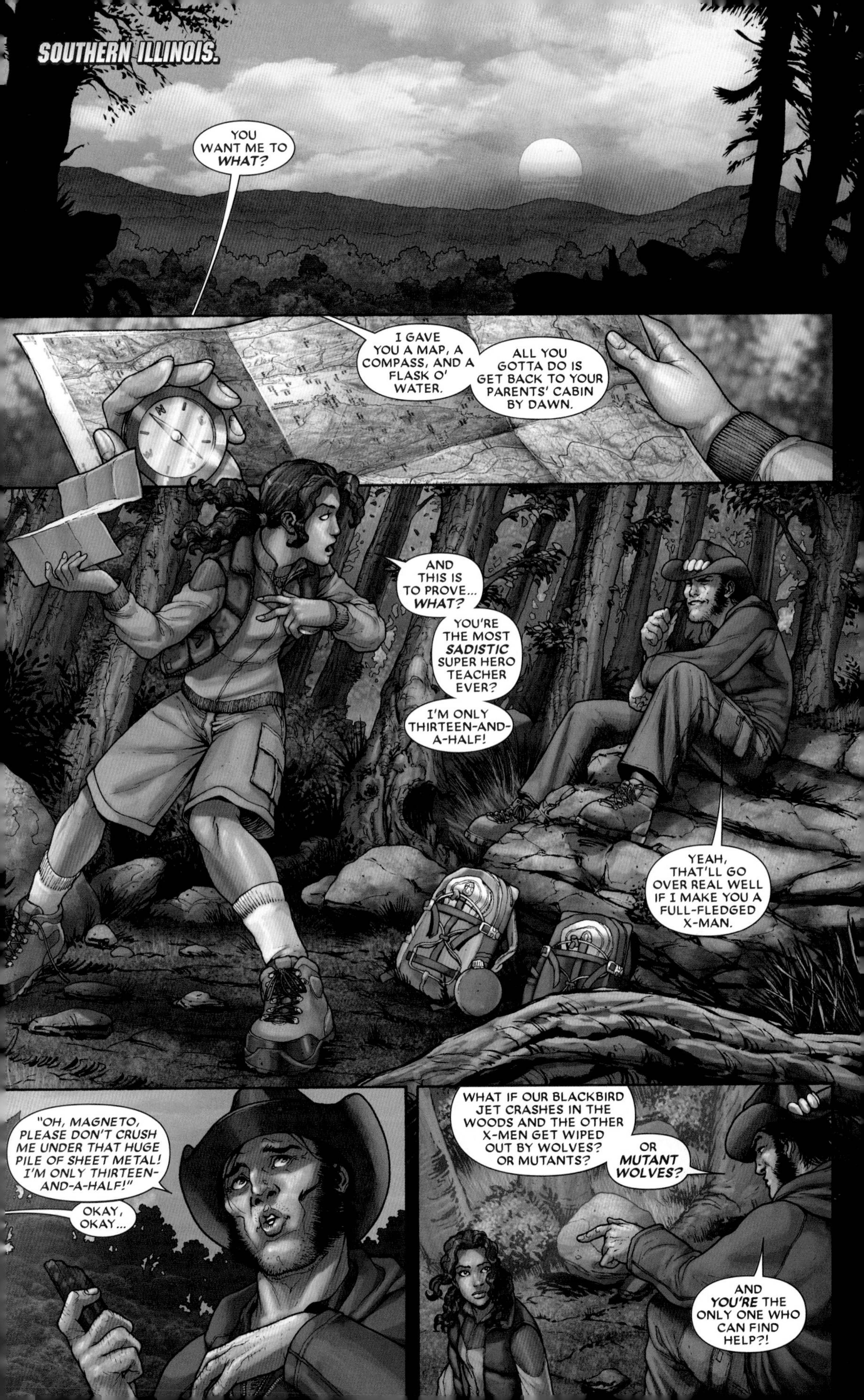
SOUTHERN ILLINOIS.
YOU WANT ME TO *WHAT?*
I GAVE YOU A MAP, A COMPASS, AND A FLASK O' WATER.
ALL YOU GOTTA DO IS GET BACK TO YOUR PARENTS' CABIN BY DAWN.
AND THIS IS TO PROVE... *WHAT?*
YOU'RE THE MOST *SADISTIC* SUPER HERO TEACHER EVER?
I'M ONLY THIRTEEN-AND-A-HALF!
YEAH, THAT'LL GO OVER REAL WELL IF I MAKE YOU A FULL-FLEDGED X-MAN.
"OH, MAGNETO, PLEASE DON'T CRUSH ME UNDER THAT HUGE PILE OF SHEET METAL! I'M ONLY THIRTEEN-AND-A-HALF!"
OKAY, OKAY...
WHAT IF OUR BLACKBIRD JET CRASHES IN THE WOODS AND THE OTHER X-MEN GET WIPED OUT BY WOLVES? OR MUTANTS?
OR *MUTANT WOLVES?*
AND *YOU'RE* THE ONLY ONE WHO CAN FIND HELP?!

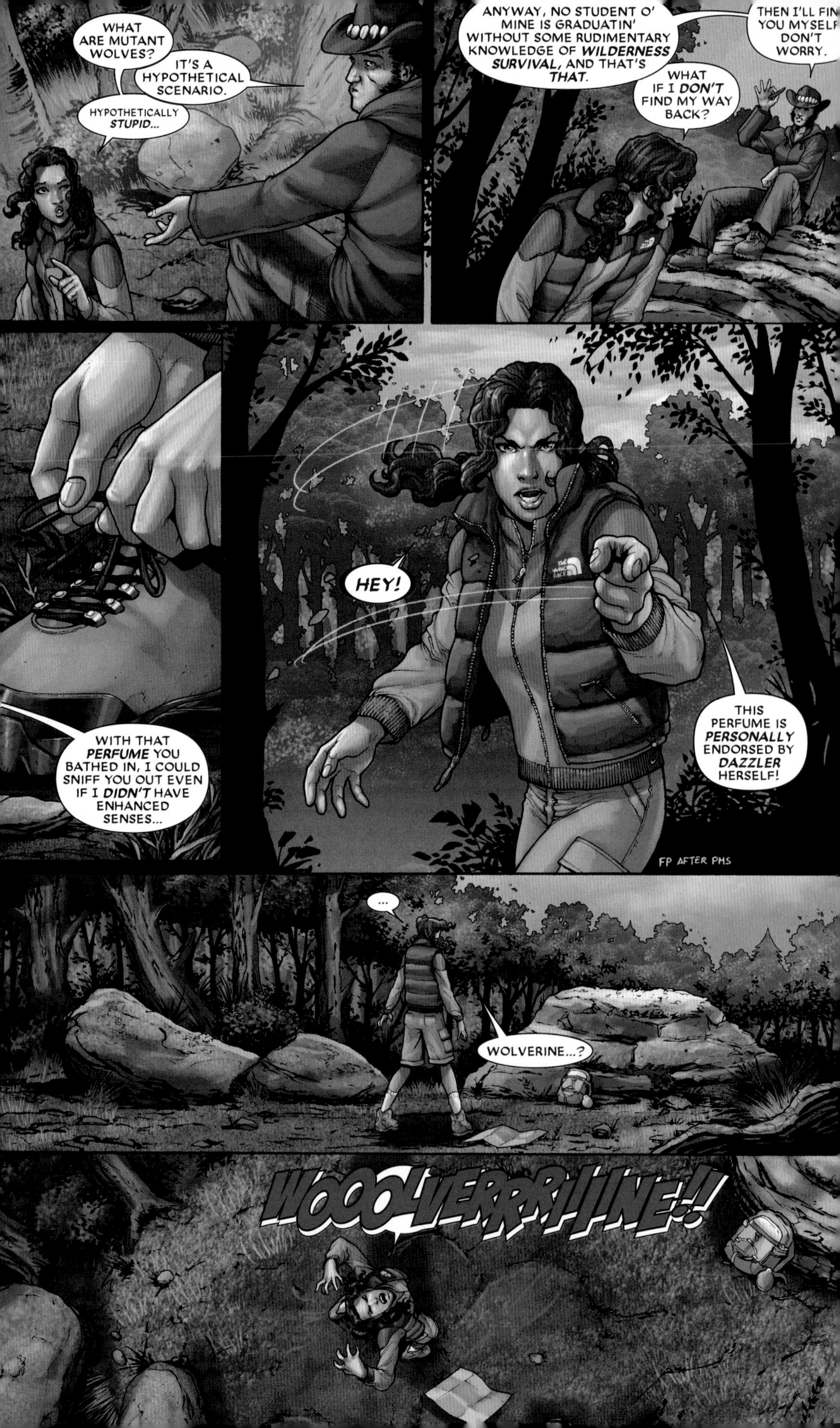
WHAT ARE MUTANT WOLVES?
IT'S A HYPOTHETICAL SCENARIO.
HYPOTHETICALLY STUPID...
ANYWAY, NO STUDENT O' MINE IS GRADUATIN' WITHOUT SOME RUDIMENTARY KNOWLEDGE OF WILDERNESS SURVIVAL, AND THAT'S THAT.
WHAT IF I DON'T FIND MY WAY BACK?
THEN I'LL FIN YOU MYSELF DON'T WORRY.
WITH THAT PERFUME YOU BATHED IN, I COULD SNIFF YOU OUT EVEN IF I DIDN'T HAVE ENHANCED SENSES...
HEY!
THIS PERFUME IS PERSONALLY ENDORSED BY DAZZLER HERSELF!
FP AFTER PHS
...
WOLVERINE...?
WOOOLVERRRIIINE!!

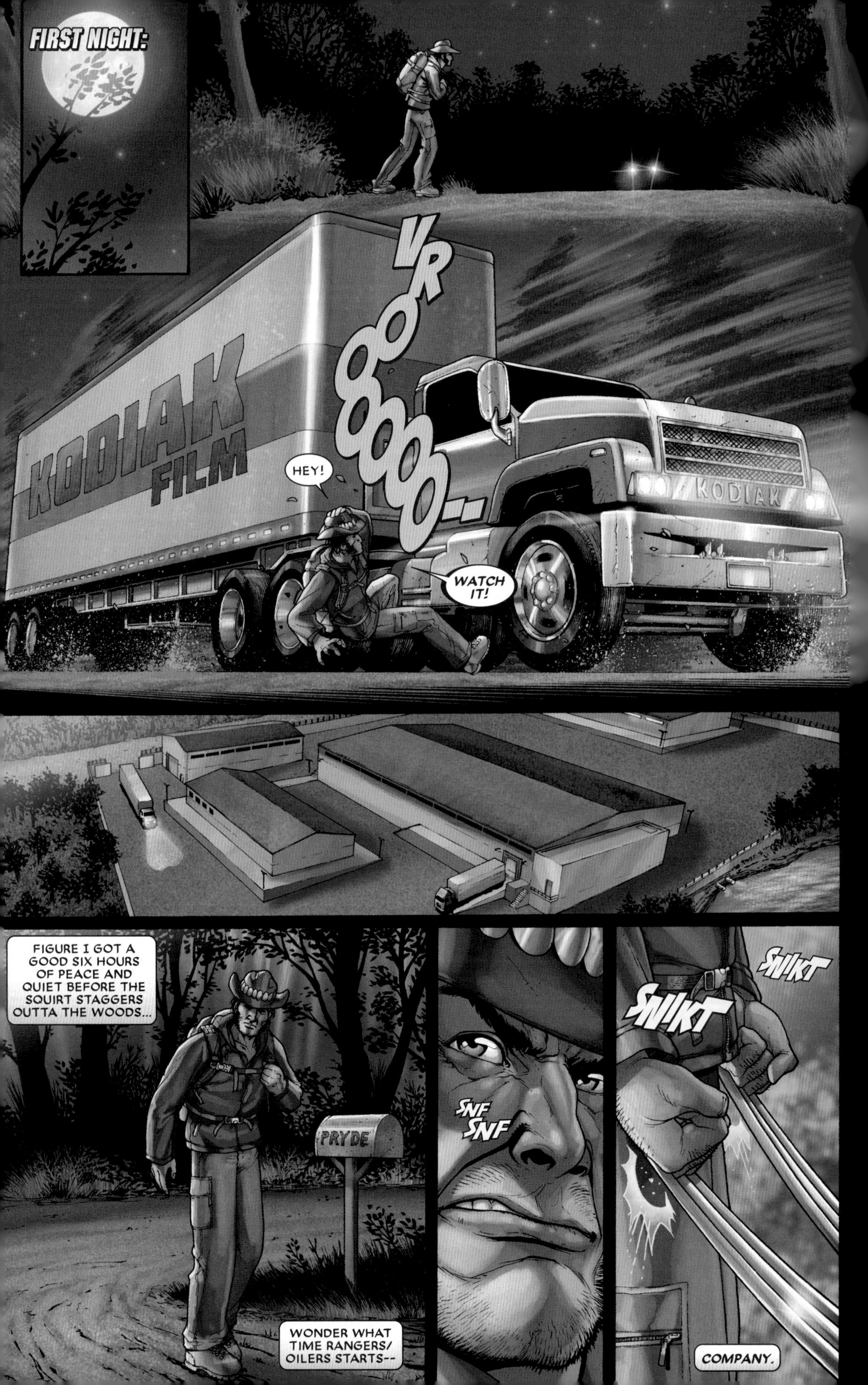

FIRST NIGHT:
KODIAK FILM
VROOOOOOM
HEY!
KODIAK
WATCH IT!
FIGURE I GOT A GOOD SIX HOURS OF PEACE AND QUIET BEFORE THE SQUIRT STAGGERS OUTTA THE WOODS...
PRYDE
WONDER WHAT TIME RANGERS/ OILERS STARTS--
SNF SNF
SNIKT
SNIKT
COMPANY.

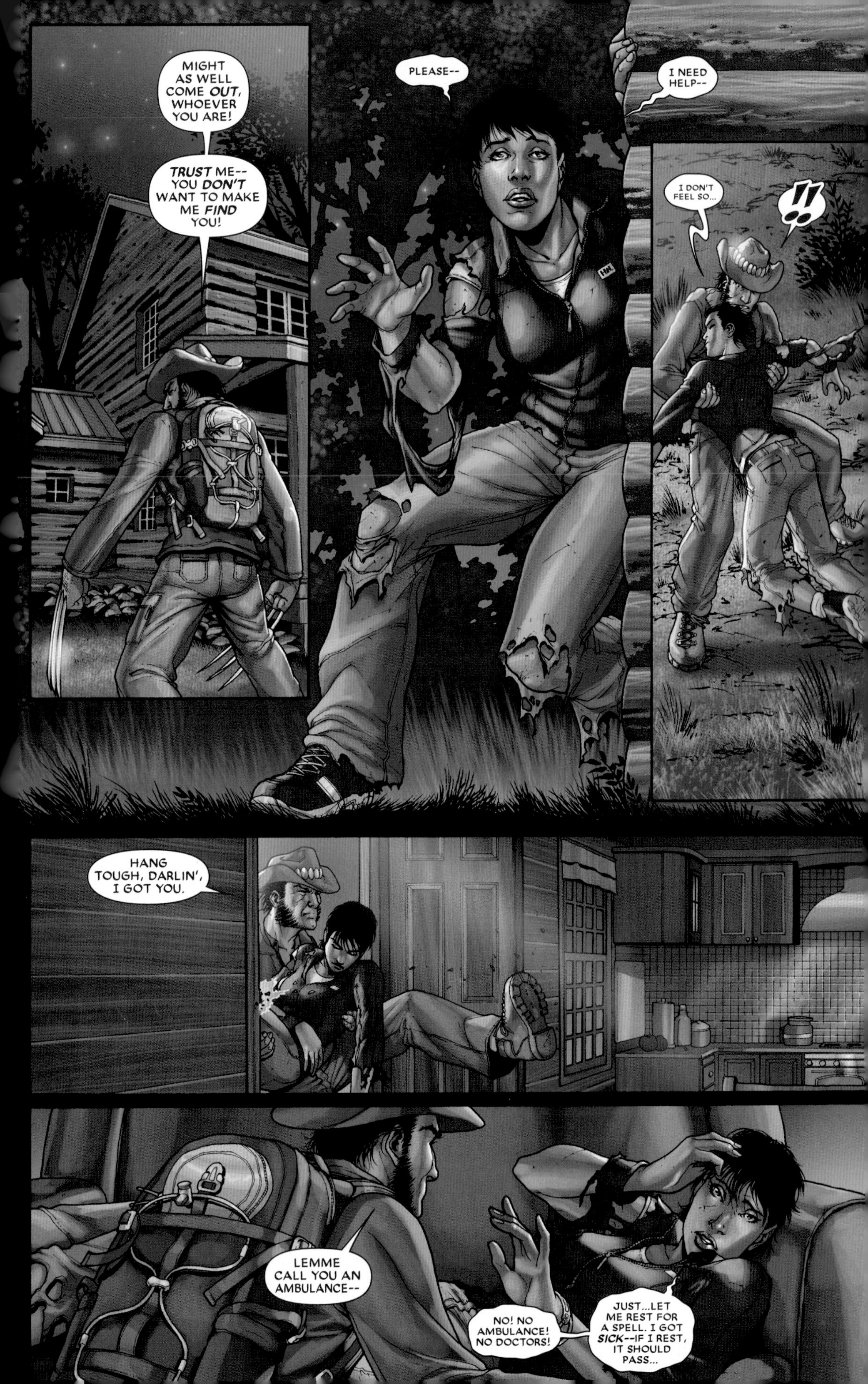
MIGHT AS WELL COME OUT, WHOEVER YOU ARE!
TRUST ME-- YOU DON'T WANT TO MAKE ME FIND YOU!
PLEASE--
I NEED HELP--
I DON'T FEEL SO...
!!
HANG TOUGH, DARLIN', I GOT YOU.
LEMME CALL YOU AN AMBULANCE--
NO! NO AMBULANCE! NO DOCTORS!
JUST...LET ME REST FOR A SPELL. I GOT SICK--IF I REST, IT SHOULD PASS...

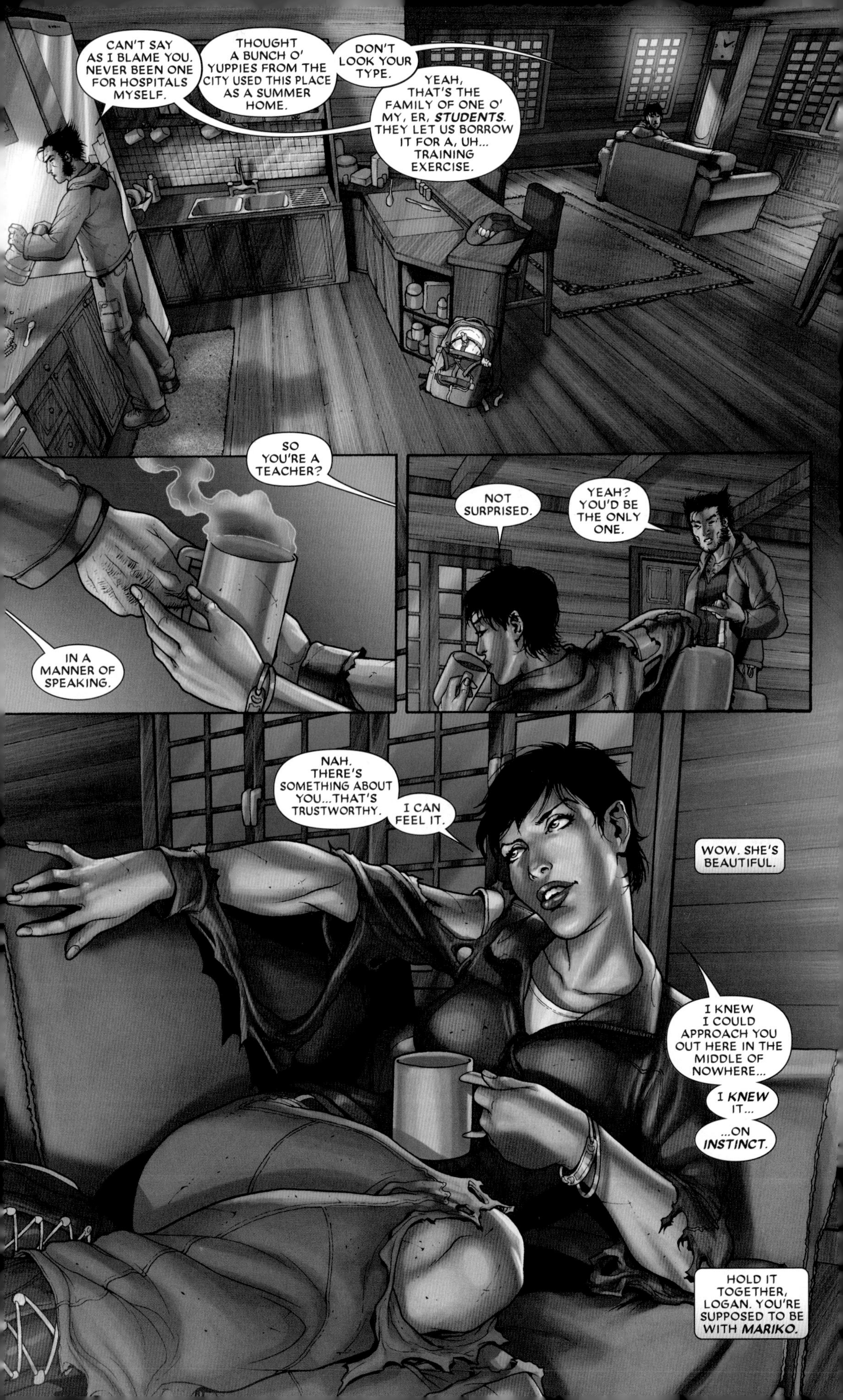
CAN'T SAY AS I BLAME YOU. NEVER BEEN ONE FOR HOSPITALS MYSELF.
THOUGHT A BUNCH O' YUPPIES FROM THE CITY USED THIS PLACE AS A SUMMER HOME.
DON'T LOOK YOUR TYPE.
YEAH, THAT'S THE FAMILY OF ONE O' MY, ER, *STUDENTS*. THEY LET US BORROW IT FOR A, UH... TRAINING EXERCISE.
SO YOU'RE A TEACHER?
IN A MANNER OF SPEAKING.
NOT SURPRISED.
YEAH? YOU'D BE THE ONLY ONE.
NAH. THERE'S SOMETHING ABOUT YOU...THAT'S TRUSTWORTHY.
I CAN FEEL IT.
WOW. SHE'S BEAUTIFUL.
I KNEW I COULD APPROACH YOU OUT HERE IN THE MIDDLE OF NOWHERE...
I *KNEW* IT...
...ON *INSTINCT*.
HOLD IT TOGETHER, LOGAN. YOU'RE SUPPOSED TO BE WITH *MARIKO*.

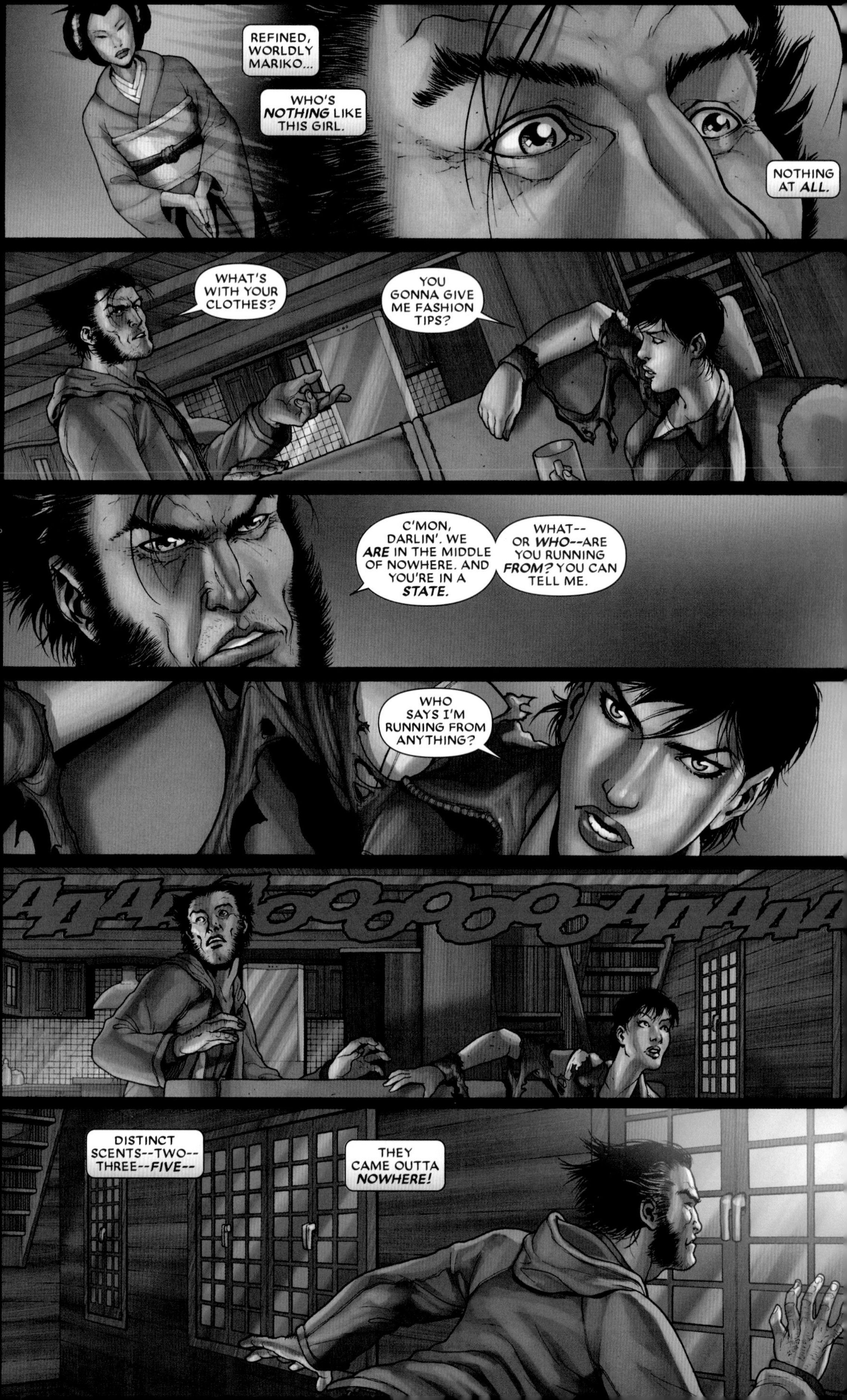
REFINED, WORLDLY MARIKO...
WHO'S NOTHING LIKE THIS GIRL.
NOTHING AT ALL.
WHAT'S WITH YOUR CLOTHES?
YOU GONNA GIVE ME FASHION TIPS?
C'MON, DARLIN'. WE ARE IN THE MIDDLE OF NOWHERE. AND YOU'RE IN A STATE.
WHAT-- OR WHO--ARE YOU RUNNING FROM? YOU CAN TELL ME.
WHO SAYS I'M RUNNING FROM ANYTHING?
AAAOOOOOOAAAAA
DISTINCT SCENTS--TWO--THREE--FIVE--
THEY CAME OUTTA NOWHERE!

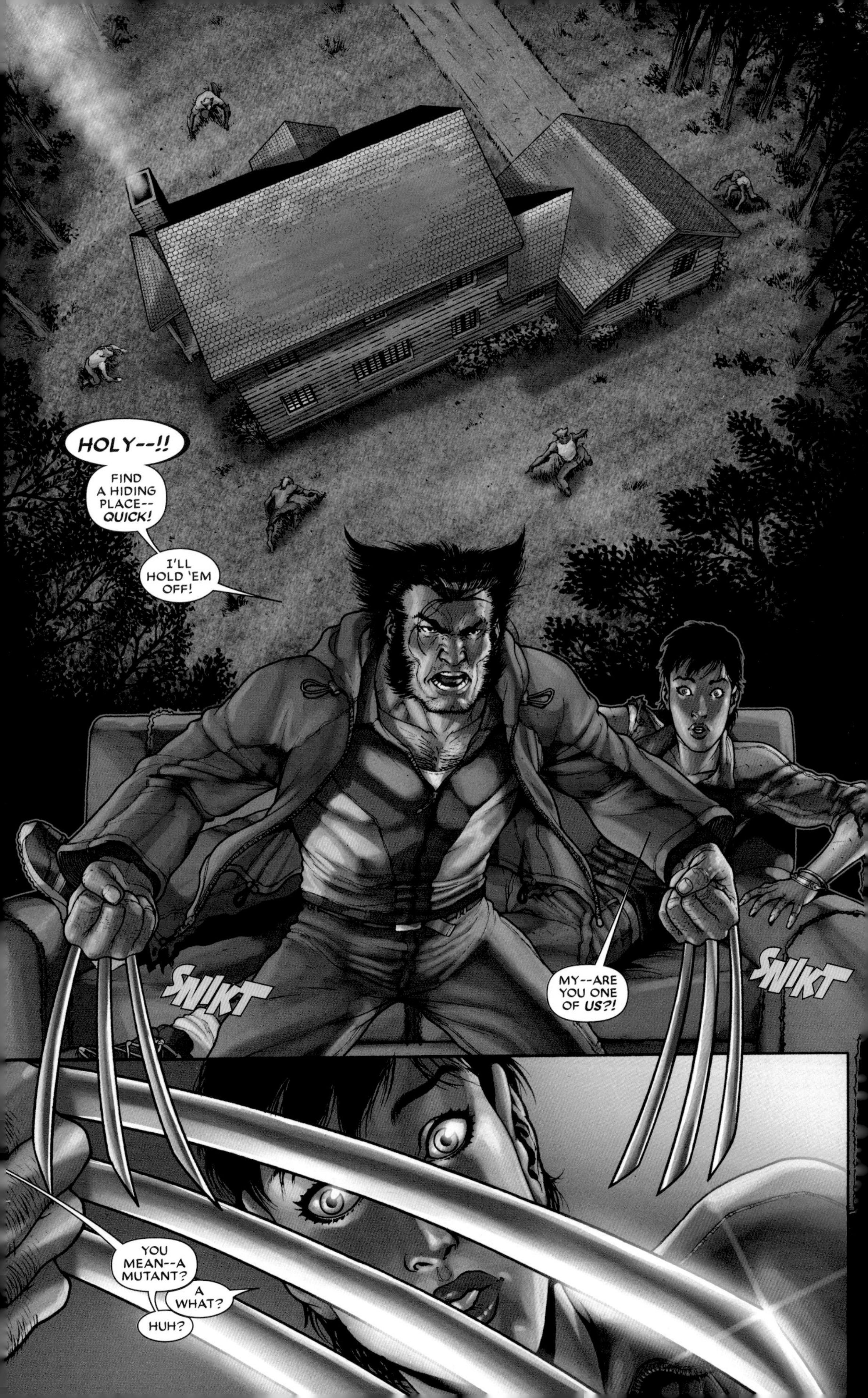
HOLY--!!
FIND A HIDING PLACE--QUICK!
I'LL HOLD 'EM OFF!
SNIKT
MY--ARE YOU ONE OF US?!
SNIKT
YOU MEAN--A MUTANT?
A WHAT?
HUH?

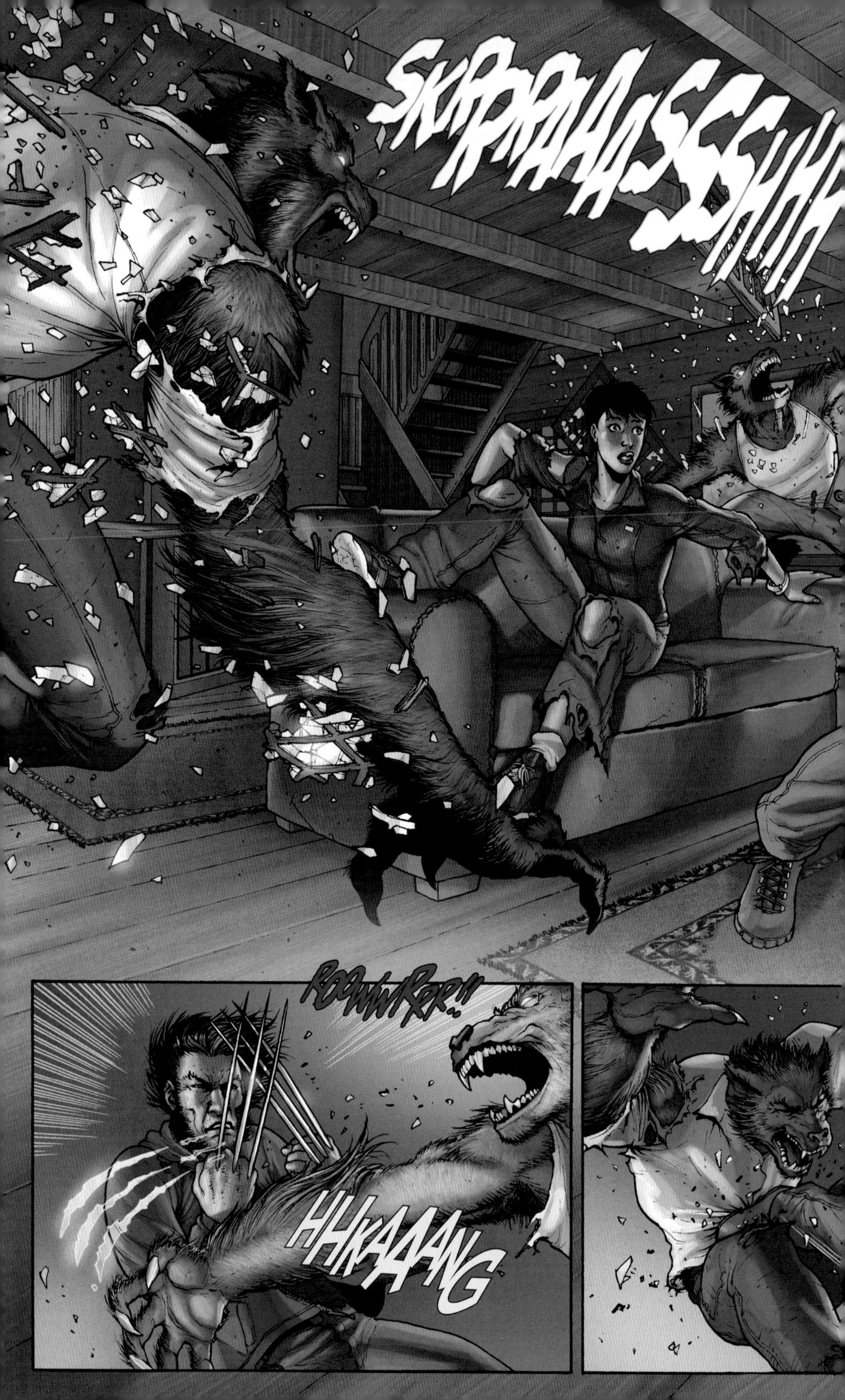
SKRRRAAA-SSHHH
ROOWWRRR!!
HHKAAANG

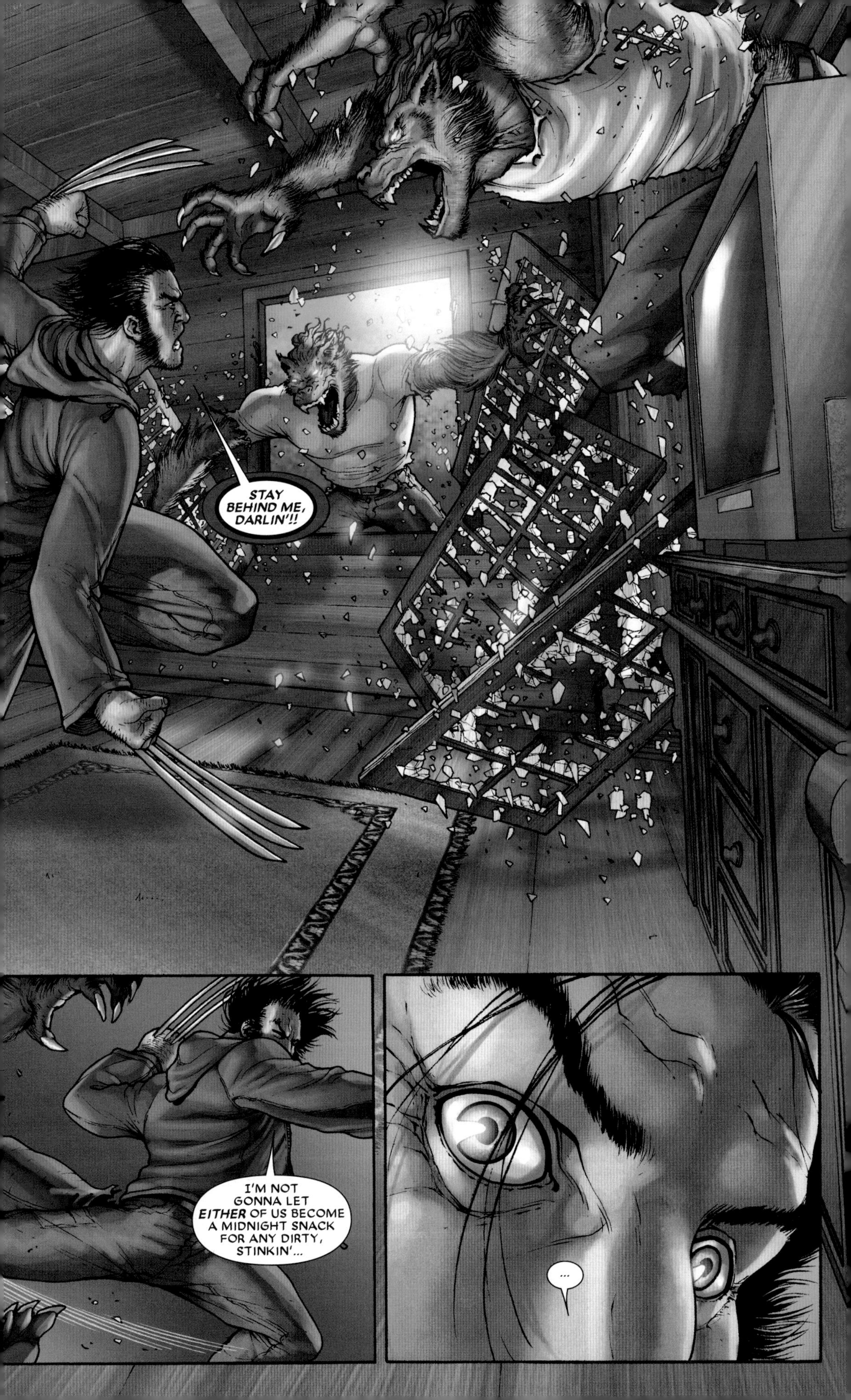
STAY BEHIND ME, DARLIN'!!
I'M NOT GONNA LET *EITHER* OF US BECOME A MIDNIGHT SNACK FOR ANY DIRTY, STINKIN'...
...

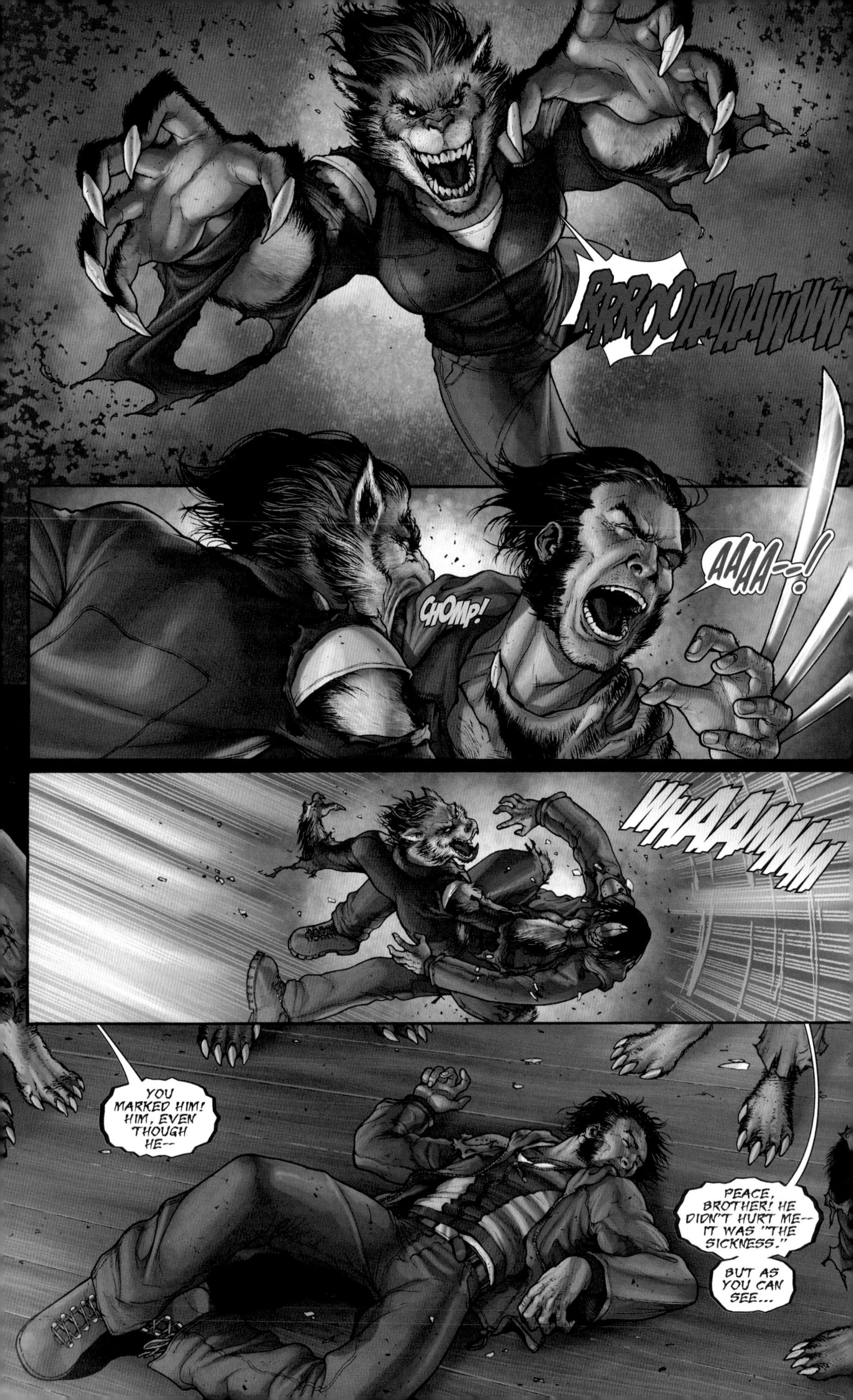
RRROOAAAAWWW
CHOMP!
AAAA--!
WHAAMM
YOU MARKED HIM! HIM, EVEN THOUGH HE--
PEACE, BROTHER! HE DIDN'T HURT ME-- IT WAS "THE SICKNESS."
BUT AS YOU CAN SEE...

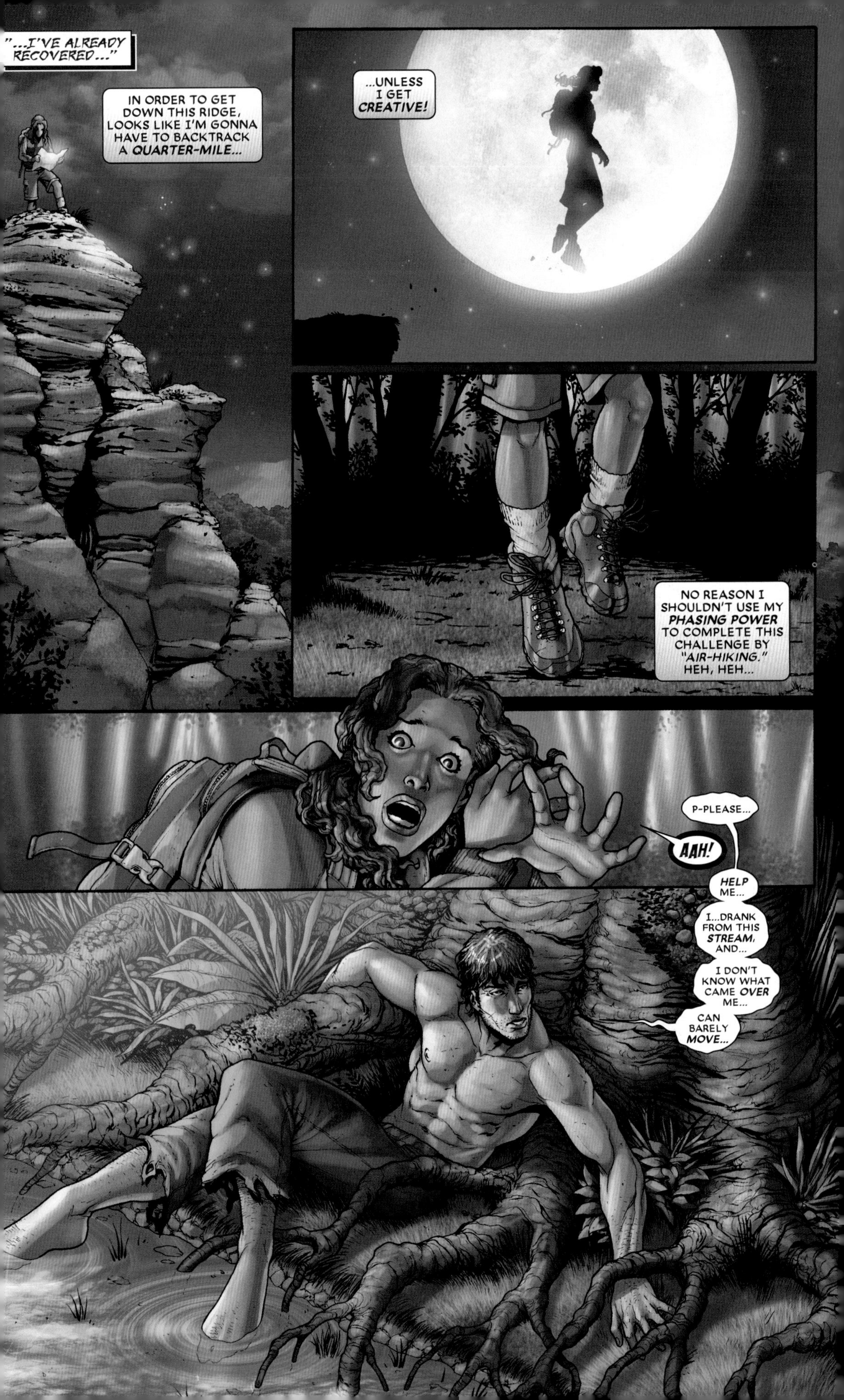
"...I'VE ALREADY RECOVERED..."
IN ORDER TO GET DOWN THIS RIDGE, LOOKS LIKE I'M GONNA HAVE TO BACKTRACK A *QUARTER-MILE*...
...UNLESS I GET *CREATIVE!*
NO REASON I SHOULDN'T USE MY *PHASING POWER* TO COMPLETE THIS CHALLENGE BY *"AIR-HIKING."* HEH, HEH...
P-PLEASE...
AAH!
HELP ME...
I...DRANK FROM THIS *STREAM*, AND...
I DON'T KNOW WHAT CAME *OVER* ME...
CAN BARELY *MOVE*...

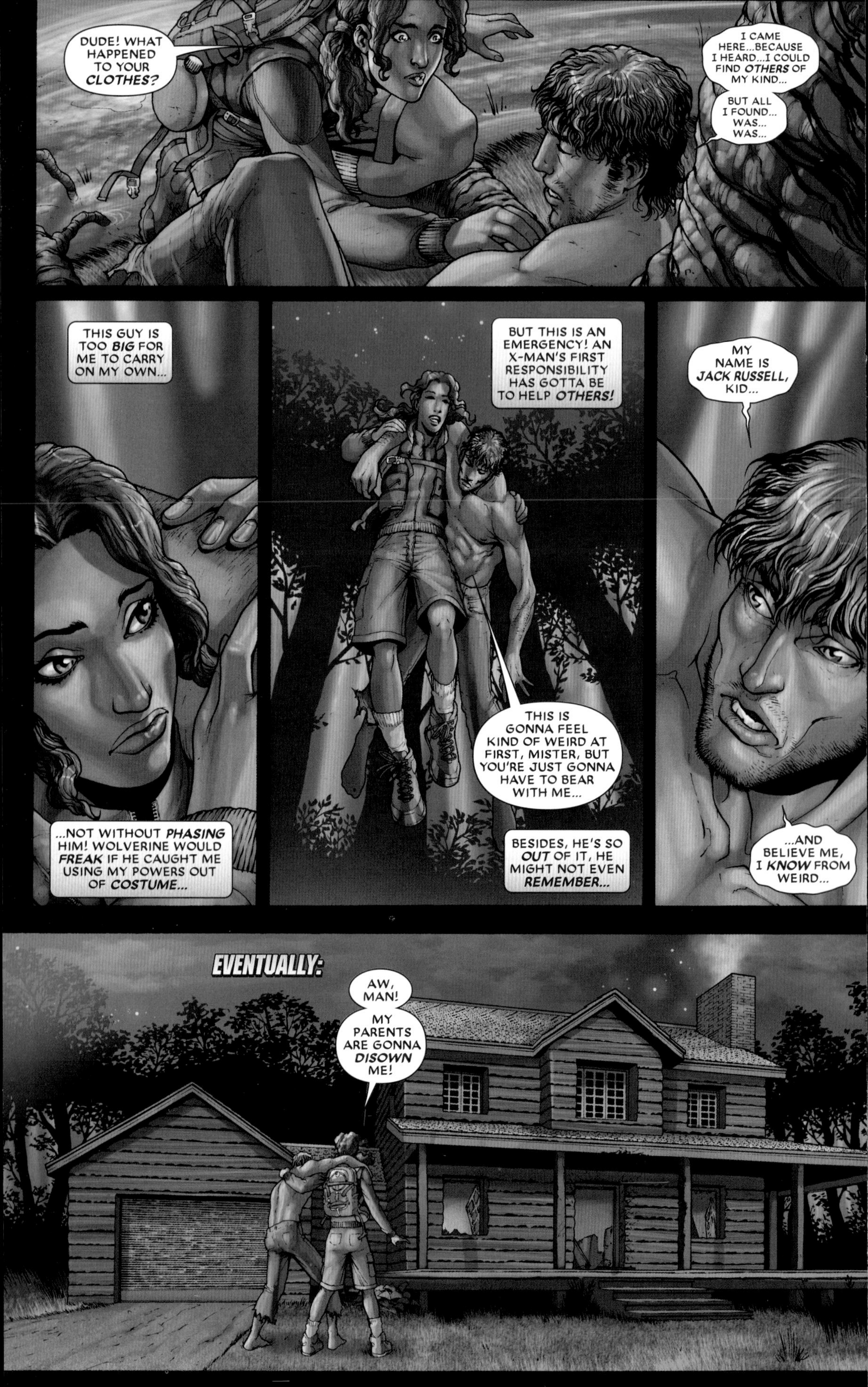
DUDE! WHAT HAPPENED TO YOUR CLOTHES?
I CAME HERE...BECAUSE I HEARD...I COULD FIND OTHERS OF MY KIND...
BUT ALL I FOUND... WAS... WAS...
THIS GUY IS TOO BIG FOR ME TO CARRY ON MY OWN...
...NOT WITHOUT PHASING HIM! WOLVERINE WOULD FREAK IF HE CAUGHT ME USING MY POWERS OUT OF COSTUME...
BUT THIS IS AN EMERGENCY! AN X-MAN'S FIRST RESPONSIBILITY HAS GOTTA BE TO HELP OTHERS!
THIS IS GONNA FEEL KIND OF WEIRD AT FIRST, MISTER, BUT YOU'RE JUST GONNA HAVE TO BEAR WITH ME...
BESIDES, HE'S SO OUT OF IT, HE MIGHT NOT EVEN REMEMBER...
MY NAME IS JACK RUSSELL, KID...
...AND BELIEVE ME, I KNOW FROM WEIRD...
EVENTUALLY:
AW, MAN!
MY PARENTS ARE GONNA DISOWN ME!

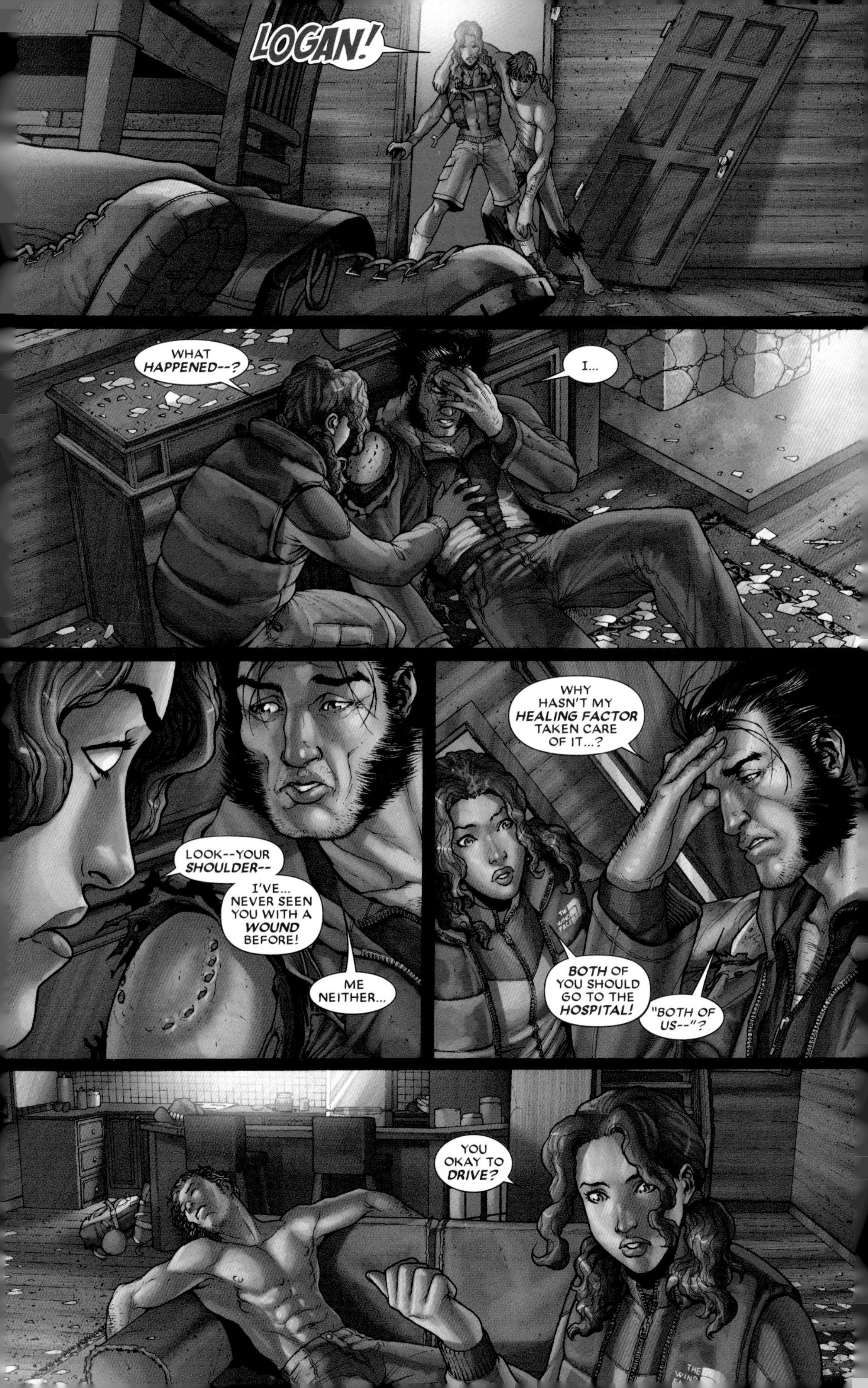
LOGAN!
WHAT HAPPENED--?
I...
LOOK--YOUR SHOULDER--
I'VE... NEVER SEEN YOU WITH A WOUND BEFORE!
ME NEITHER...
WHY HASN'T MY HEALING FACTOR TAKEN CARE OF IT...?
BOTH OF YOU SHOULD GO TO THE HOSPITAL!
"BOTH OF US--"?
YOU OKAY TO DRIVE?

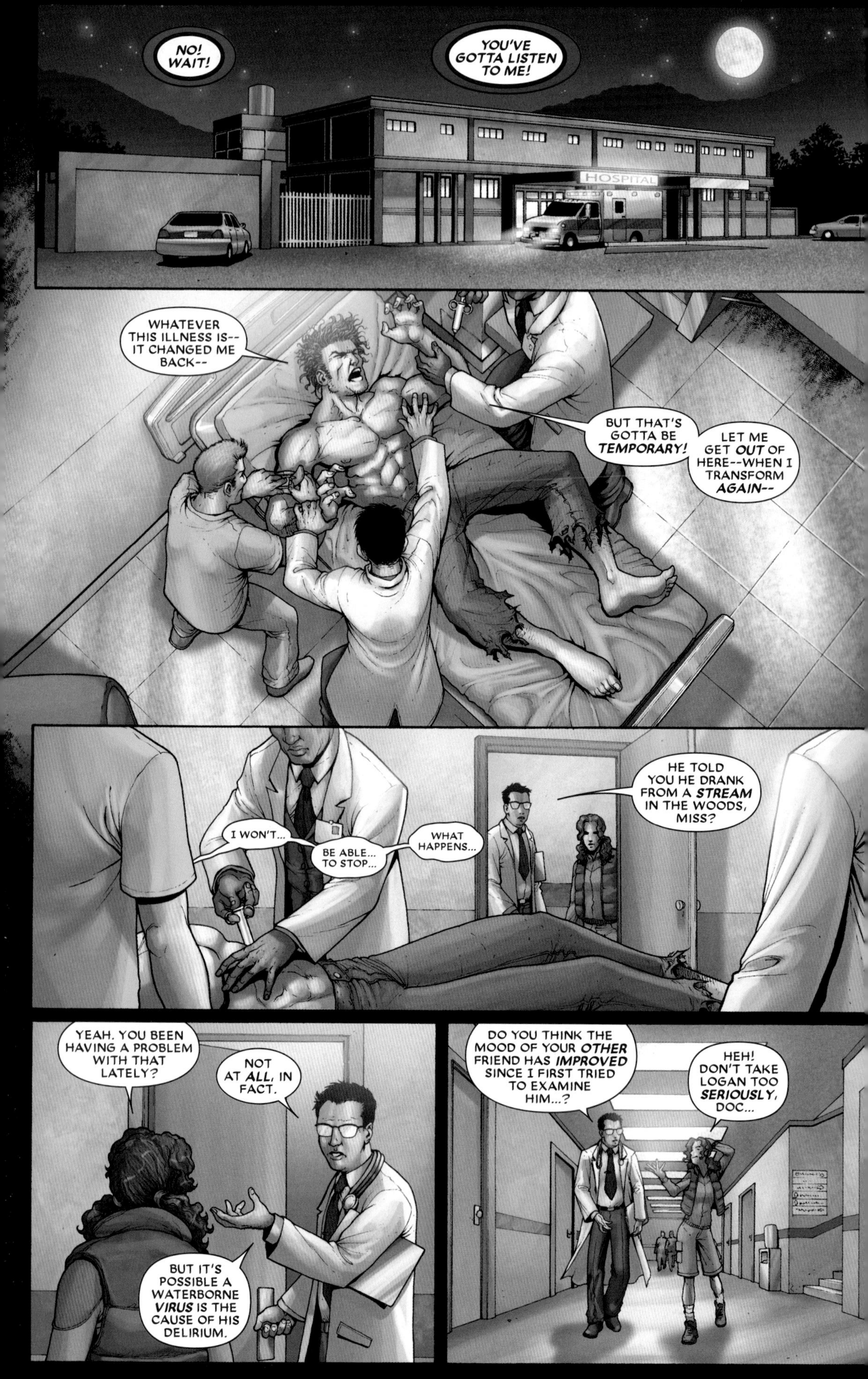
NO! WAIT!
YOU'VE GOTTA LISTEN TO ME!
HOSPITAL
WHATEVER THIS ILLNESS IS-- IT CHANGED ME BACK--
BUT THAT'S GOTTA BE TEMPORARY!
LET ME GET OUT OF HERE--WHEN I TRANSFORM AGAIN--
I WON'T...
BE ABLE... TO STOP...
WHAT HAPPENS...
HE TOLD YOU HE DRANK FROM A STREAM IN THE WOODS, MISS?
YEAH. YOU BEEN HAVING A PROBLEM WITH THAT LATELY?
NOT AT ALL, IN FACT.
BUT IT'S POSSIBLE A WATERBORNE VIRUS IS THE CAUSE OF HIS DELIRIUM.
DO YOU THINK THE MOOD OF YOUR OTHER FRIEND HAS IMPROVED SINCE I FIRST TRIED TO EXAMINE HIM...?
HEH! DON'T TAKE LOGAN TOO SERIOUSLY, DOC...

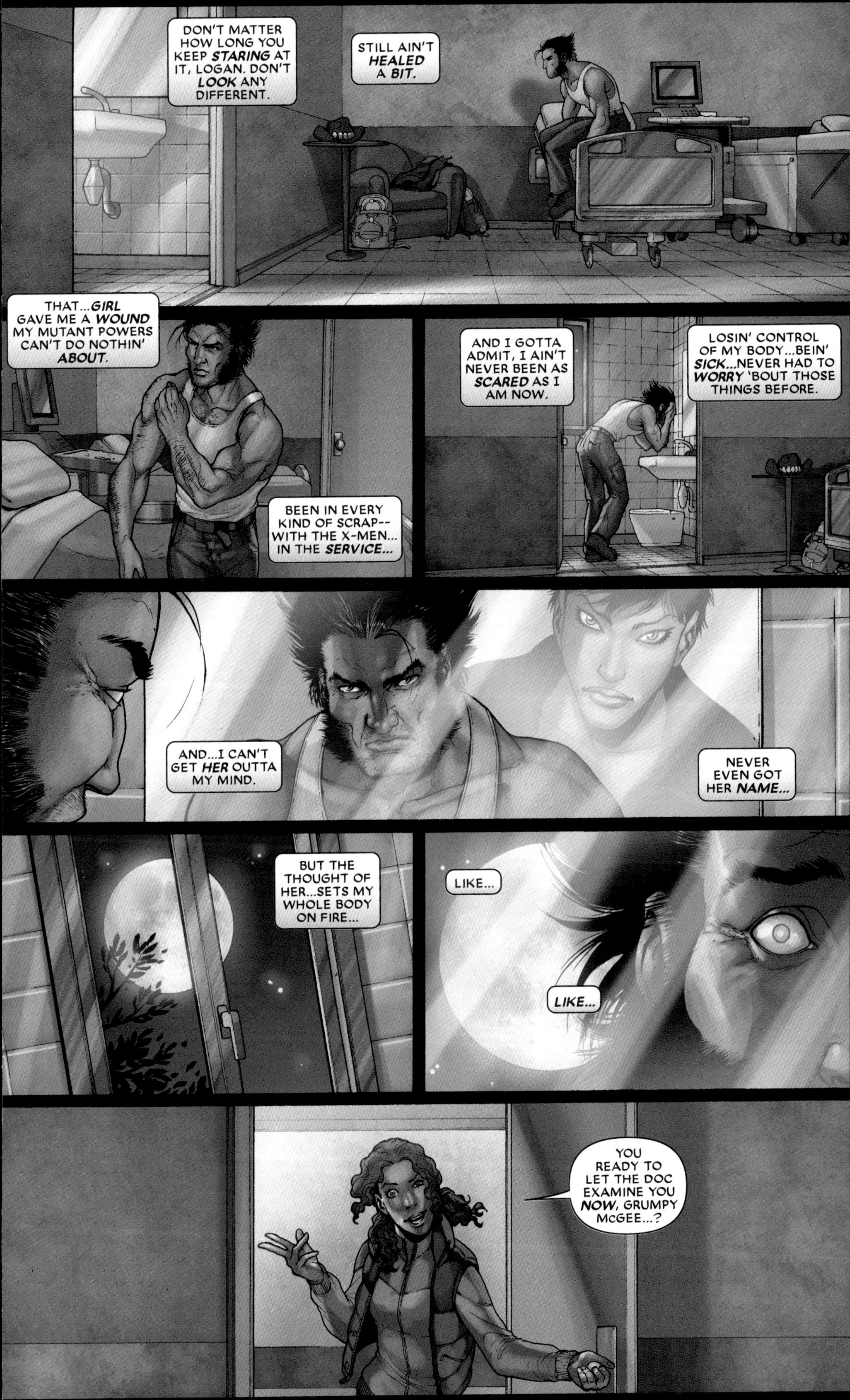
DON'T MATTER HOW LONG YOU KEEP STARING AT IT, LOGAN. DON'T LOOK ANY DIFFERENT.
STILL AIN'T HEALED A BIT.
THAT...GIRL GAVE ME A WOUND MY MUTANT POWERS CAN'T DO NOTHIN' ABOUT.
BEEN IN EVERY KIND OF SCRAP-- WITH THE X-MEN... IN THE SERVICE...
AND I GOTTA ADMIT, I AIN'T NEVER BEEN AS SCARED AS I AM NOW.
LOSIN' CONTROL OF MY BODY...BEIN' SICK...NEVER HAD TO WORRY 'BOUT THOSE THINGS BEFORE.
AND...I CAN'T GET HER OUTTA MY MIND.
NEVER EVEN GOT HER NAME...
BUT THE THOUGHT OF HER...SETS MY WHOLE BODY ON FIRE...
LIKE...
LIKE...
YOU READY TO LET THE DOC EXAMINE YOU NOW, GRUMPY McGEE...?

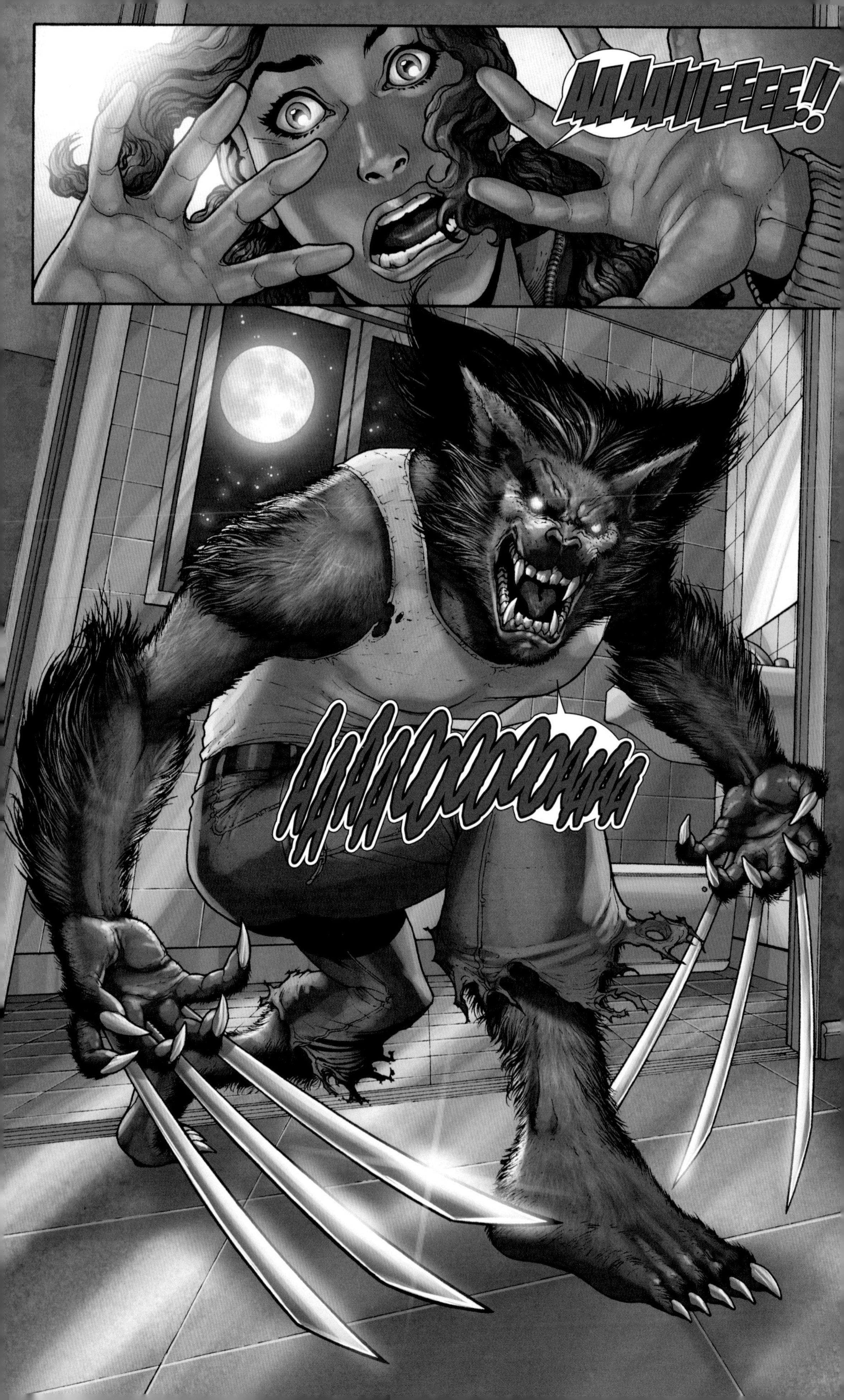
AAAAIIIEEEEE!!
AAAAOOOOOAAAA

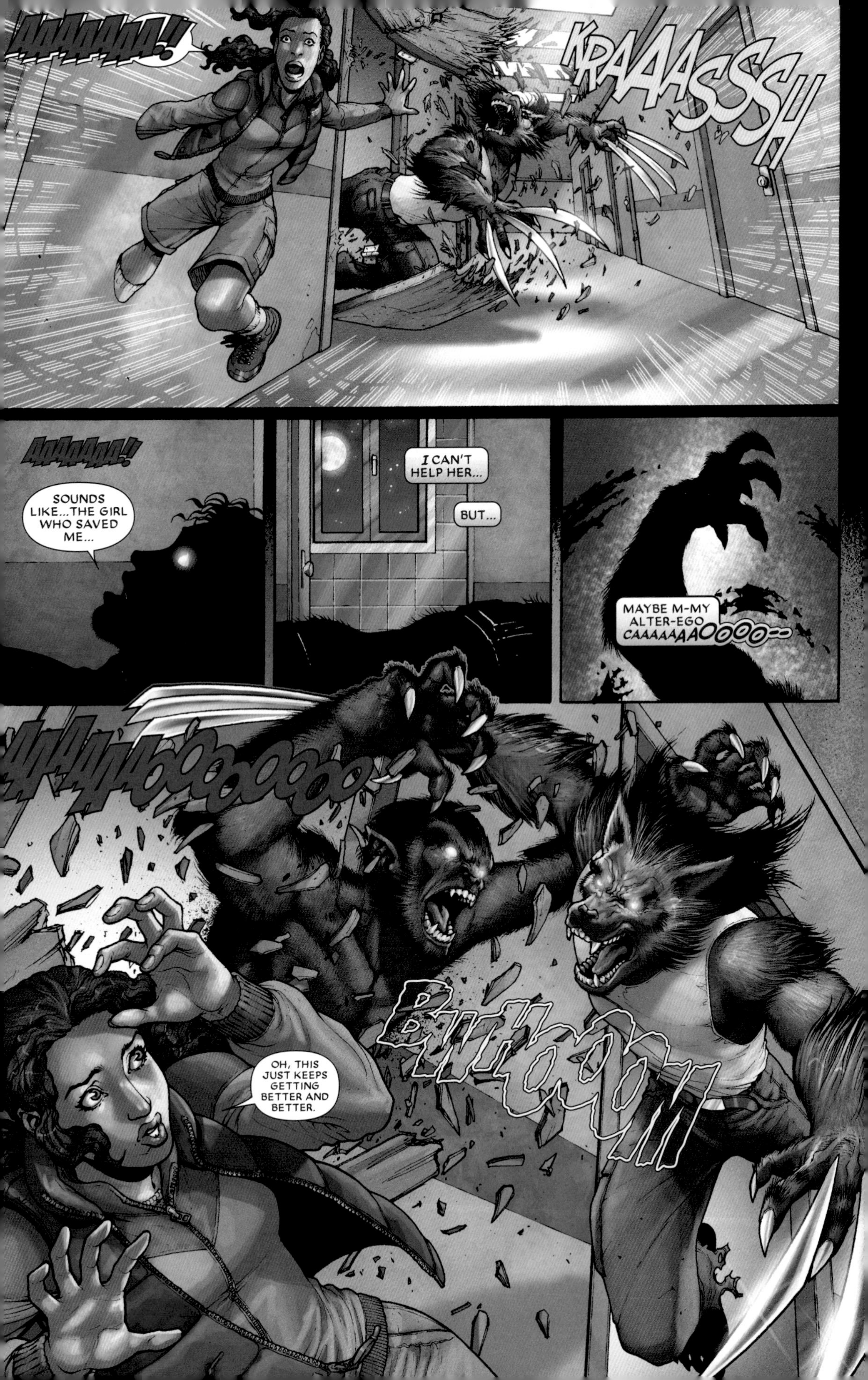
AAAAAAA!!
KRAAASSSH
AAAAAAA!!
SOUNDS LIKE...THE GIRL WHO SAVED ME...
I CAN'T HELP HER...
BUT...
MAYBE M-MY ALTER-EGO CAAAAAAAOOOO--
AAAAOOOOOOOOO
BUDOOOM
OH, THIS JUST KEEPS GETTING BETTER AND BETTER.

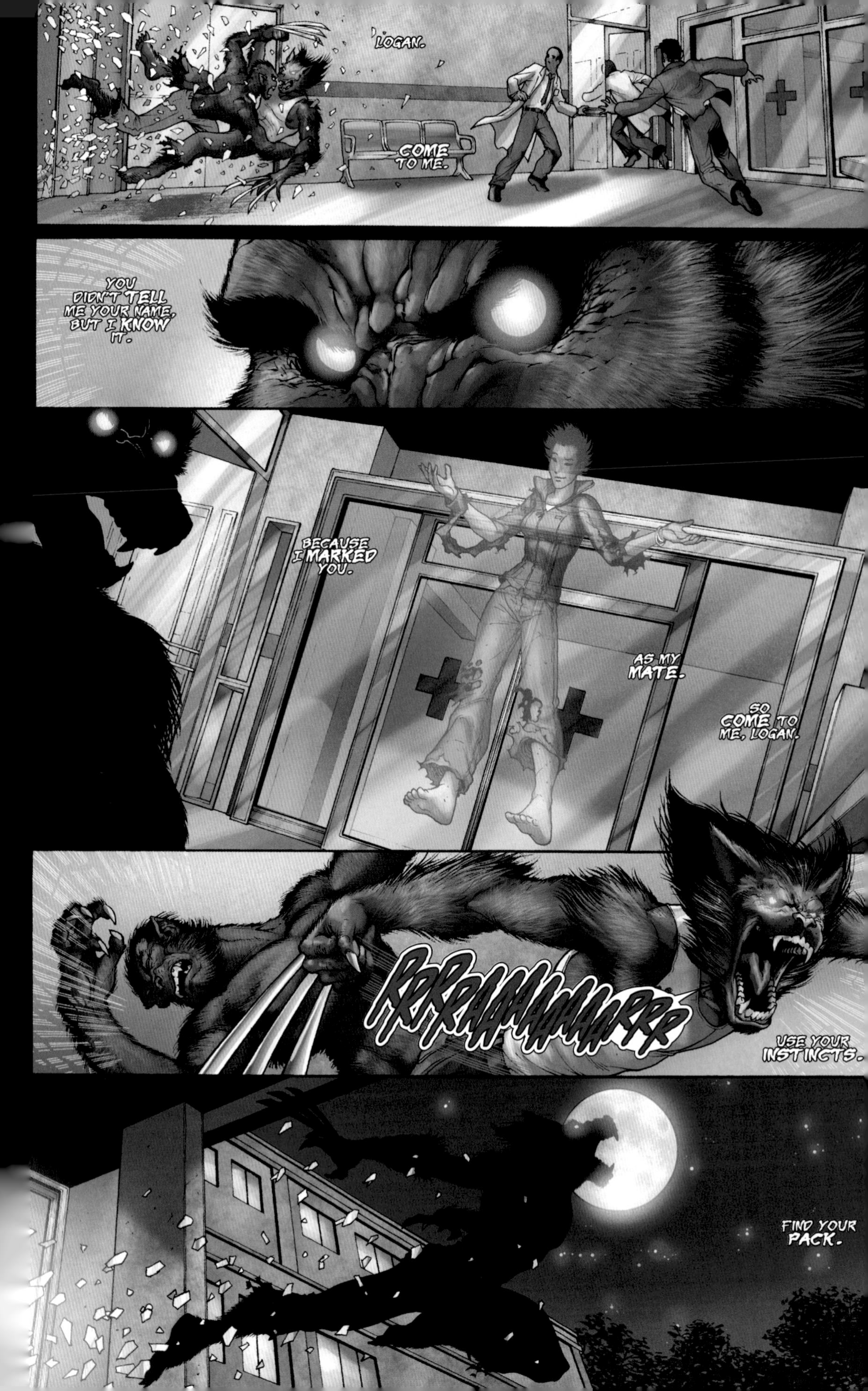
LOGAN.
COME TO ME.
YOU DIDN'T TELL ME YOUR NAME, BUT I KNOW IT.
BECAUSE I MARKED YOU.
AS MY MATE.
SO COME TO ME, LOGAN.
RRRRAAAAAAAAAARRR
USE YOUR INSTINCTS.
FIND YOUR PACK.

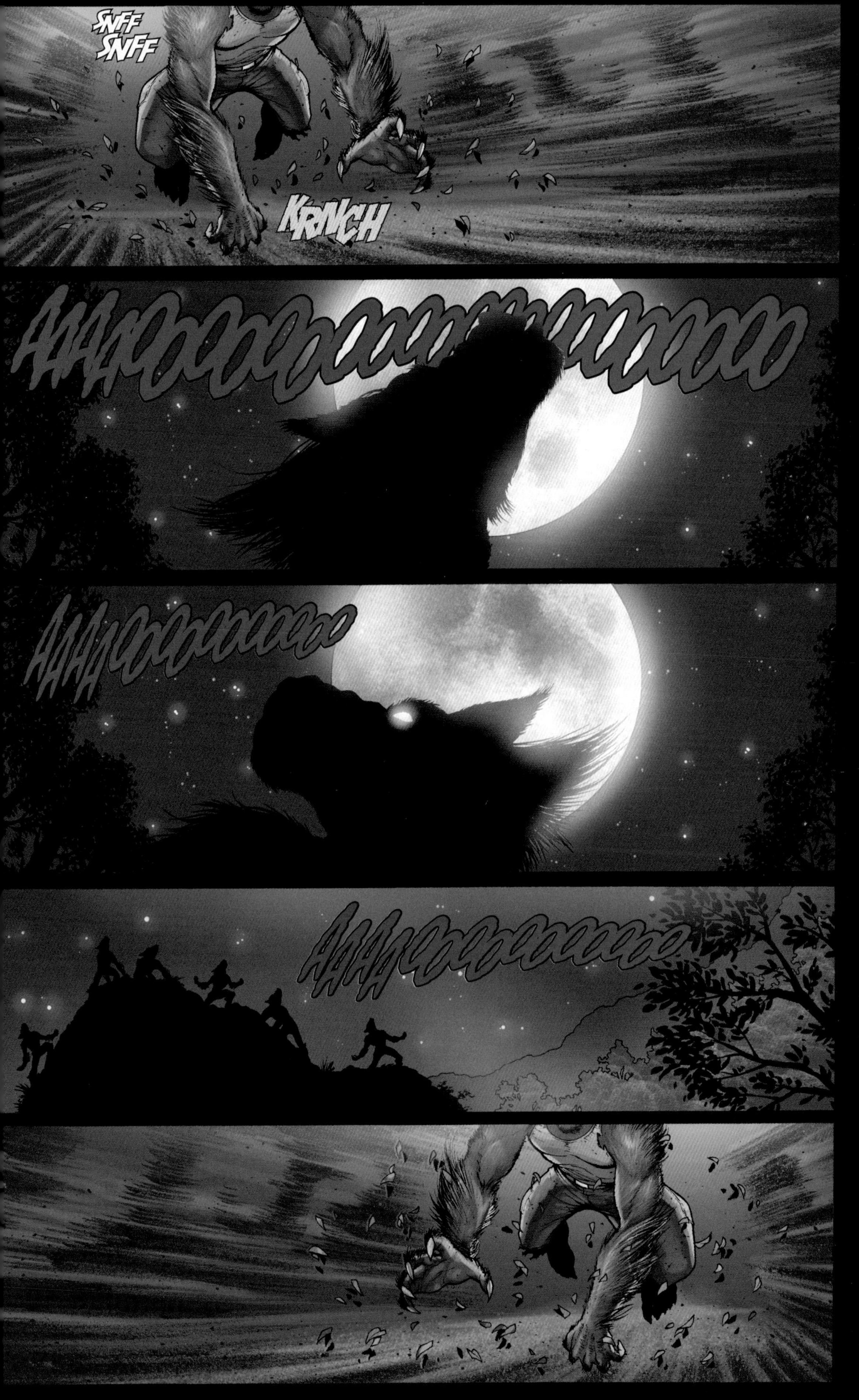
SNFF
SNFF
KRNCH
AAAHOOOOOOOOOOOOOOOO
AAAHOOOOOOOOOOO
AAAHOOOOOOOOOOO

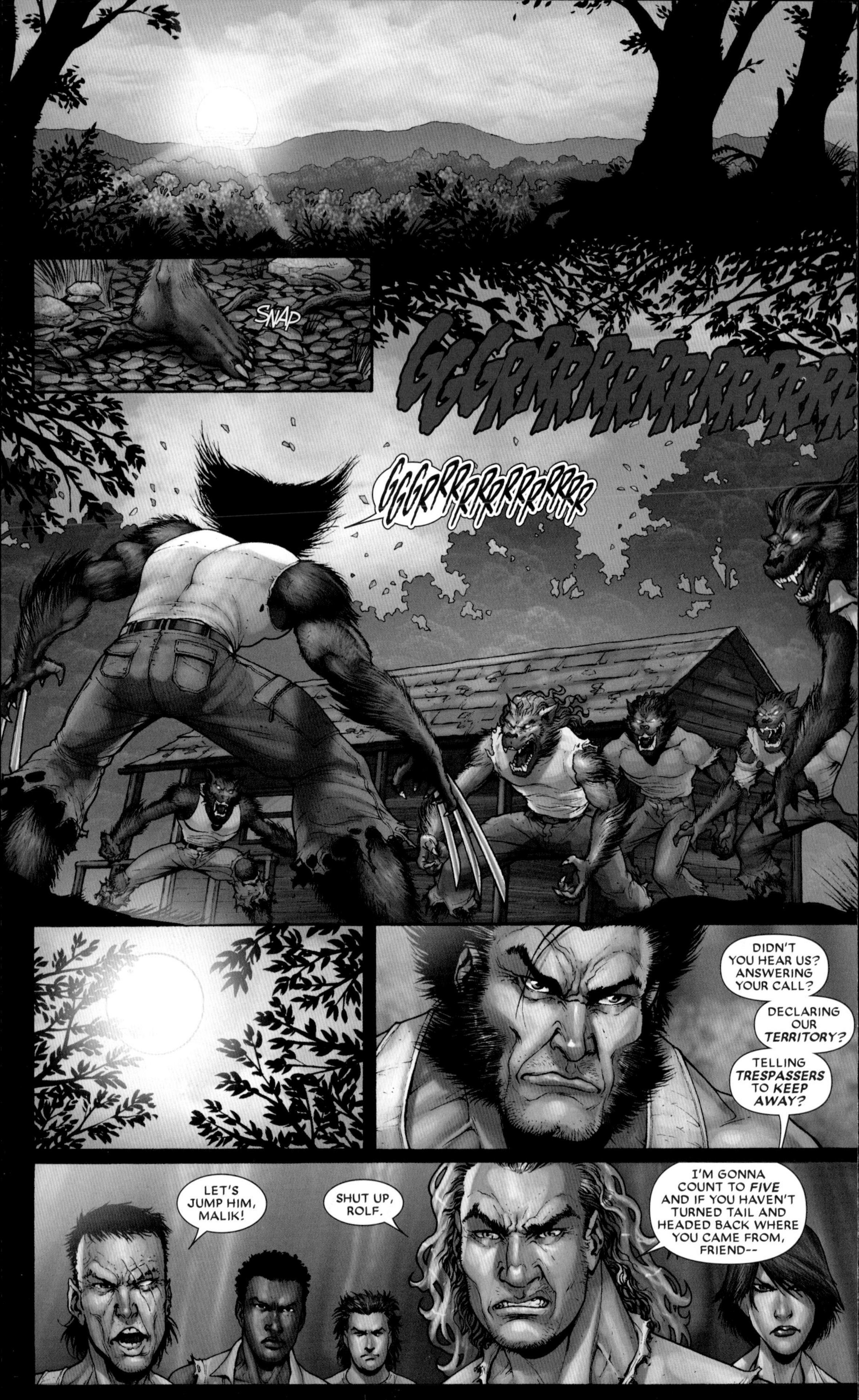
SNAP
GGRRRRRRRRRRRRR
GGRRRRRRRRRRRR
DIDN'T YOU HEAR US? ANSWERING YOUR CALL?
DECLARING OUR *TERRITORY*?
TELLING ***TRESPASSERS*** TO ***KEEP AWAY?***
LET'S JUMP HIM, MALIK!
SHUT UP, ROLF.
I'M GONNA COUNT TO *FIVE* AND IF YOU HAVEN'T TURNED TAIL AND HEADED BACK WHERE YOU CAME FROM, FRIEND--

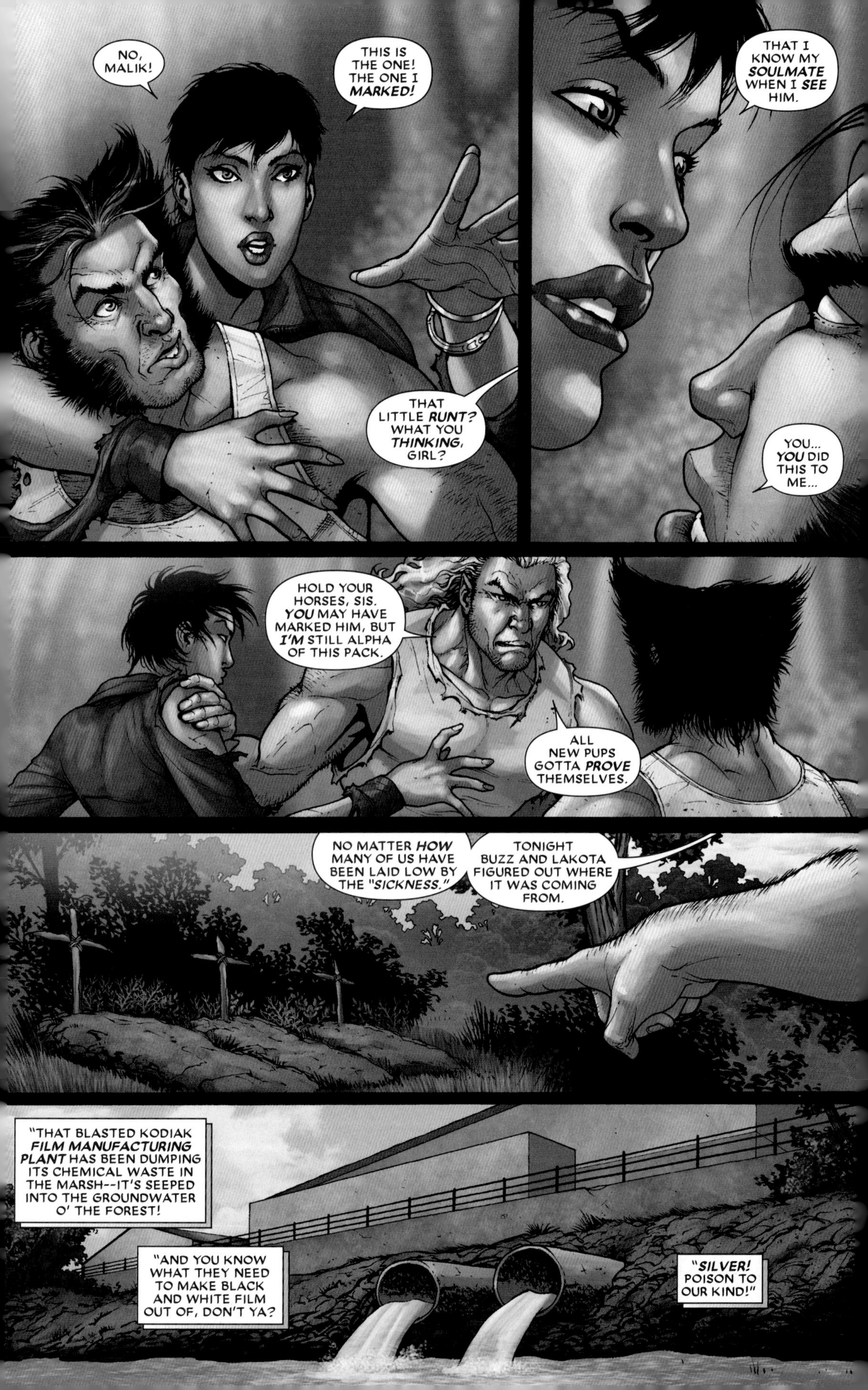
NO, MALIK!
THIS IS THE ONE! THE ONE I MARKED!
THAT LITTLE RUNT? WHAT YOU THINKING, GIRL?
THAT I KNOW MY SOULMATE WHEN I SEE HIM.
YOU... YOU DID THIS TO ME...
HOLD YOUR HORSES, SIS. YOU MAY HAVE MARKED HIM, BUT I'M STILL ALPHA OF THIS PACK.
ALL NEW PUPS GOTTA PROVE THEMSELVES.
NO MATTER HOW MANY OF US HAVE BEEN LAID LOW BY THE "SICKNESS."
TONIGHT BUZZ AND LAKOTA FIGURED OUT WHERE IT WAS COMING FROM.
"THAT BLASTED KODIAK FILM MANUFACTURING PLANT HAS BEEN DUMPING ITS CHEMICAL WASTE IN THE MARSH--IT'S SEEPED INTO THE GROUNDWATER O' THE FOREST!
"AND YOU KNOW WHAT THEY NEED TO MAKE BLACK AND WHITE FILM OUT OF, DON'T YA?
"SILVER! POISON TO OUR KIND!"

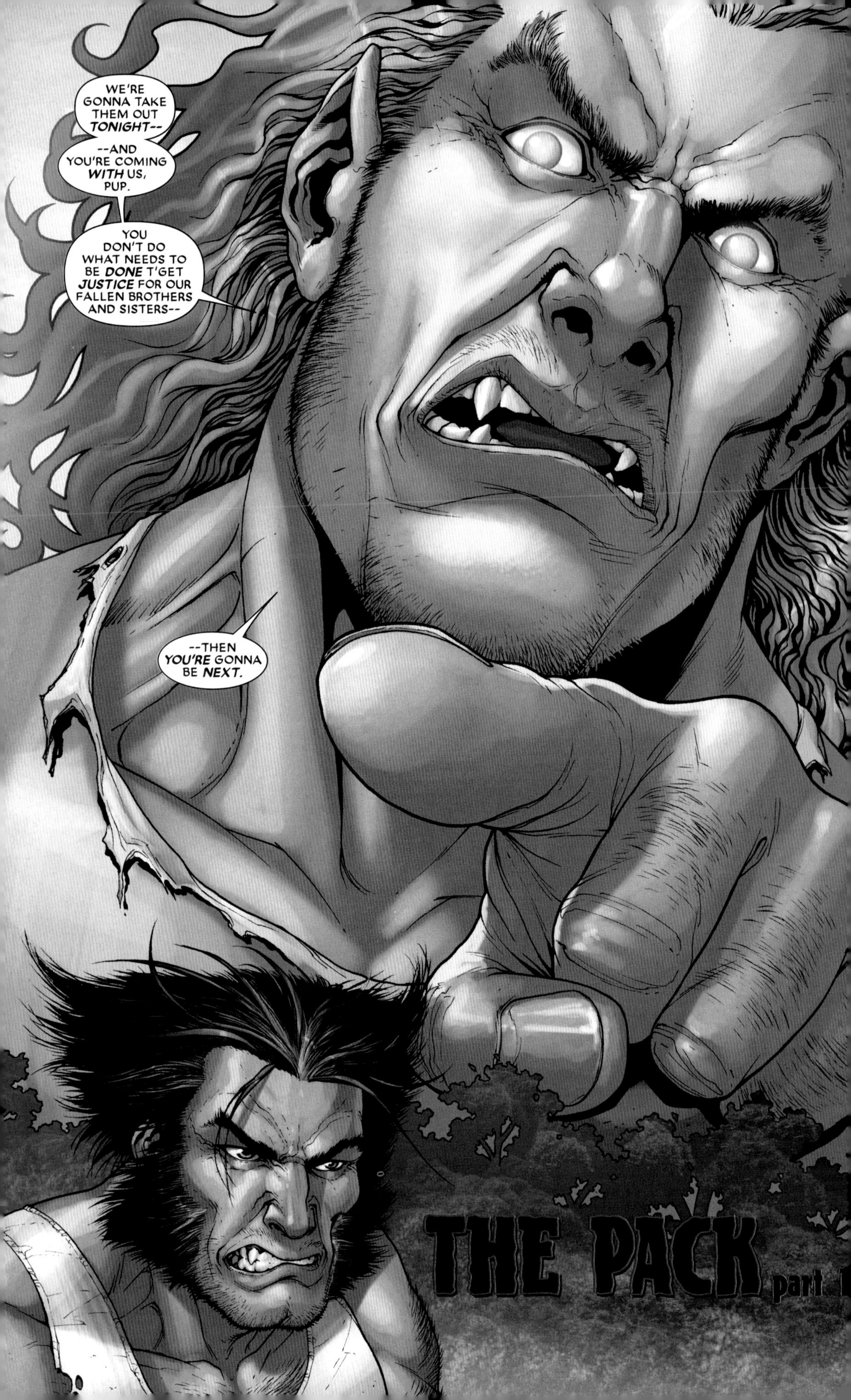
WE'RE GONNA TAKE THEM OUT *TONIGHT*--
--AND YOU'RE COMING *WITH* US, PUP.
YOU DON'T DO WHAT NEEDS TO BE *DONE* T'GET *JUSTICE* FOR OUR FALLEN BROTHERS AND SISTERS--
--THEN *YOU'RE* GONNA BE *NEXT.*
THE PACK part

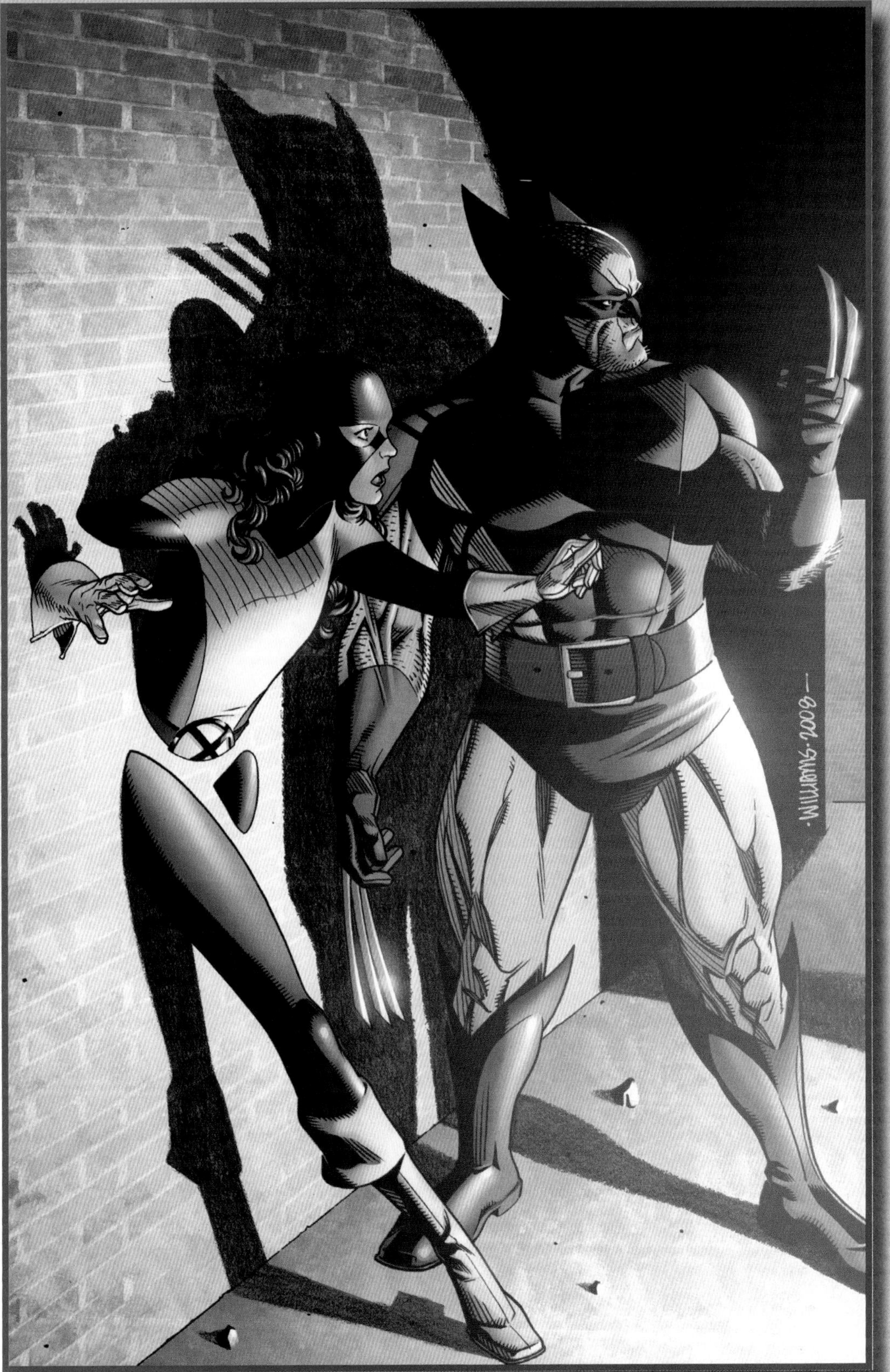
WILLIAMS·2008

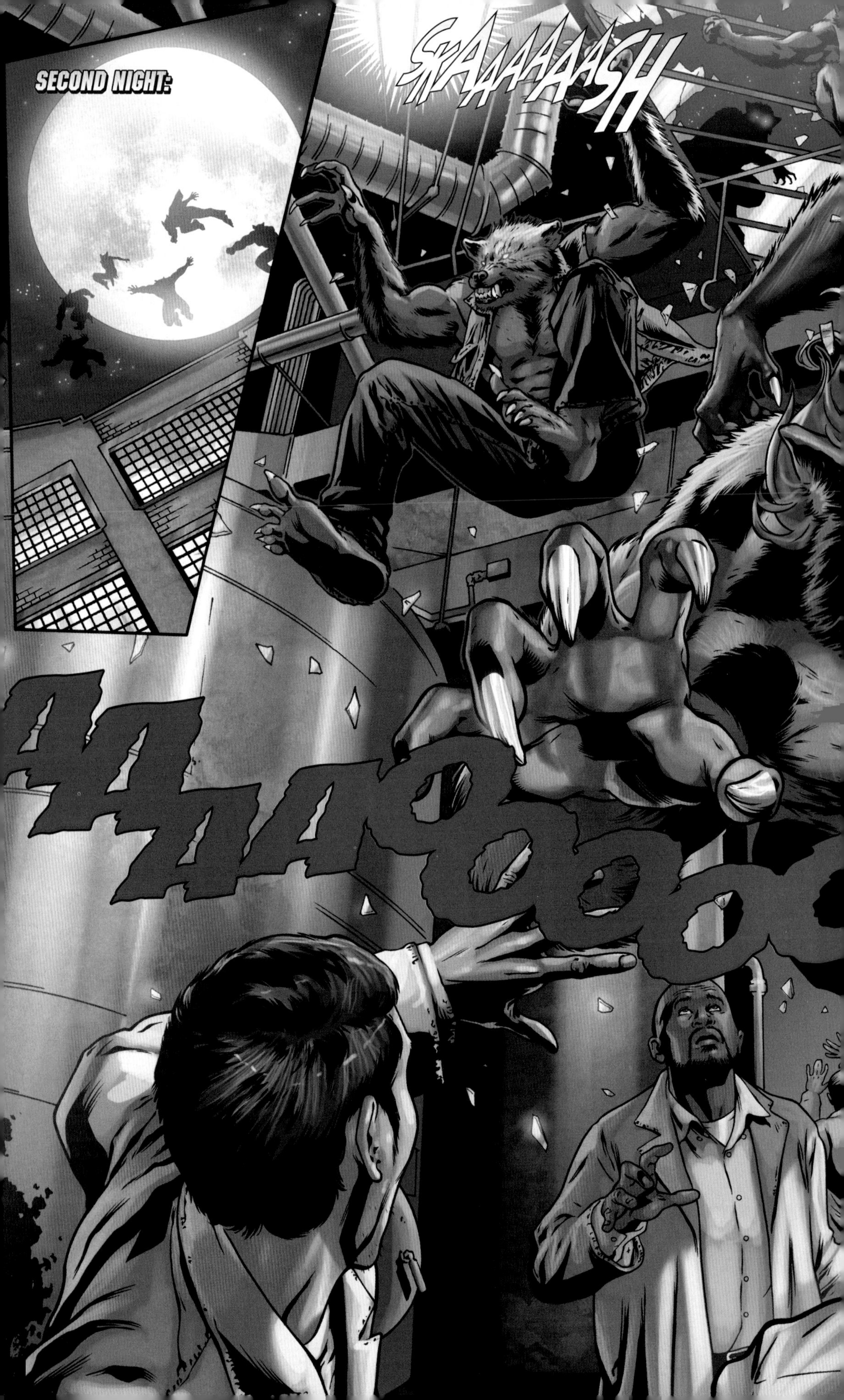
SECOND NIGHT:
SKRAAAAAASH
AHHROOOO

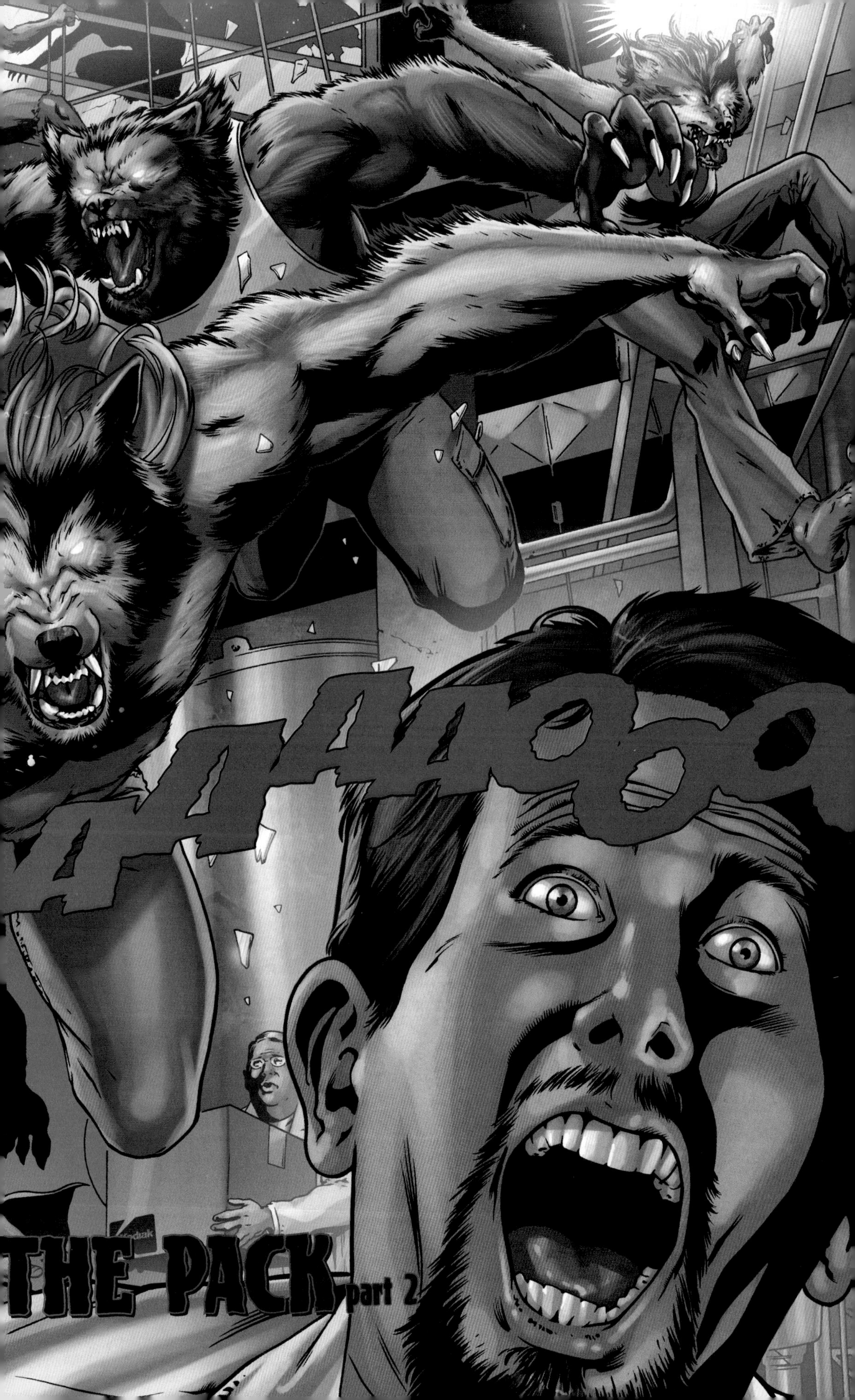
THE PACK, part 2

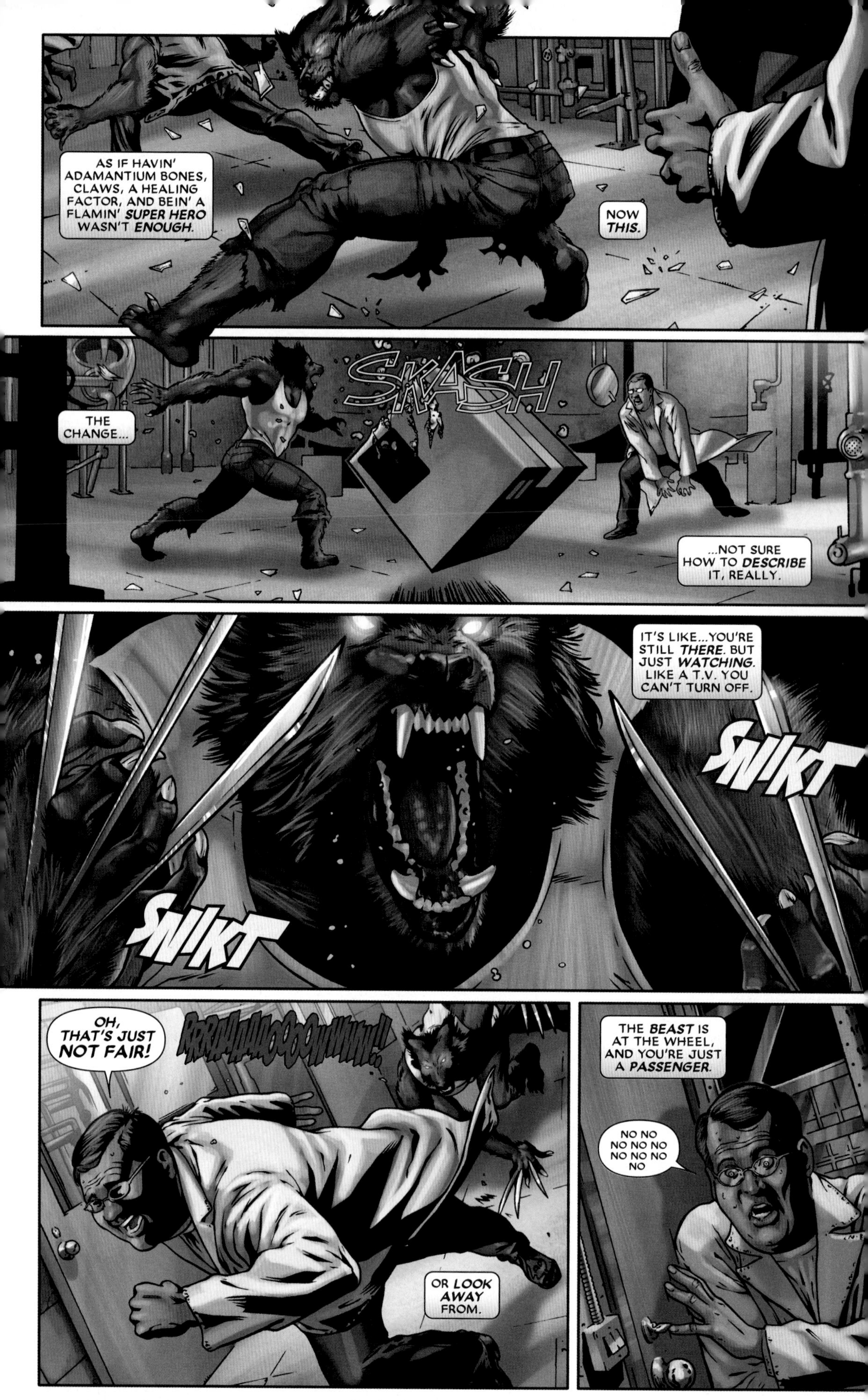
AS IF HAVIN' ADAMANTIUM BONES, CLAWS, A HEALING FACTOR, AND BEIN' A FLAMIN' *SUPER HERO* WASN'T *ENOUGH*.
NOW *THIS*.
THE CHANGE...
SKASH
...NOT SURE HOW TO *DESCRIBE* IT, REALLY.
IT'S LIKE...YOU'RE STILL *THERE*. BUT JUST *WATCHING*. LIKE A T.V. YOU CAN'T TURN OFF.
SNIKT
SNIKT
OH, THAT'S JUST **NOT FAIR!**
RRRAAAAAOOOOWWWW!!
OR *LOOK AWAY* FROM.
THE *BEAST* IS AT THE WHEEL, AND YOU'RE JUST A *PASSENGER*.
NO NO NO NO NO NO NO NO NO

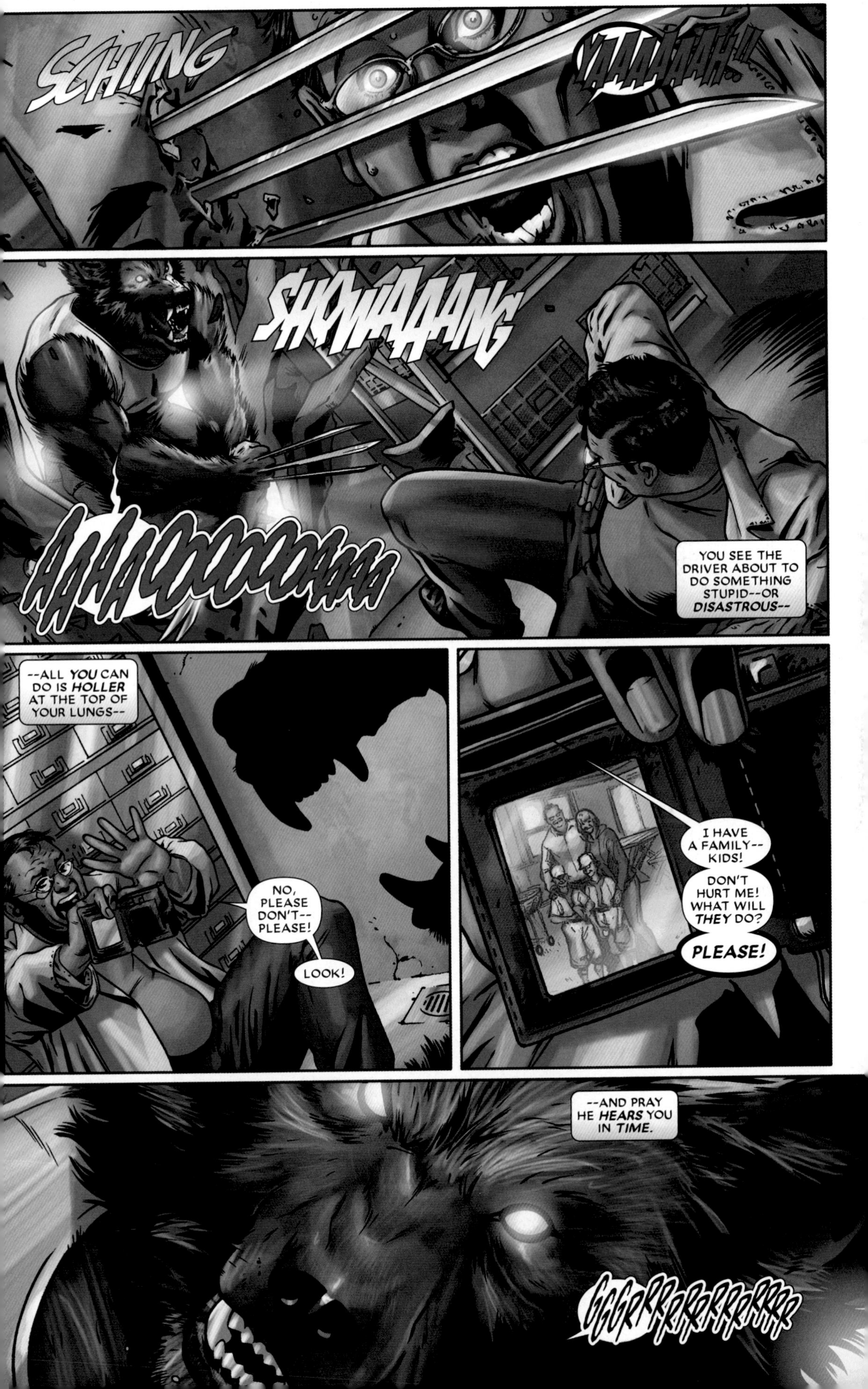
SCHIING
YAAAAAAH!!
SHOWAAANG
AAAAOOOOOAAAA
YOU SEE THE DRIVER ABOUT TO DO SOMETHING STUPID--OR DISASTROUS--
--ALL YOU CAN DO IS HOLLER AT THE TOP OF YOUR LUNGS--
NO, PLEASE DON'T--PLEASE!
LOOK!
I HAVE A FAMILY--KIDS!
DON'T HURT ME! WHAT WILL THEY DO?
PLEASE!
--AND PRAY HE HEARS YOU IN TIME.
GGGRRRRRRRRRRRR

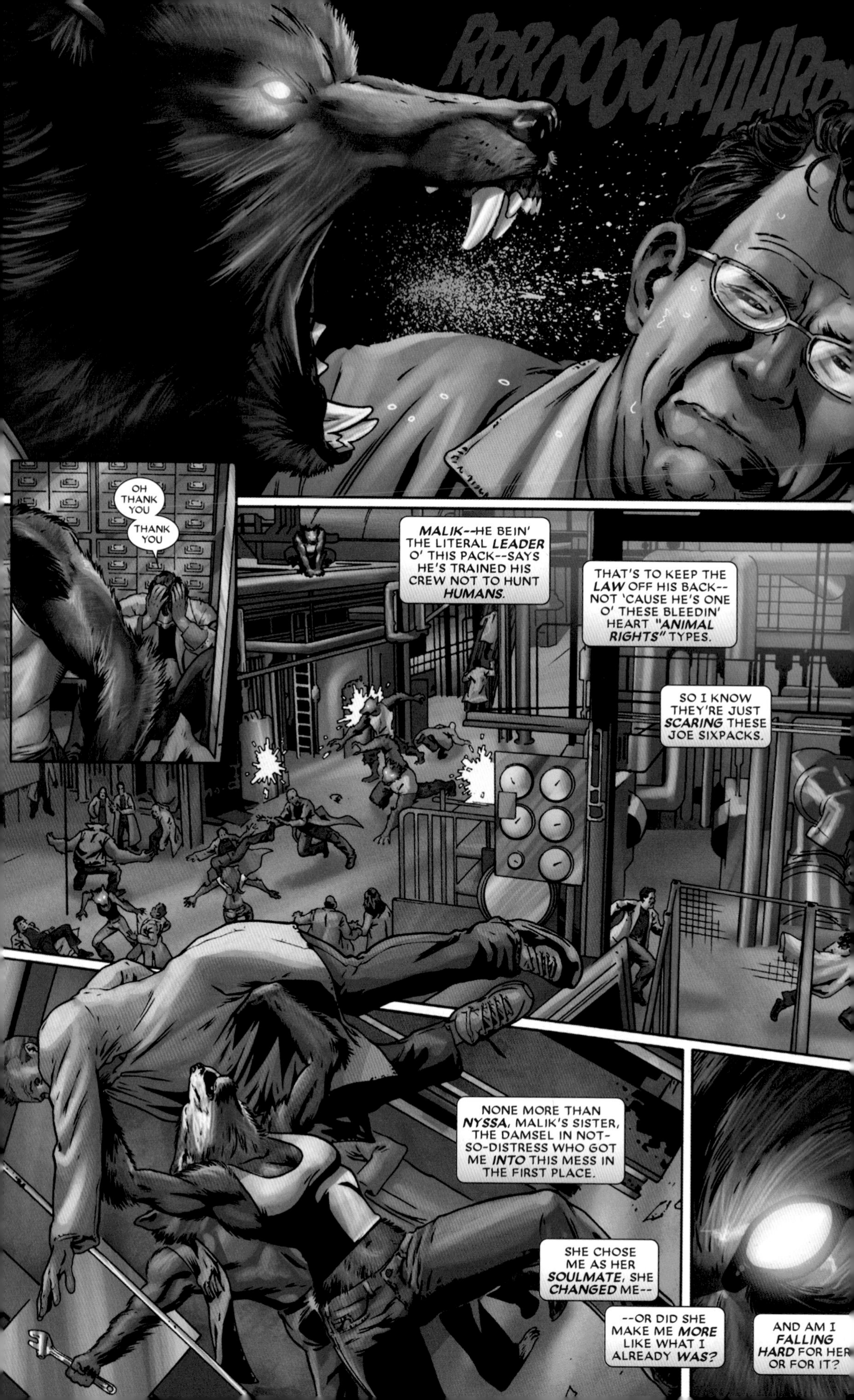
RRROOOOAAARR
OH THANK YOU
THANK YOU
MALIK--HE BEIN' THE LITERAL LEADER O' THIS PACK--SAYS HE'S TRAINED HIS CREW NOT TO HUNT HUMANS.
THAT'S TO KEEP THE LAW OFF HIS BACK--NOT 'CAUSE HE'S ONE O' THESE BLEEDIN' HEART "ANIMAL RIGHTS" TYPES.
SO I KNOW THEY'RE JUST SCARING THESE JOE SIXPACKS.
NONE MORE THAN NYSSA, MALIK'S SISTER, THE DAMSEL IN NOT-SO-DISTRESS WHO GOT ME INTO THIS MESS IN THE FIRST PLACE.
SHE CHOSE ME AS HER SOULMATE, SHE CHANGED ME--
--OR DID SHE MAKE ME MORE LIKE WHAT I ALREADY WAS?
AND AM I FALLING HARD FOR HER OR FOR IT?

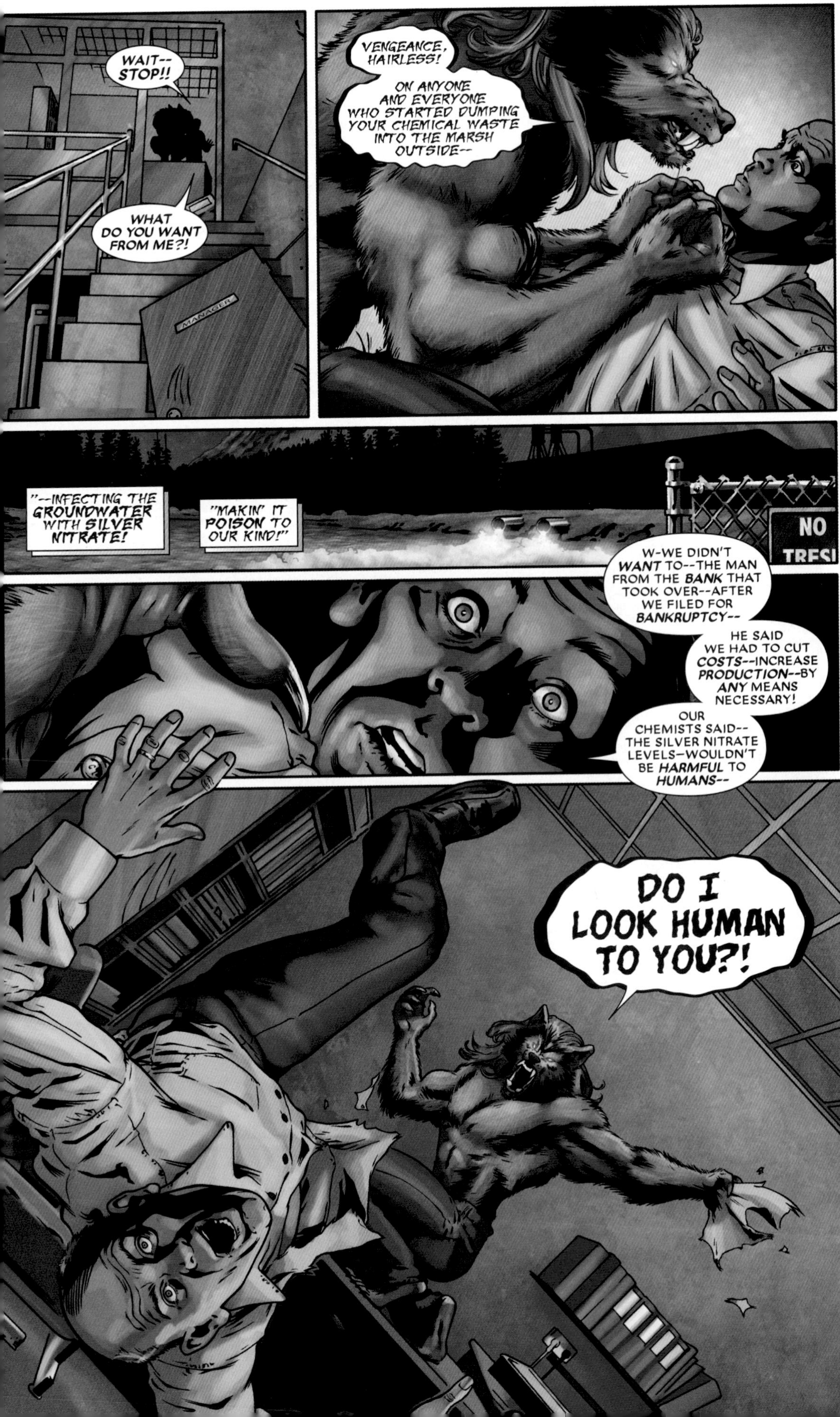
WAIT--
STOP!!
WHAT
DO YOU WANT
FROM ME?!
MANAGER
VENGEANCE,
HAIRLESS!
ON ANYONE
AND EVERYONE
WHO STARTED DUMPING
YOUR CHEMICAL WASTE
INTO THE MARSH
OUTSIDE--
"--INFECTING THE GROUNDWATER WITH SILVER NITRATE!
"MAKIN' IT POISON TO OUR KIND!"
NO
W-WE DIDN'T WANT TO--THE MAN FROM THE BANK THAT TOOK OVER--AFTER WE FILED FOR BANKRUPTCY--
HE SAID WE HAD TO CUT COSTS--INCREASE PRODUCTION--BY ANY MEANS NECESSARY!
OUR CHEMISTS SAID-- THE SILVER NITRATE LEVELS--WOULDN'T BE HARMFUL TO HUMANS--
DO I LOOK HUMAN TO YOU?!

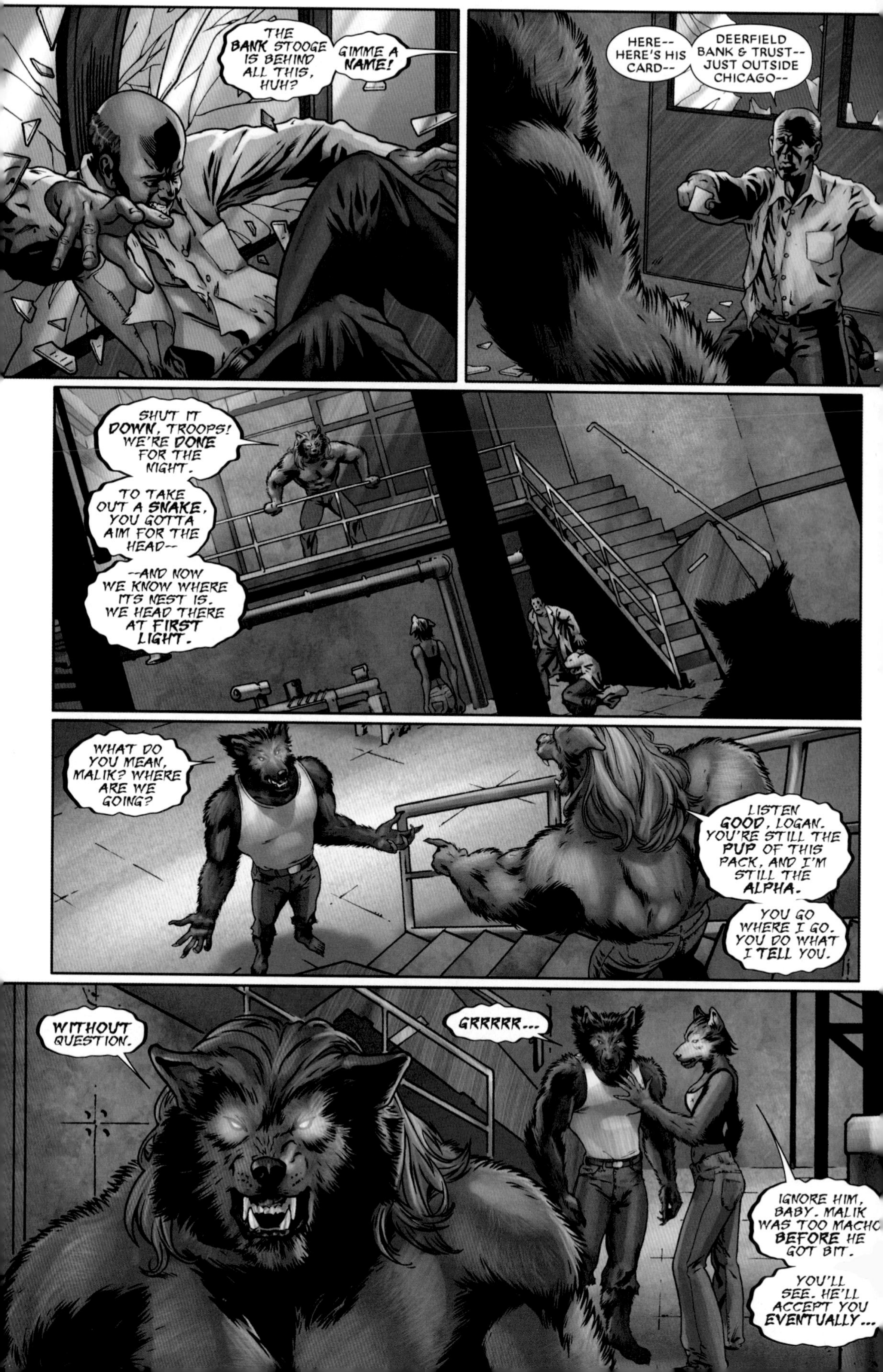
THE BANK STOOGE IS BEHIND ALL THIS, HUH?
GIMME A NAME!
HERE-- HERE'S HIS CARD--
DEERFIELD BANK & TRUST-- JUST OUTSIDE CHICAGO--
SHUT IT DOWN, TROOPS! WE'RE DONE FOR THE NIGHT.
TO TAKE OUT A SNAKE, YOU GOTTA AIM FOR THE HEAD--
--AND NOW WE KNOW WHERE ITS NEST IS. WE HEAD THERE AT FIRST LIGHT.
WHAT DO YOU MEAN, MALIK? WHERE ARE WE GOING?
LISTEN GOOD, LOGAN. YOU'RE STILL THE PUP OF THIS PACK, AND I'M STILL THE ALPHA.
YOU GO WHERE I GO. YOU DO WHAT I TELL YOU.
WITHOUT QUESTION.
GRRRRR...
IGNORE HIM, BABY. MALIK WAS TOO MACHO BEFORE HE GOT BIT.
YOU'LL SEE. HE'LL ACCEPT YOU EVENTUALLY...

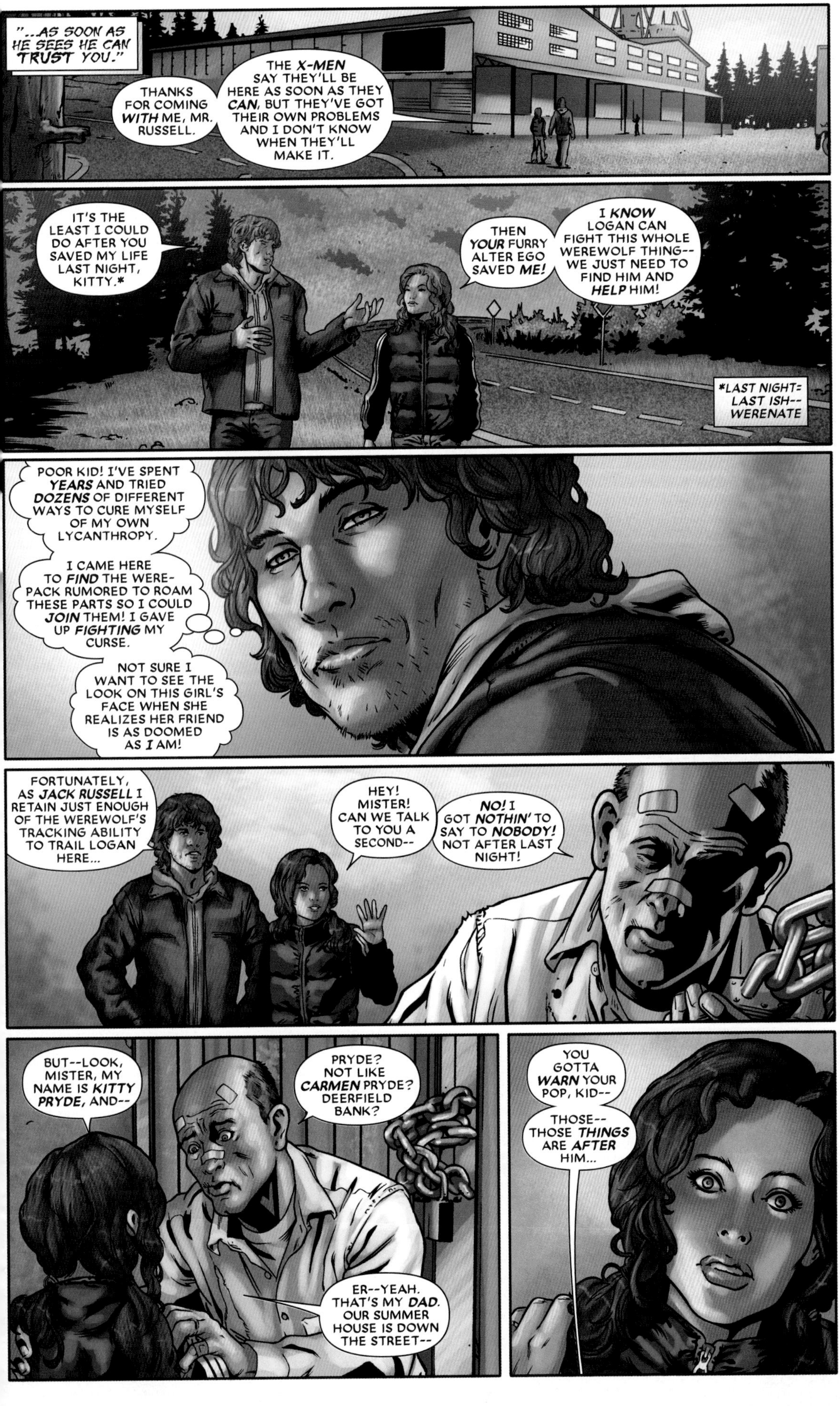
"...AS SOON AS HE SEES HE CAN TRUST YOU."
THANKS FOR COMING WITH ME, MR. RUSSELL.
THE X-MEN SAY THEY'LL BE HERE AS SOON AS THEY CAN, BUT THEY'VE GOT THEIR OWN PROBLEMS AND I DON'T KNOW WHEN THEY'LL MAKE IT.
IT'S THE LEAST I COULD DO AFTER YOU SAVED MY LIFE LAST NIGHT, KITTY.*
THEN YOUR FURRY ALTER EGO SAVED ME!
I KNOW LOGAN CAN FIGHT THIS WHOLE WEREWOLF THING-- WE JUST NEED TO FIND HIM AND HELP HIM!
*LAST NIGHT= LAST ISH-- WERENATE
POOR KID! I'VE SPENT YEARS AND TRIED DOZENS OF DIFFERENT WAYS TO CURE MYSELF OF MY OWN LYCANTHROPY.
I CAME HERE TO FIND THE WERE-PACK RUMORED TO ROAM THESE PARTS SO I COULD JOIN THEM! I GAVE UP FIGHTING MY CURSE.
NOT SURE I WANT TO SEE THE LOOK ON THIS GIRL'S FACE WHEN SHE REALIZES HER FRIEND IS AS DOOMED AS I AM!
FORTUNATELY, AS JACK RUSSELL I RETAIN JUST ENOUGH OF THE WEREWOLF'S TRACKING ABILITY TO TRAIL LOGAN HERE...
HEY! MISTER! CAN WE TALK TO YOU A SECOND--
NO! I GOT NOTHIN' TO SAY TO NOBODY! NOT AFTER LAST NIGHT!
BUT--LOOK, MISTER, MY NAME IS KITTY PRYDE, AND--
PRYDE? NOT LIKE CARMEN PRYDE? DEERFIELD BANK?
ER--YEAH. THAT'S MY DAD. OUR SUMMER HOUSE IS DOWN THE STREET--
YOU GOTTA WARN YOUR POP, KID--
THOSE-- THOSE THINGS ARE AFTER HIM...

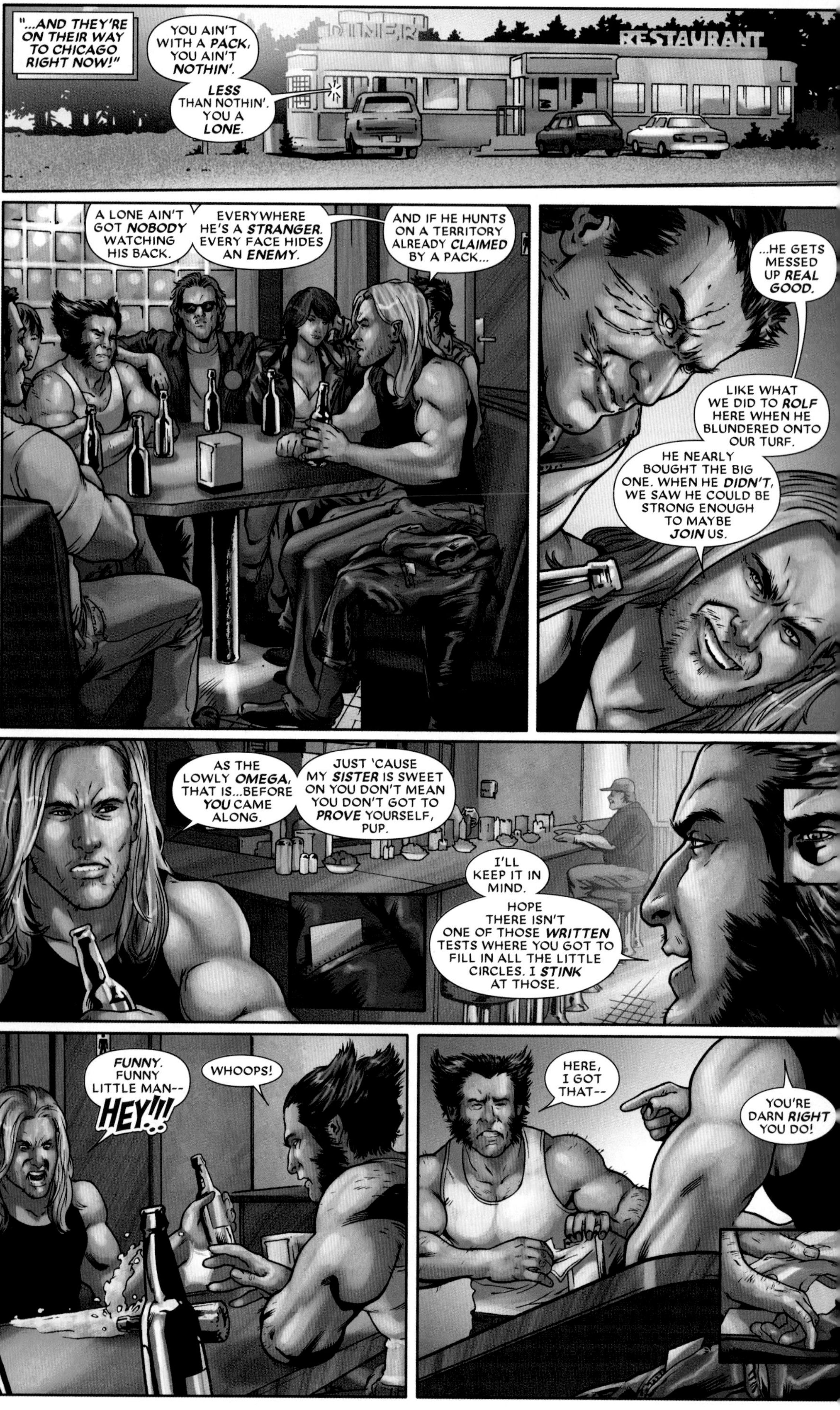

"...AND THEY'RE ON THEIR WAY TO CHICAGO RIGHT NOW!"
YOU AIN'T WITH A PACK, YOU AIN'T NOTHIN'.
LESS THAN NOTHIN'. YOU A LONE.
RESTAURANT
A LONE AIN'T GOT NOBODY WATCHING HIS BACK.
EVERYWHERE HE'S A STRANGER. EVERY FACE HIDES AN ENEMY.
AND IF HE HUNTS ON A TERRITORY ALREADY CLAIMED BY A PACK...
...HE GETS MESSED UP REAL GOOD.
LIKE WHAT WE DID TO ROLF HERE WHEN HE BLUNDERED ONTO OUR TURF.
HE NEARLY BOUGHT THE BIG ONE. WHEN HE DIDN'T, WE SAW HE COULD BE STRONG ENOUGH TO MAYBE JOIN US.
AS THE LOWLY OMEGA, THAT IS...BEFORE YOU CAME ALONG.
JUST 'CAUSE MY SISTER IS SWEET ON YOU DON'T MEAN YOU DON'T GOT TO PROVE YOURSELF, PUP.
I'LL KEEP IT IN MIND.
HOPE THERE ISN'T ONE OF THOSE WRITTEN TESTS WHERE YOU GOT TO FILL IN ALL THE LITTLE CIRCLES. I STINK AT THOSE.
FUNNY. FUNNY LITTLE MAN--
HEY!!!
WHOOPS!
HERE, I GOT THAT--
YOU'RE DARN RIGHT YOU DO!

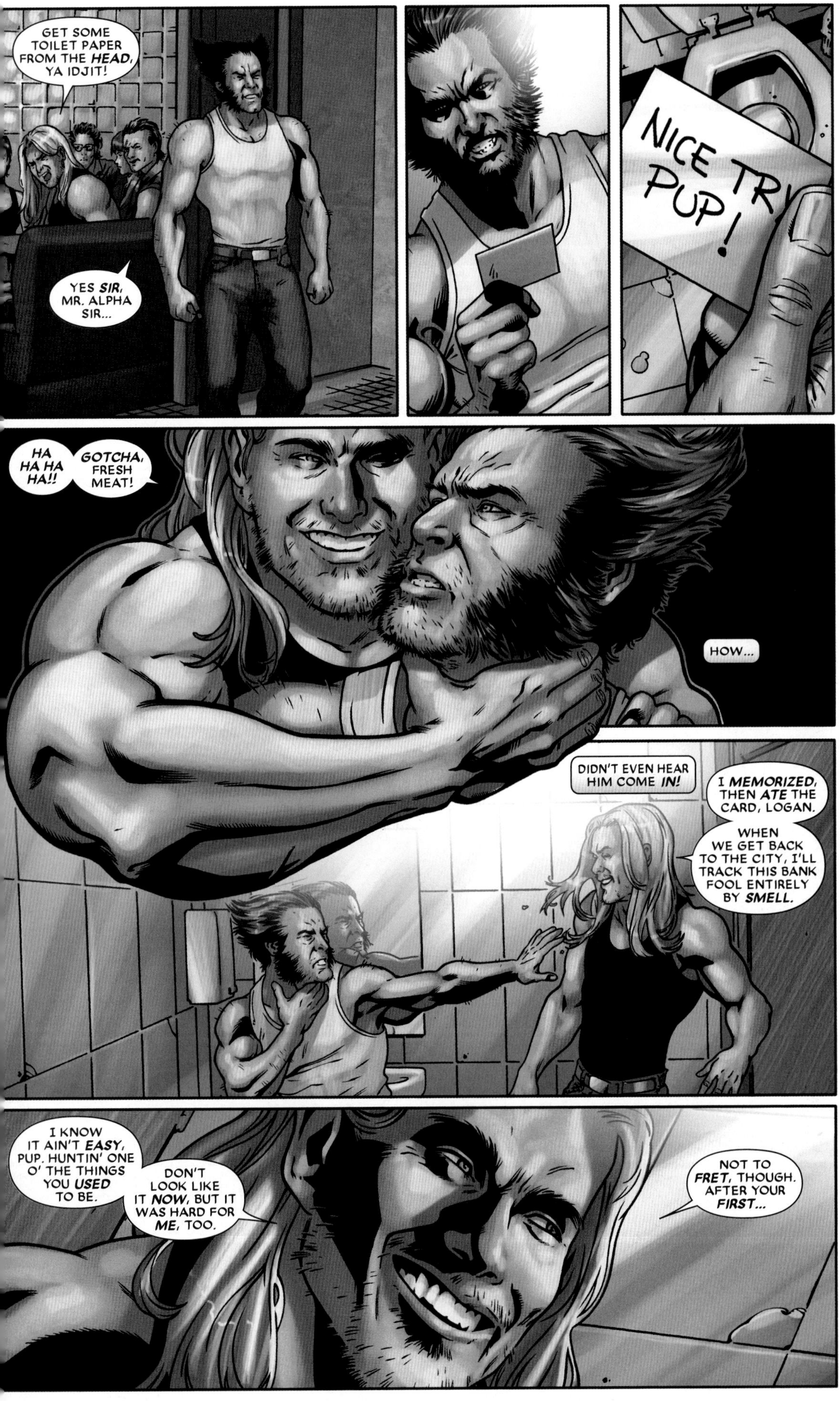
GET SOME TOILET PAPER FROM THE HEAD, YA IDJIT!
YES SIR, MR. ALPHA SIR...
NICE TRY PUP!
HA HA HA HA!!
GOTCHA, FRESH MEAT!
HOW...
DIDN'T EVEN HEAR HIM COME IN!
I MEMORIZED, THEN ATE THE CARD, LOGAN.
WHEN WE GET BACK TO THE CITY, I'LL TRACK THIS BANK FOOL ENTIRELY BY SMELL.
I KNOW IT AIN'T EASY, PUP. HUNTIN' ONE O' THE THINGS YOU USED TO BE.
DON'T LOOK LIKE IT NOW, BUT IT WAS HARD FOR ME, TOO.
NOT TO FRET, THOUGH. AFTER YOUR FIRST...

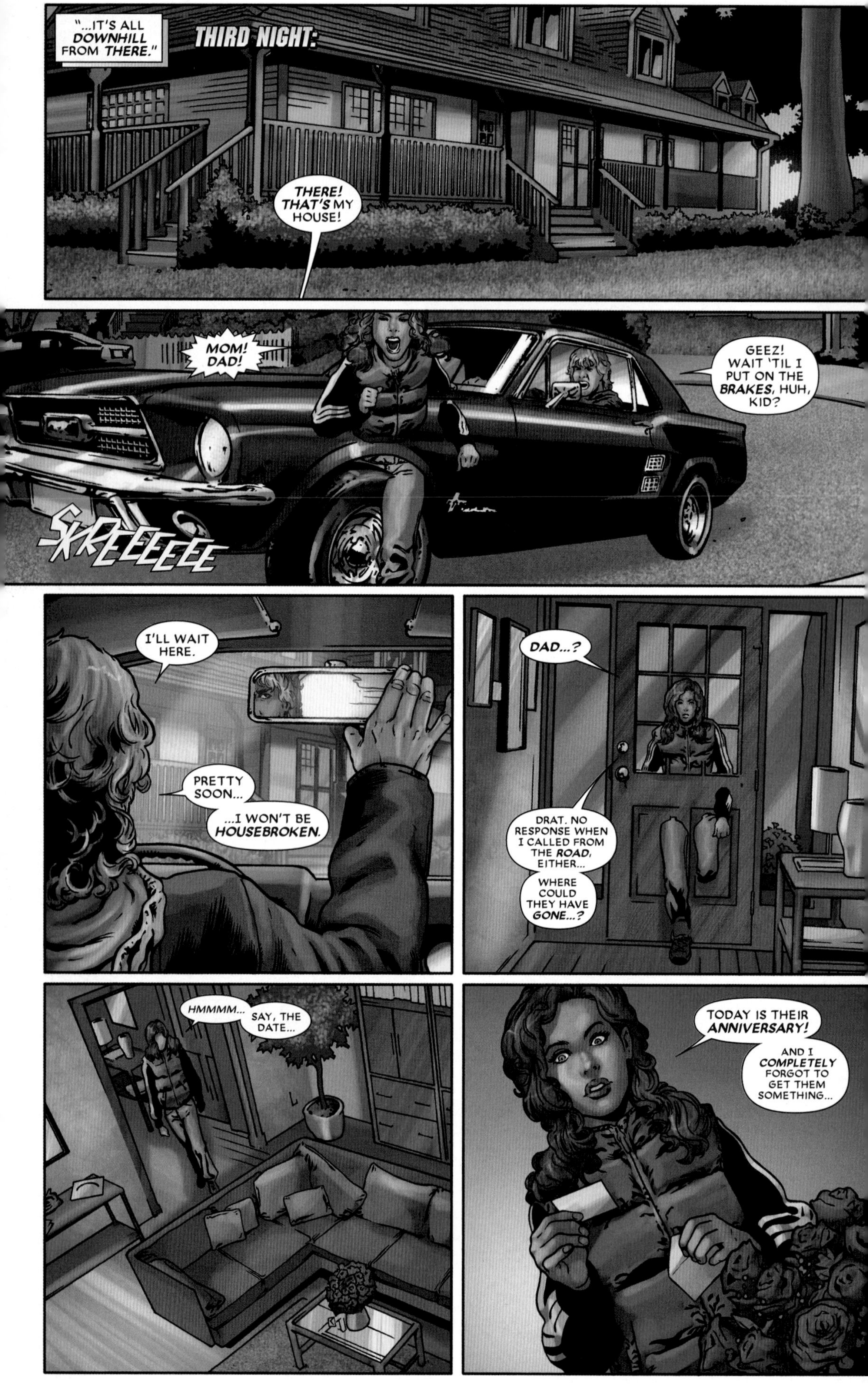

"...IT'S ALL DOWNHILL FROM THERE."
THIRD NIGHT:
THERE! THAT'S MY HOUSE!
MOM! DAD!
GEEZ! WAIT 'TIL I PUT ON THE BRAKES, HUH, KID?
SKREEEEEEE
I'LL WAIT HERE.
PRETTY SOON...
...I WON'T BE HOUSEBROKEN.
DAD...?
DRAT. NO RESPONSE WHEN I CALLED FROM THE ROAD, EITHER...
WHERE COULD THEY HAVE GONE...?
HMMMM...
SAY, THE DATE...
TODAY IS THEIR ANNIVERSARY!
AND I COMPLETELY FORGOT TO GET THEM SOMETHING...

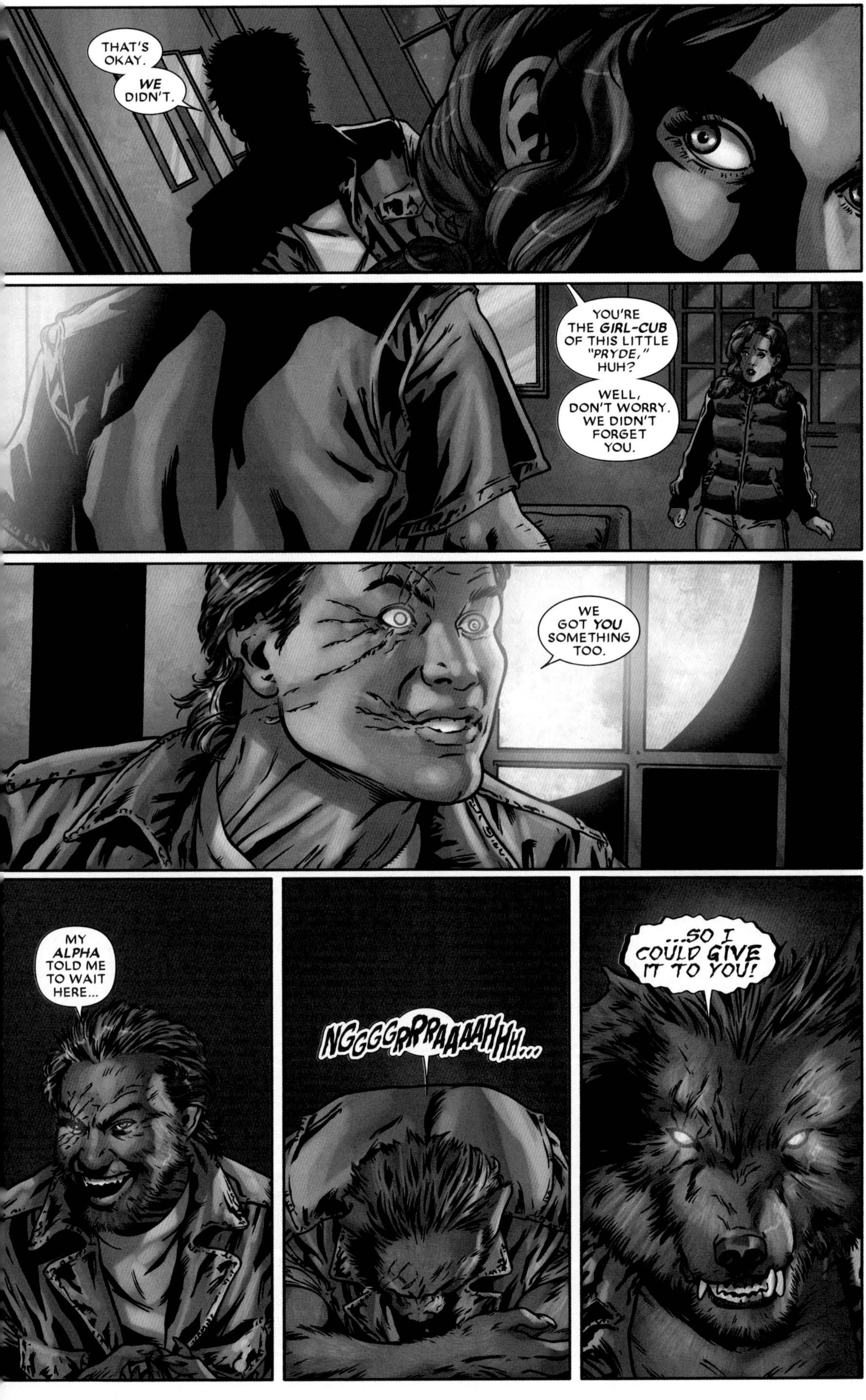
THAT'S OKAY. WE DIDN'T.
YOU'RE THE GIRL-CUB OF THIS LITTLE "PRYDE," HUH?
WELL, DON'T WORRY. WE DIDN'T FORGET YOU.
WE GOT YOU SOMETHING TOO.
MY ALPHA TOLD ME TO WAIT HERE...
NGGGGRRRAAAAHHH...
...SO I COULD GIVE IT TO YOU!

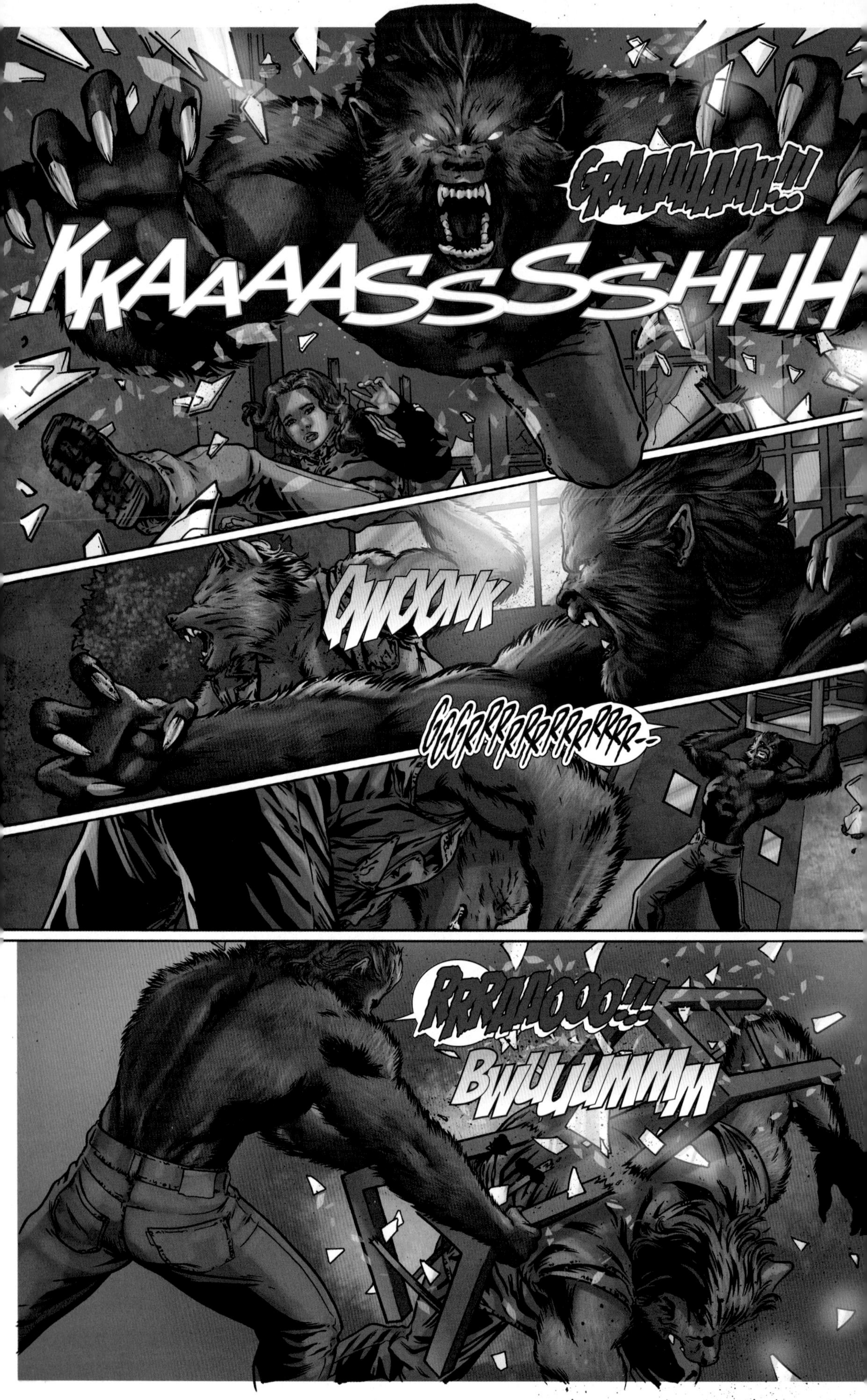
GRAAAAAAAH!!!
KKAAAASSSSHHH
OWOOONK
GGGRRRRRRRRRRRR--
RRRAAOOOO!!!
BWUUUMMM

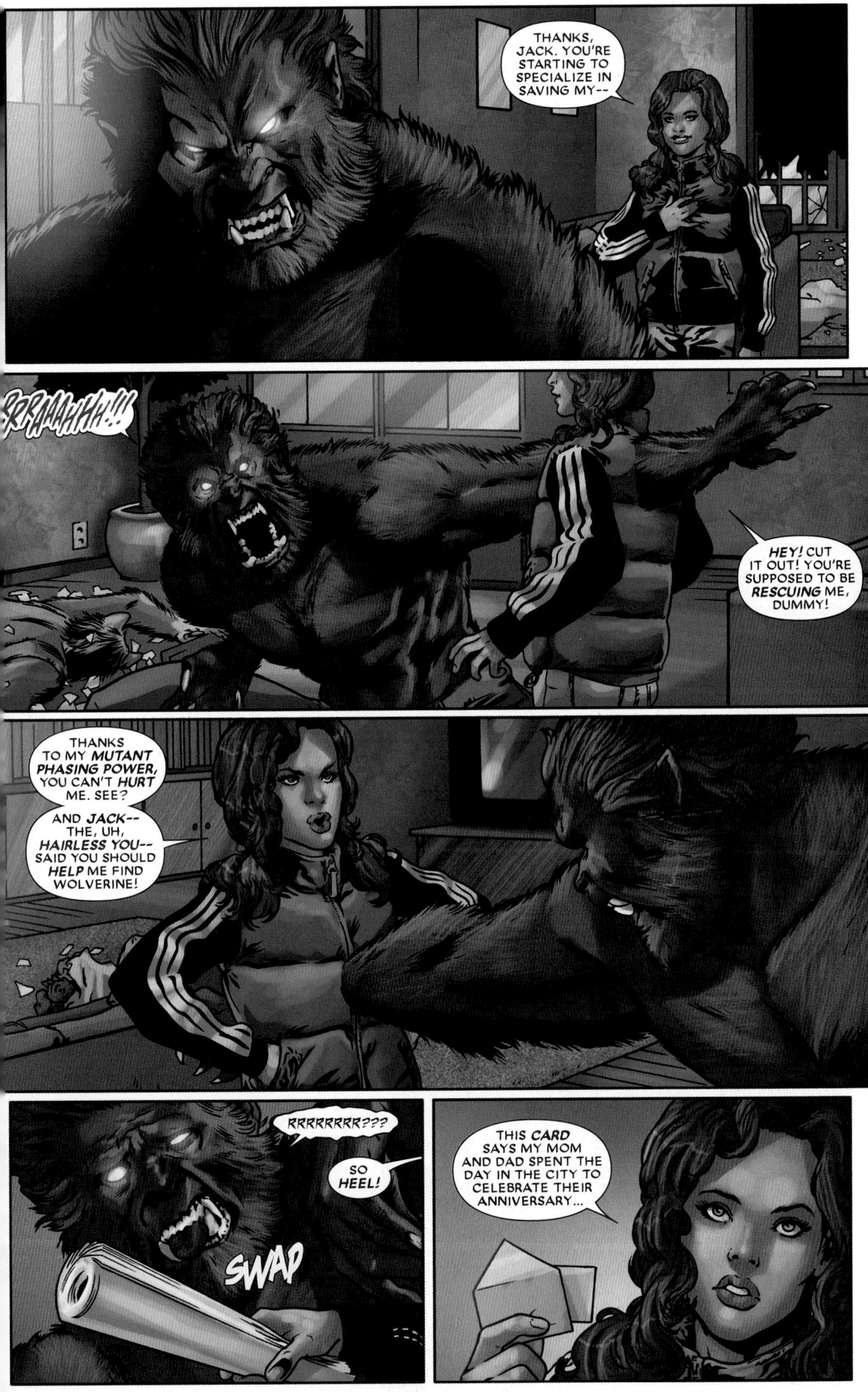
THANKS, JACK. YOU'RE STARTING TO SPECIALIZE IN SAVING MY--
RRAAAHHH!!!
HEY! CUT IT OUT! YOU'RE SUPPOSED TO BE RESCUING ME, DUMMY!
THANKS TO MY MUTANT PHASING POWER, YOU CAN'T HURT ME. SEE?
AND JACK-- THE, UH, HAIRLESS YOU-- SAID YOU SHOULD HELP ME FIND WOLVERINE!
RRRRRRRR???
SO HEEL!
SWAP
THIS CARD SAYS MY MOM AND DAD SPENT THE DAY IN THE CITY TO CELEBRATE THEIR ANNIVERSARY...

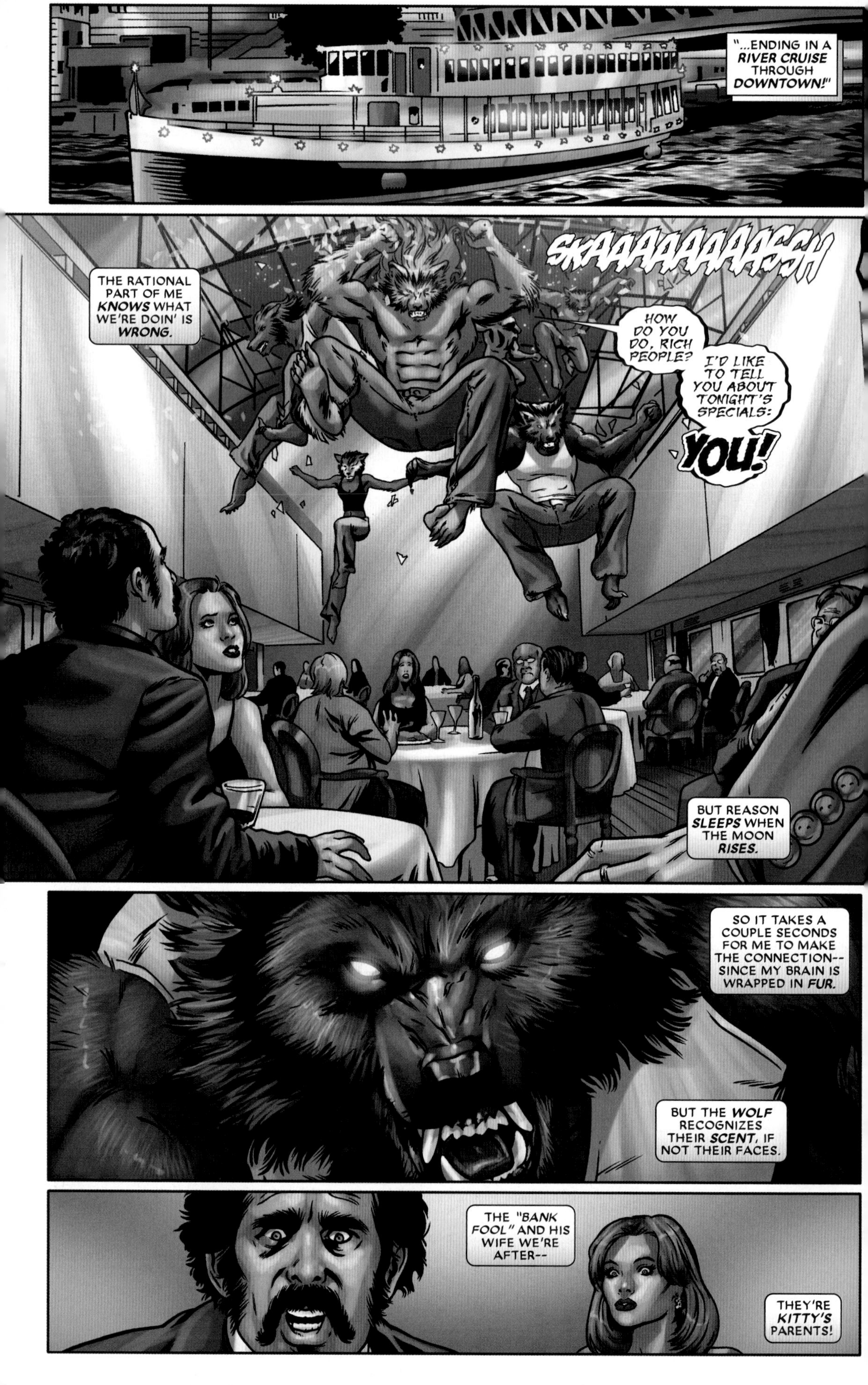
"...ENDING IN A RIVER CRUISE THROUGH DOWNTOWN!"
SKAAAAAAAAASH
THE RATIONAL PART OF ME KNOWS WHAT WE'RE DOIN' IS WRONG.
HOW DO YOU DO, RICH PEOPLE?
I'D LIKE TO TELL YOU ABOUT TONIGHT'S SPECIALS:
YOU!
BUT REASON SLEEPS WHEN THE MOON RISES.
SO IT TAKES A COUPLE SECONDS FOR ME TO MAKE THE CONNECTION-- SINCE MY BRAIN IS WRAPPED IN FUR.
BUT THE WOLF RECOGNIZES THEIR SCENT, IF NOT THEIR FACES.
THE "BANK FOOL" AND HIS WIFE WE'RE AFTER--
THEY'RE KITTY'S PARENTS!

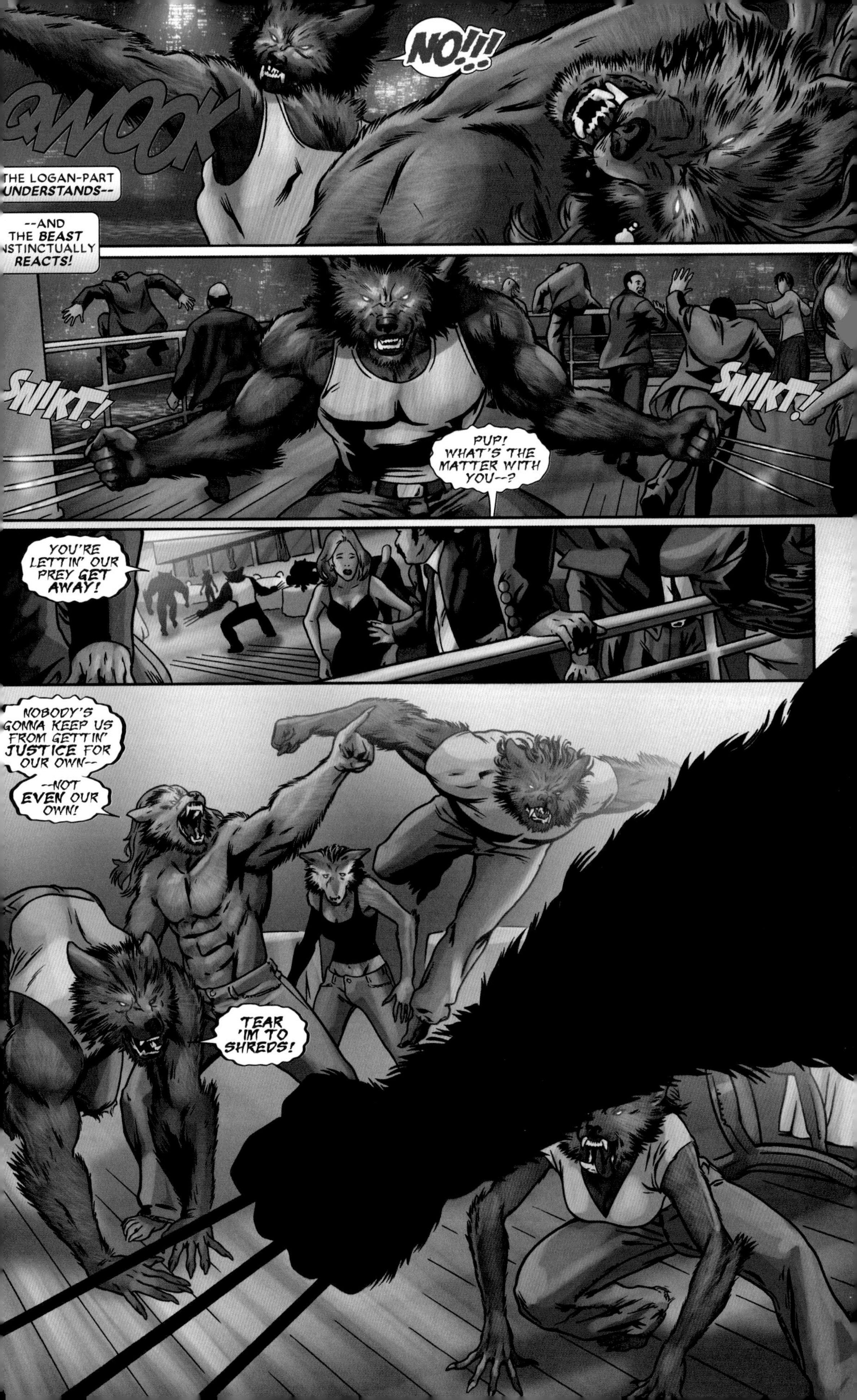
NO!!!
QWOOK
THE LOGAN-PART UNDERSTANDS--
--AND THE BEAST INSTINCTUALLY REACTS!
SNIKT!
SNIKT!
PUP! WHAT'S THE MATTER WITH YOU--?
YOU'RE LETTIN' OUR PREY GET AWAY!
NOBODY'S GONNA KEEP US FROM GETTIN' JUSTICE FOR OUR OWN--
--NOT EVEN OUR OWN!
TEAR 'IM TO SHREDS!

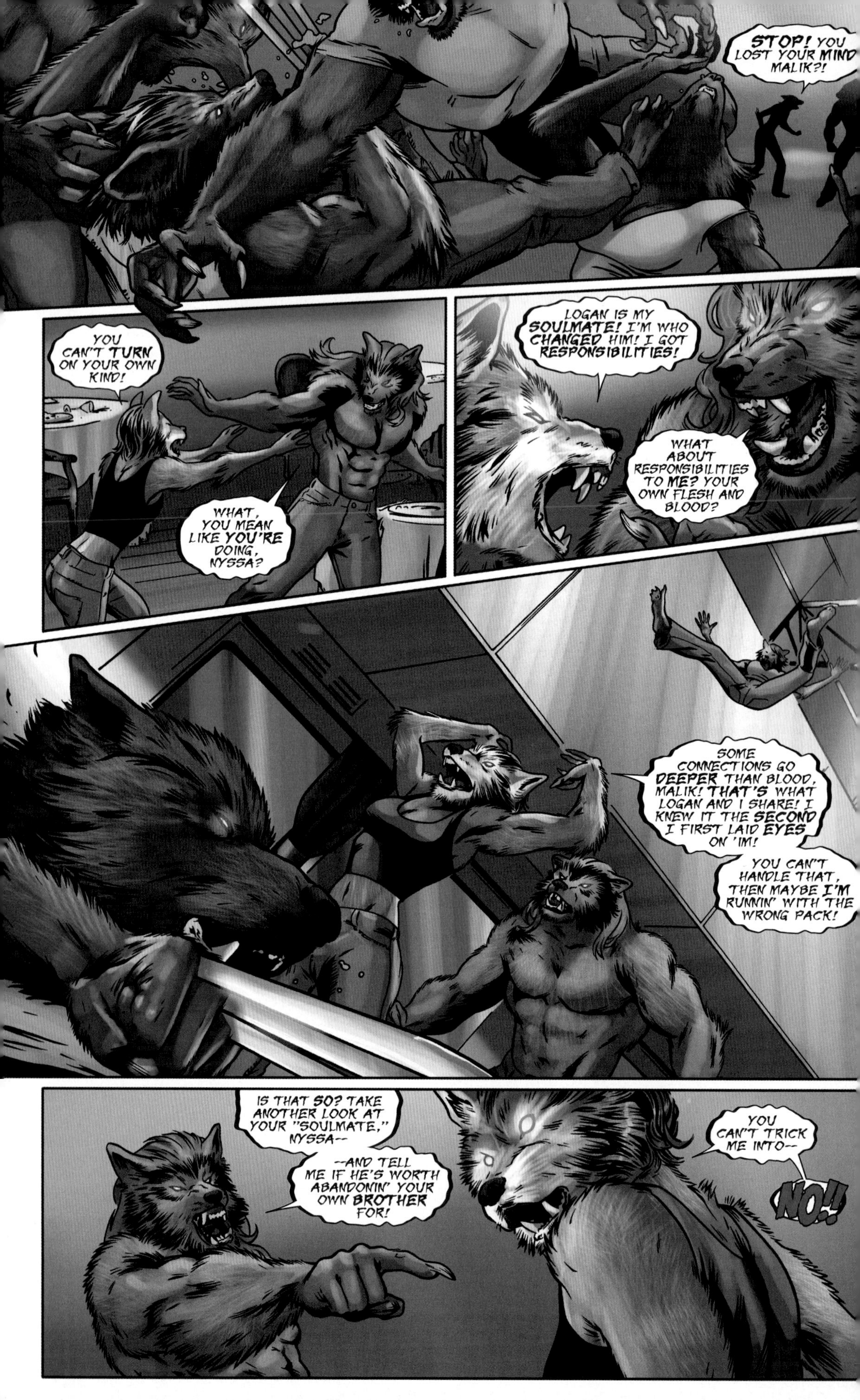
STOP! YOU LOST YOUR MIND MALIK?!
YOU CAN'T TURN ON YOUR OWN KIND!
WHAT, YOU MEAN LIKE YOU'RE DOING, NYSSA?
LOGAN IS MY SOULMATE! I'M WHO CHANGED HIM! I GOT RESPONSIBILITIES!
WHAT ABOUT RESPONSIBILITIES TO ME? YOUR OWN FLESH AND BLOOD?
SOME CONNECTIONS GO DEEPER THAN BLOOD, MALIK! THAT'S WHAT LOGAN AND I SHARE! I KNEW IT THE SECOND I FIRST LAID EYES ON 'IM!
YOU CAN'T HANDLE THAT, THEN MAYBE I'M RUNNIN' WITH THE WRONG PACK!
IS THAT SO? TAKE ANOTHER LOOK AT YOUR "SOULMATE," NYSSA--
--AND TELL ME IF HE'S WORTH ABANDONIN' YOUR OWN BROTHER FOR!
YOU CAN'T TRICK ME INTO--
NO!!

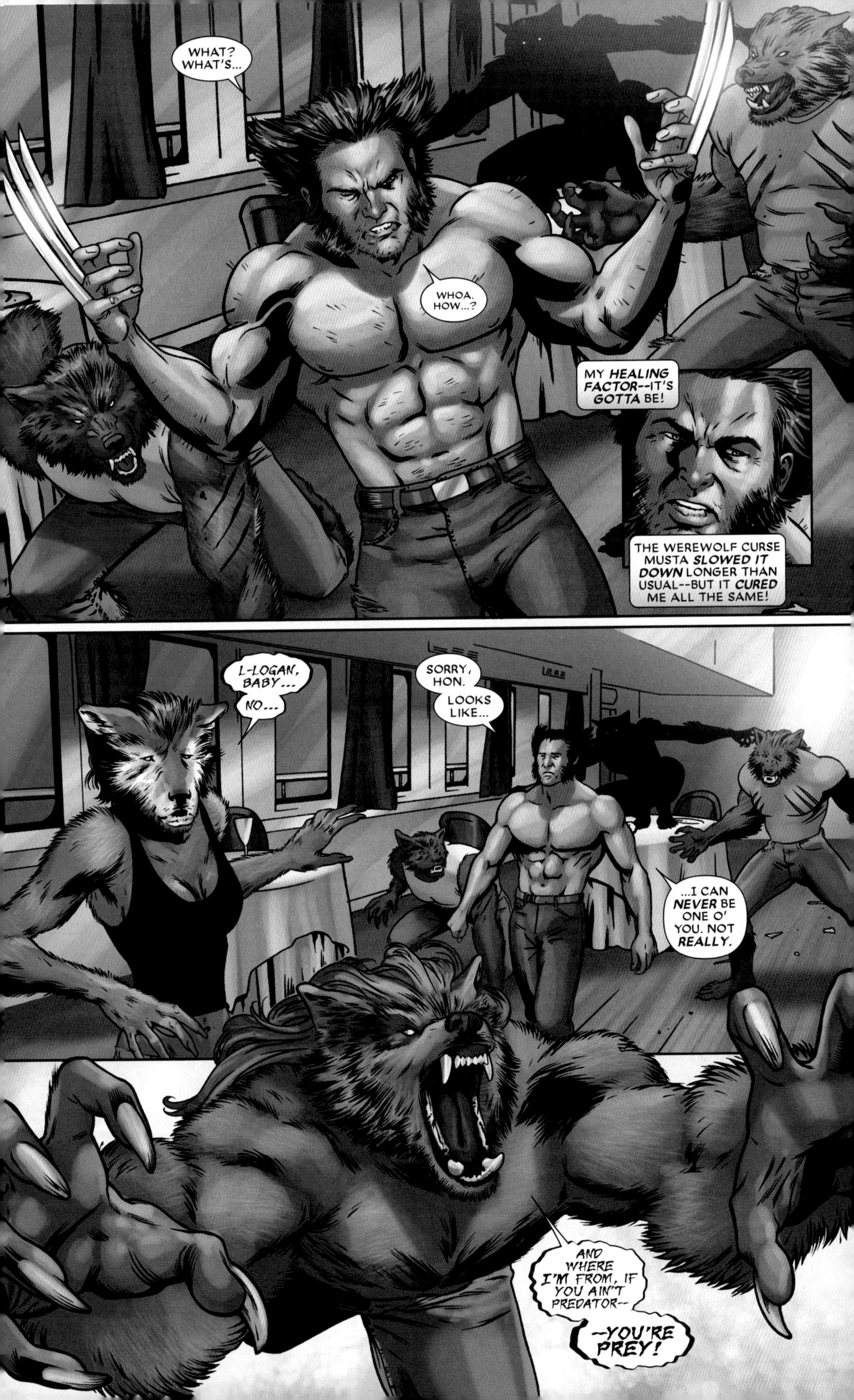
WHAT? WHAT'S...
WHOA. HOW...?
MY HEALING FACTOR--IT'S GOTTA BE!
THE WEREWOLF CURSE MUSTA SLOWED IT DOWN LONGER THAN USUAL--BUT IT CURED ME ALL THE SAME!
L-LOGAN, BABY...
NO...
SORRY, HON.
LOOKS LIKE...
...I CAN NEVER BE ONE O' YOU. NOT REALLY.
AND WHERE I'M FROM, IF YOU AIN'T PREDATOR--
--YOU'RE PREY!

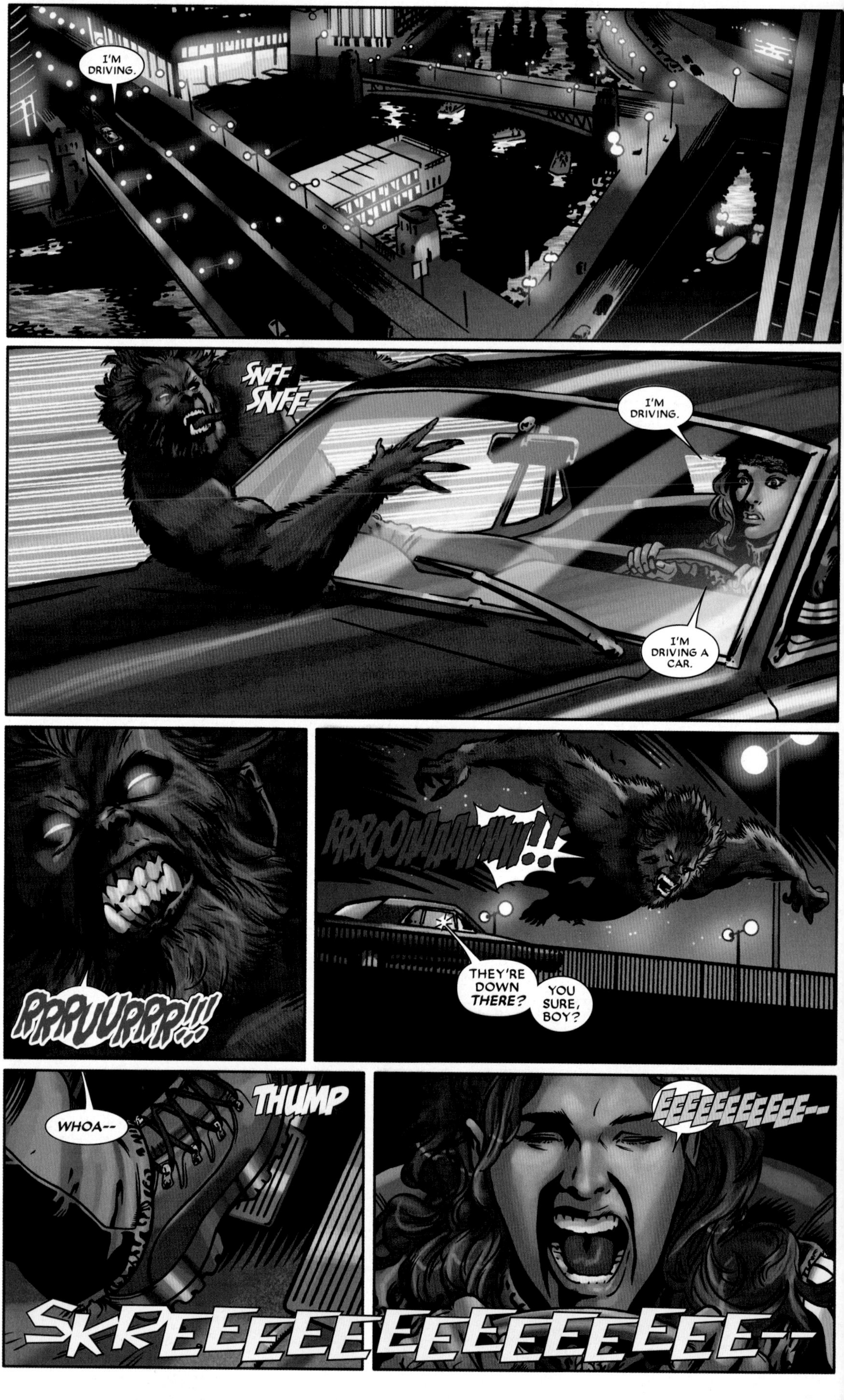
I'M DRIVING.
SNFF SNFF
I'M DRIVING.
I'M DRIVING A CAR.
RRRUURRR!!!
RRROOAAAWWW!!
THEY'RE DOWN THERE?
YOU SURE, BOY?
WHOA--
THUMP
EEEEEEEEEE--
SKREEEEEEEEEEEEEEE--

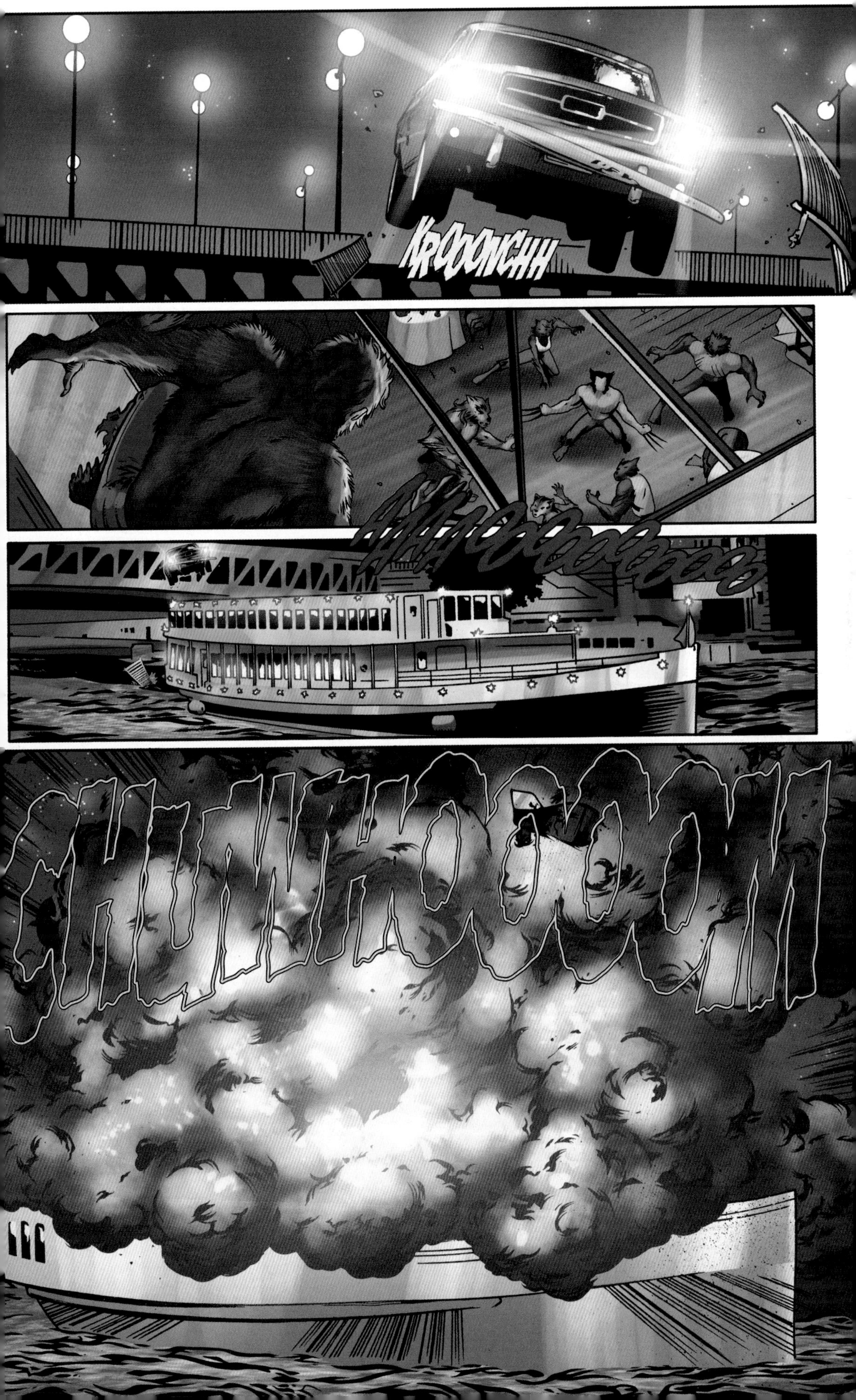

KROOONCHH
AAAOOOOOoooo
CHUNKOOOOM

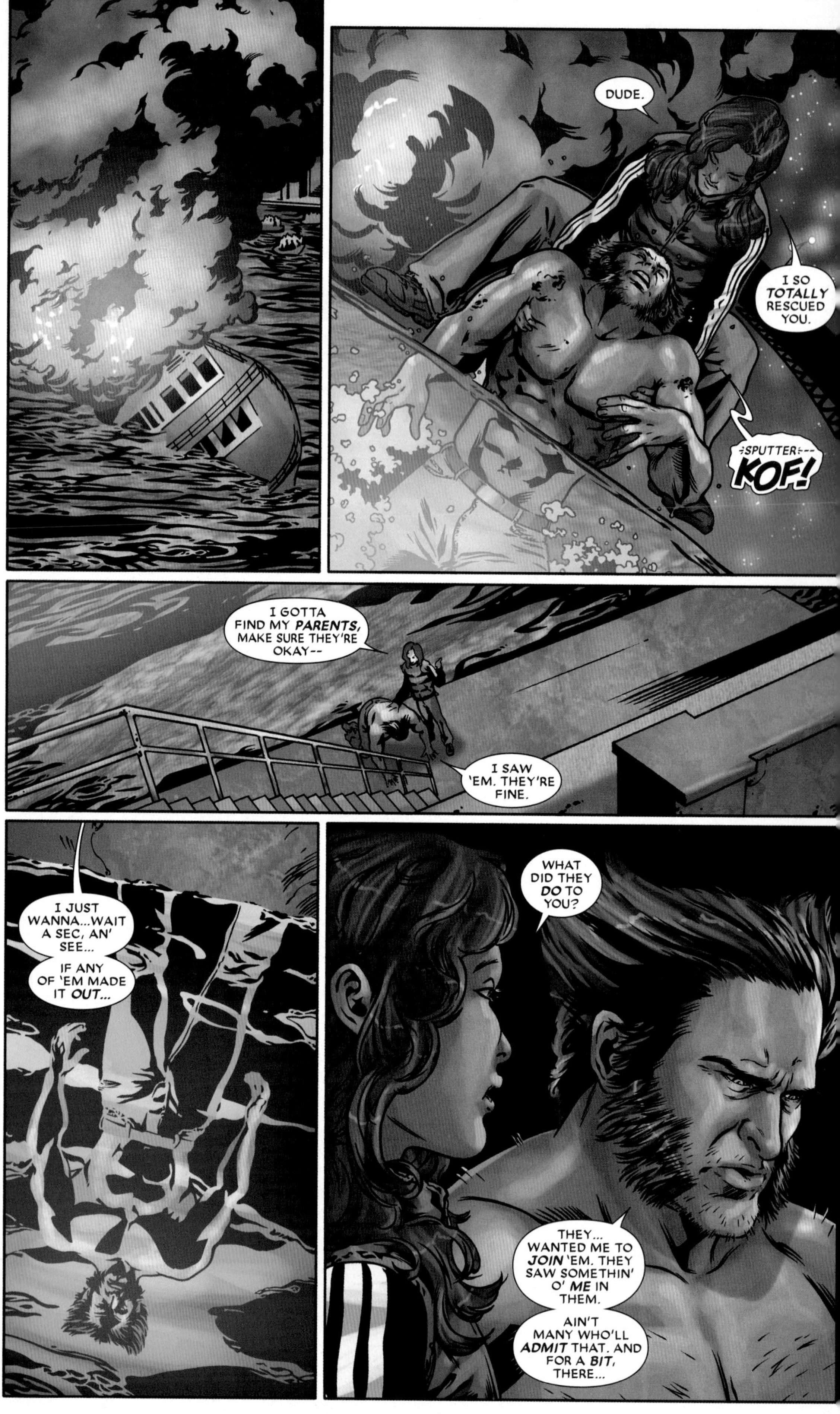
DUDE.
I SO TOTALLY RESCUED YOU.
SPUTTER--
KOF!
I GOTTA FIND MY PARENTS, MAKE SURE THEY'RE OKAY--
I SAW 'EM. THEY'RE FINE.
I JUST WANNA...WAIT A SEC, AN' SEE...
IF ANY OF 'EM MADE IT OUT...
WHAT DID THEY DO TO YOU?
THEY... WANTED ME TO JOIN 'EM. THEY SAW SOMETHIN' O' ME IN THEM.
AIN'T MANY WHO'LL ADMIT THAT. AND FOR A BIT, THERE...

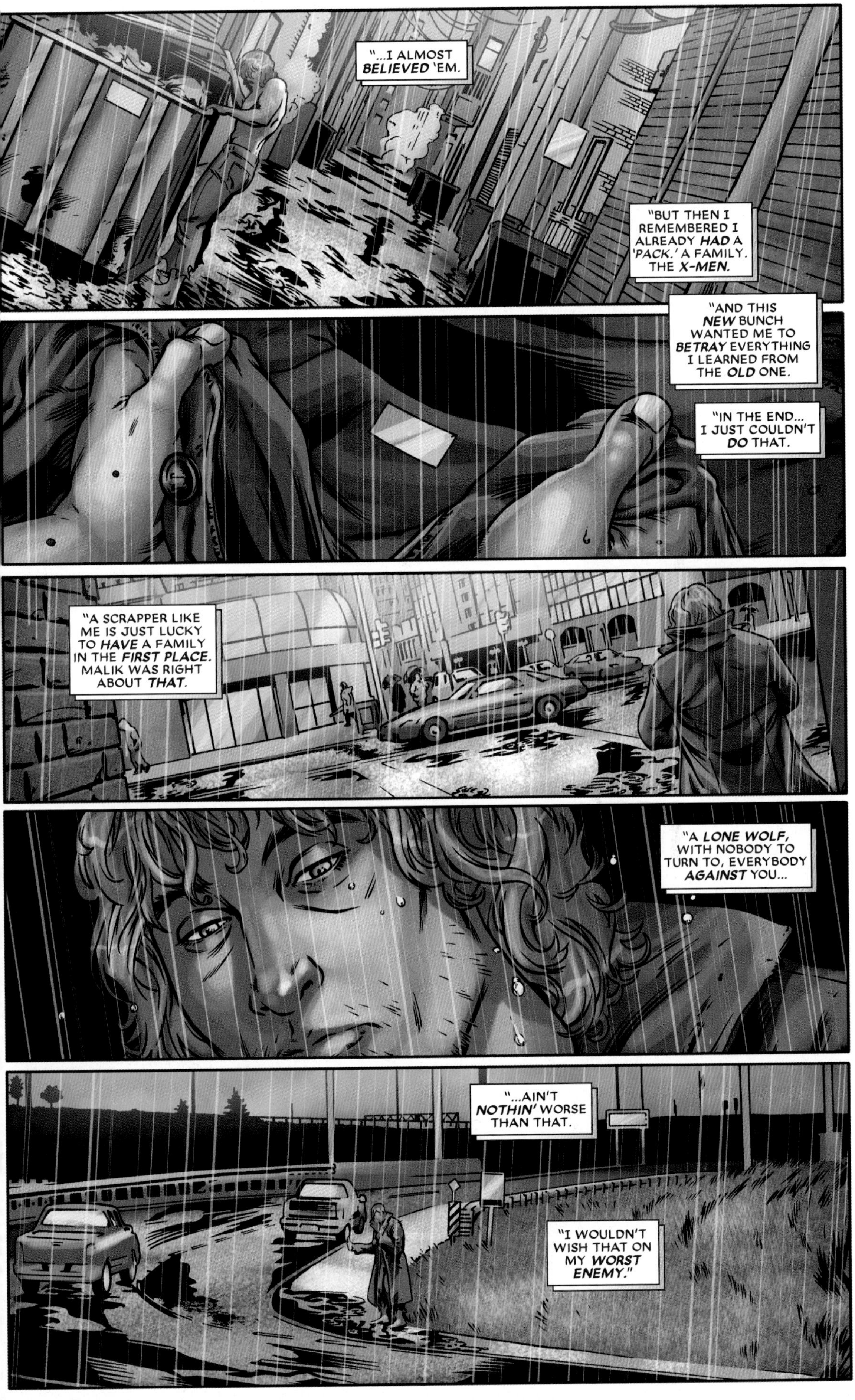
"...I ALMOST BELIEVED 'EM.
"BUT THEN I REMEMBERED I ALREADY HAD A 'PACK.' A FAMILY. THE X-MEN.
"AND THIS NEW BUNCH WANTED ME TO BETRAY EVERYTHING I LEARNED FROM THE OLD ONE.
"IN THE END... I JUST COULDN'T DO THAT.
"A SCRAPPER LIKE ME IS JUST LUCKY TO HAVE A FAMILY IN THE FIRST PLACE. MALIK WAS RIGHT ABOUT THAT.
"A LONE WOLF, WITH NOBODY TO TURN TO, EVERYBODY AGAINST YOU...
"...AIN'T NOTHIN' WORSE THAN THAT.
"I WOULDN'T WISH THAT ON MY WORST ENEMY."

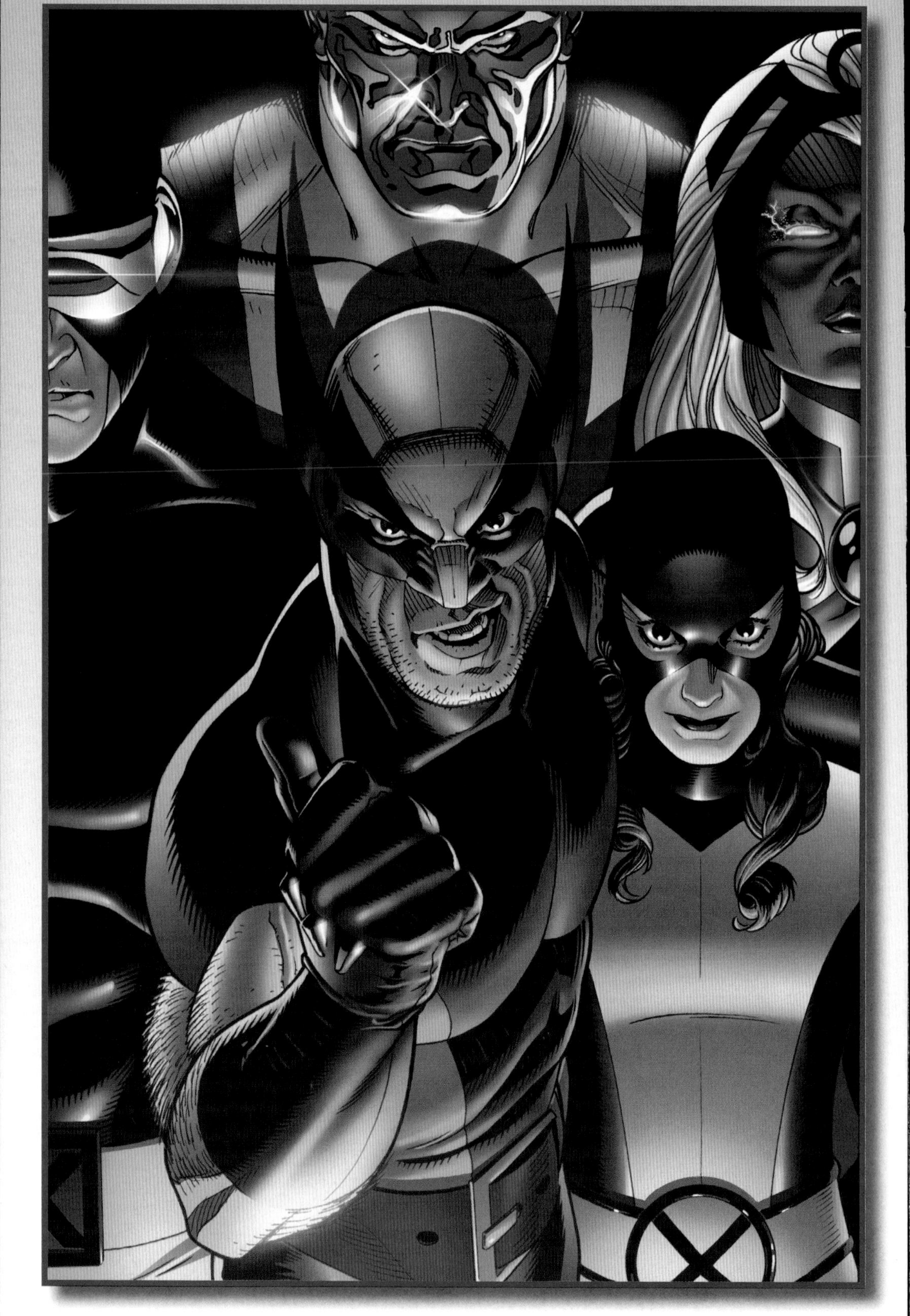

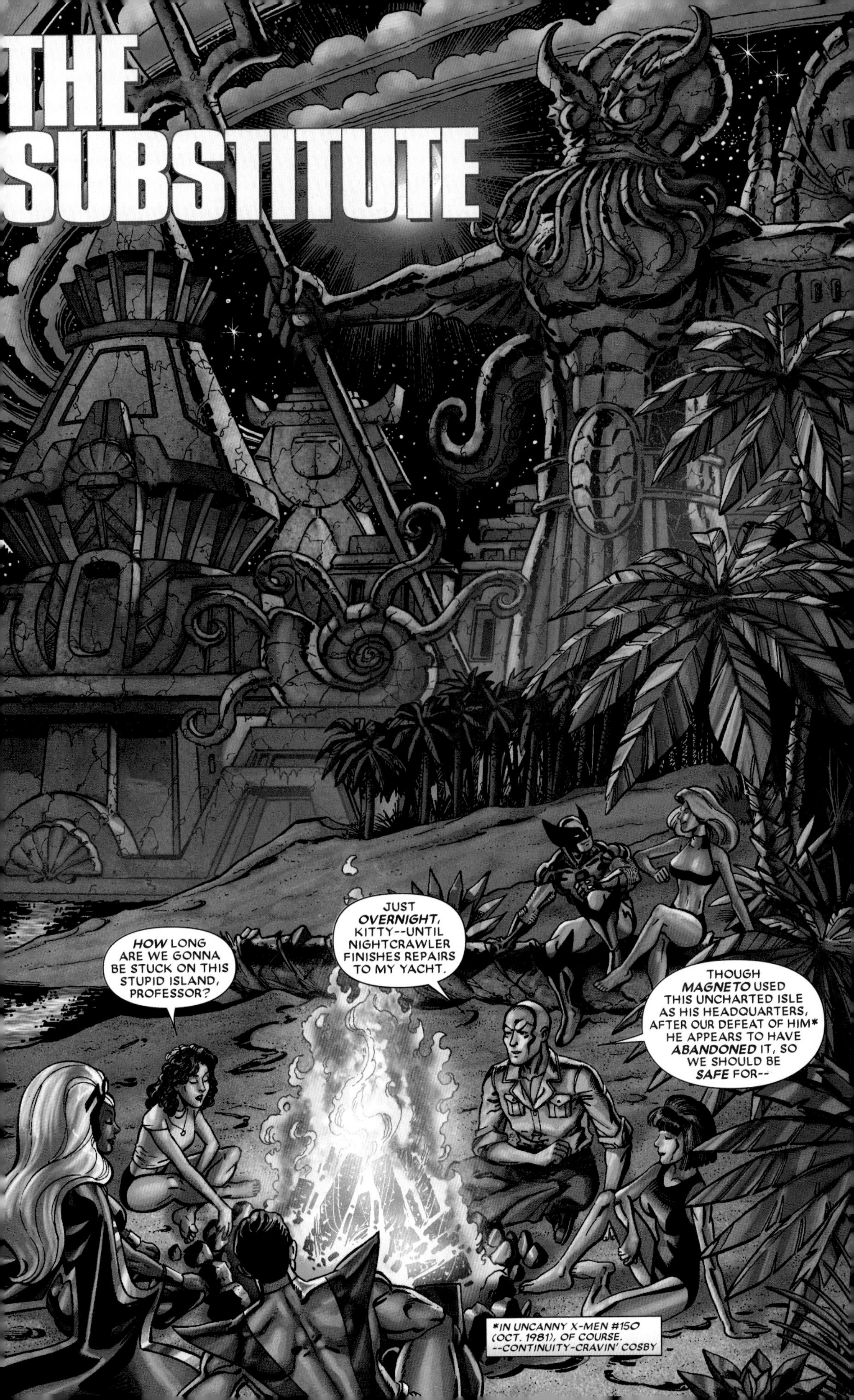
THE SUBSTITUTE
HOW LONG ARE WE GONNA BE STUCK ON THIS STUPID ISLAND, PROFESSOR?
JUST OVERNIGHT, KITTY--UNTIL NIGHTCRAWLER FINISHES REPAIRS TO MY YACHT.
THOUGH MAGNETO USED THIS UNCHARTED ISLE AS HIS HEADQUARTERS, AFTER OUR DEFEAT OF HIM* HE APPEARS TO HAVE ABANDONED IT, SO WE SHOULD BE SAFE FOR--
*IN UNCANNY X-MEN #150 (OCT. 1981), OF COURSE. --CONTINUITY-CRAVIN' COSBY

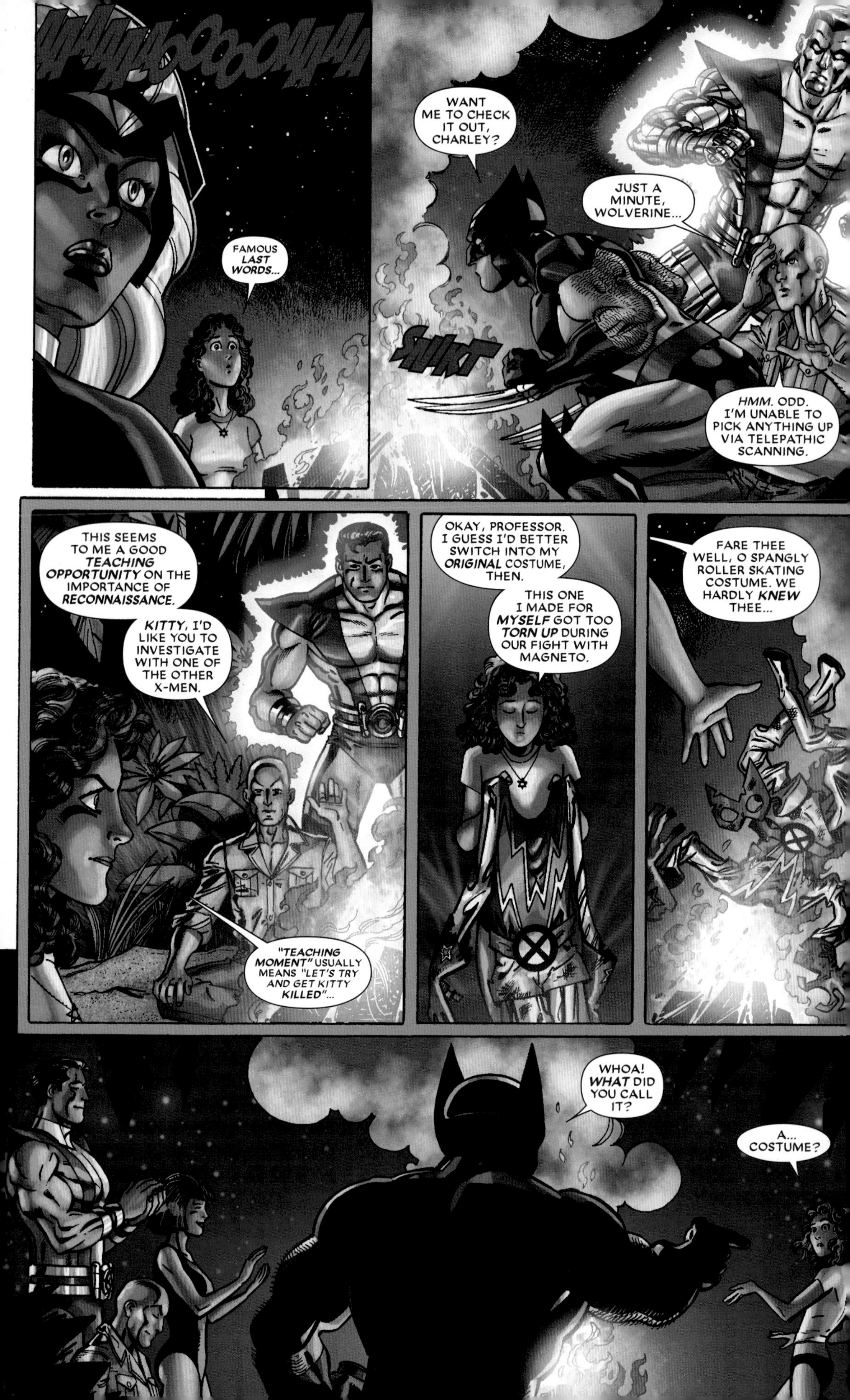
WHHHHOOOOOOMMM
FAMOUS LAST WORDS...
WANT ME TO CHECK IT OUT, CHARLEY?
SNIKT
JUST A MINUTE, WOLVERINE...
HMM. ODD. I'M UNABLE TO PICK ANYTHING UP VIA TELEPATHIC SCANNING.
THIS SEEMS TO ME A GOOD TEACHING OPPORTUNITY ON THE IMPORTANCE OF RECONNAISSANCE.
KITTY, I'D LIKE YOU TO INVESTIGATE WITH ONE OF THE OTHER X-MEN.
"TEACHING MOMENT" USUALLY MEANS "LET'S TRY AND GET KITTY KILLED"...
OKAY, PROFESSOR. I GUESS I'D BETTER SWITCH INTO MY ORIGINAL COSTUME, THEN.
THIS ONE I MADE FOR MYSELF GOT TOO TORN UP DURING OUR FIGHT WITH MAGNETO.
FARE THEE WELL, O SPANGLY ROLLER SKATING COSTUME. WE HARDLY KNEW THEE...
WHOA! WHAT DID YOU CALL IT?
A... COSTUME?

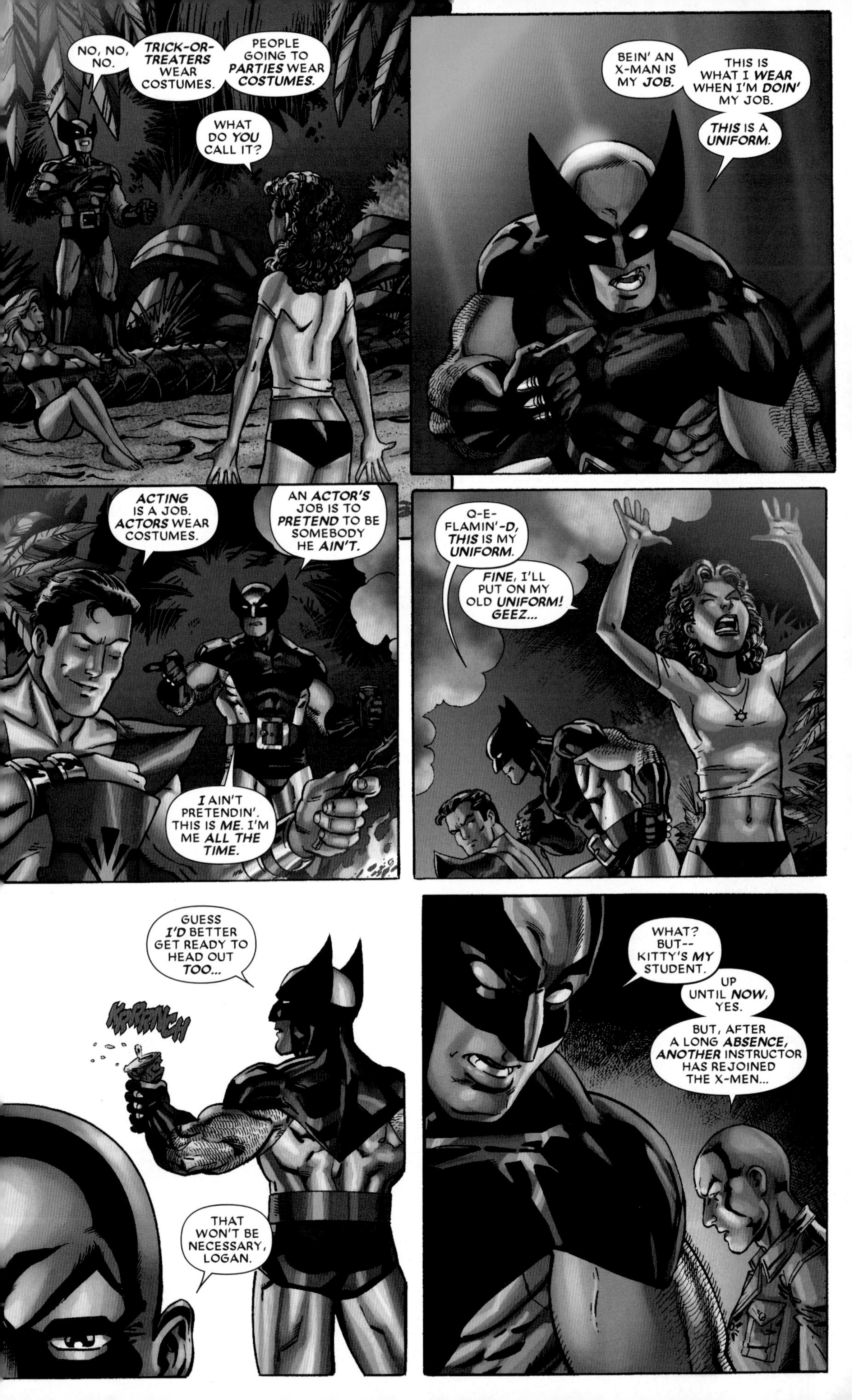
NO, NO, NO.
TRICK-OR-TREATERS WEAR COSTUMES.
PEOPLE GOING TO PARTIES WEAR COSTUMES.
WHAT DO YOU CALL IT?
BEIN' AN X-MAN IS MY JOB.
THIS IS WHAT I WEAR WHEN I'M DOIN' MY JOB.
THIS IS A UNIFORM.
ACTING IS A JOB. ACTORS WEAR COSTUMES.
AN ACTOR'S JOB IS TO PRETEND TO BE SOMEBODY HE AIN'T.
I AIN'T PRETENDIN'. THIS IS ME. I'M ME ALL THE TIME.
Q-E-FLAMIN'-D, THIS IS MY UNIFORM.
FINE, I'LL PUT ON MY OLD UNIFORM! GEEZ...
GUESS I'D BETTER GET READY TO HEAD OUT TOO...
KRRRNCH
THAT WON'T BE NECESSARY, LOGAN.
WHAT? BUT-- KITTY'S MY STUDENT.
UP UNTIL NOW, YES.
BUT, AFTER A LONG ABSENCE, ANOTHER INSTRUCTOR HAS REJOINED THE X-MEN...

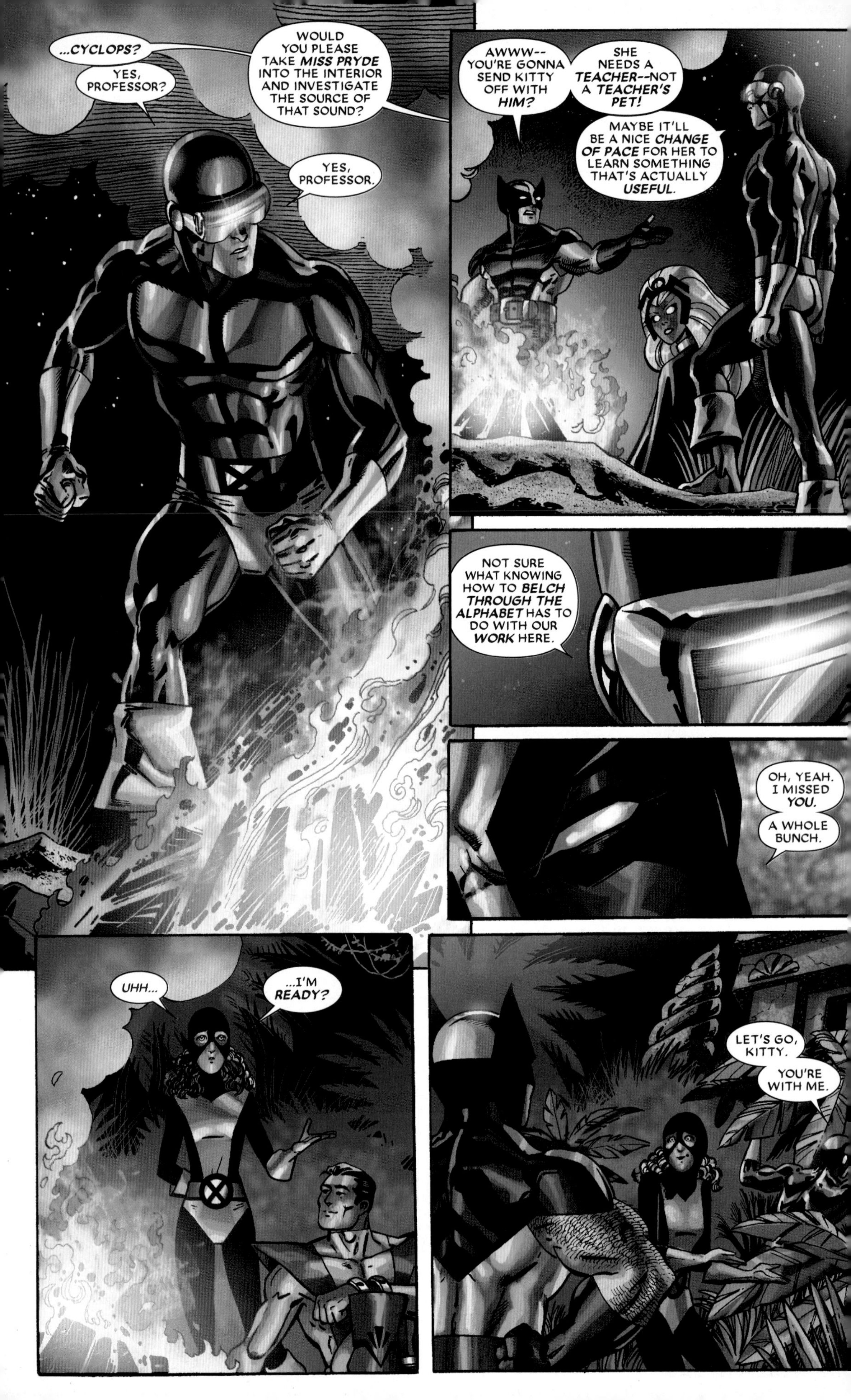

...CYCLOPS?
YES, PROFESSOR?
WOULD YOU PLEASE TAKE MISS PRYDE INTO THE INTERIOR AND INVESTIGATE THE SOURCE OF THAT SOUND?
YES, PROFESSOR.
AWWW-- YOU'RE GONNA SEND KITTY OFF WITH HIM?
SHE NEEDS A TEACHER--NOT A TEACHER'S PET!
MAYBE IT'LL BE A NICE CHANGE OF PACE FOR HER TO LEARN SOMETHING THAT'S ACTUALLY USEFUL.
NOT SURE WHAT KNOWING HOW TO BELCH THROUGH THE ALPHABET HAS TO DO WITH OUR WORK HERE.
OH, YEAH. I MISSED YOU.
A WHOLE BUNCH.
UHH...
...I'M READY?
LET'S GO, KITTY.
YOU'RE WITH ME.

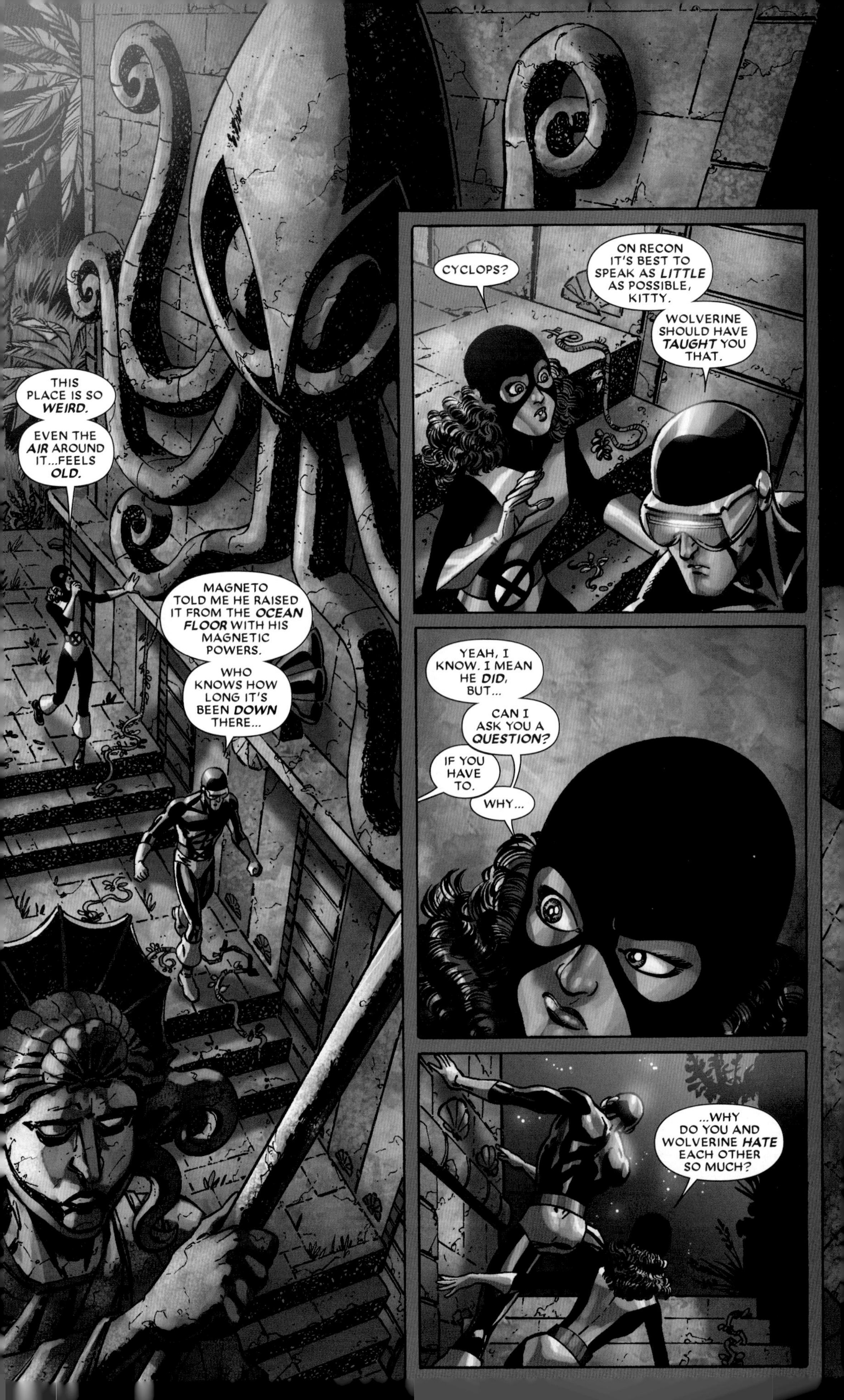
THIS PLACE IS SO WEIRD.
EVEN THE AIR AROUND IT...FEELS OLD.
MAGNETO TOLD ME HE RAISED IT FROM THE OCEAN FLOOR WITH HIS MAGNETIC POWERS.
WHO KNOWS HOW LONG IT'S BEEN DOWN THERE...
CYCLOPS?
ON RECON IT'S BEST TO SPEAK AS LITTLE AS POSSIBLE, KITTY.
WOLVERINE SHOULD HAVE TAUGHT YOU THAT.
YEAH, I KNOW. I MEAN HE DID, BUT...
CAN I ASK YOU A QUESTION?
IF YOU HAVE TO.
WHY...
...WHY DO YOU AND WOLVERINE HATE EACH OTHER SO MUCH?

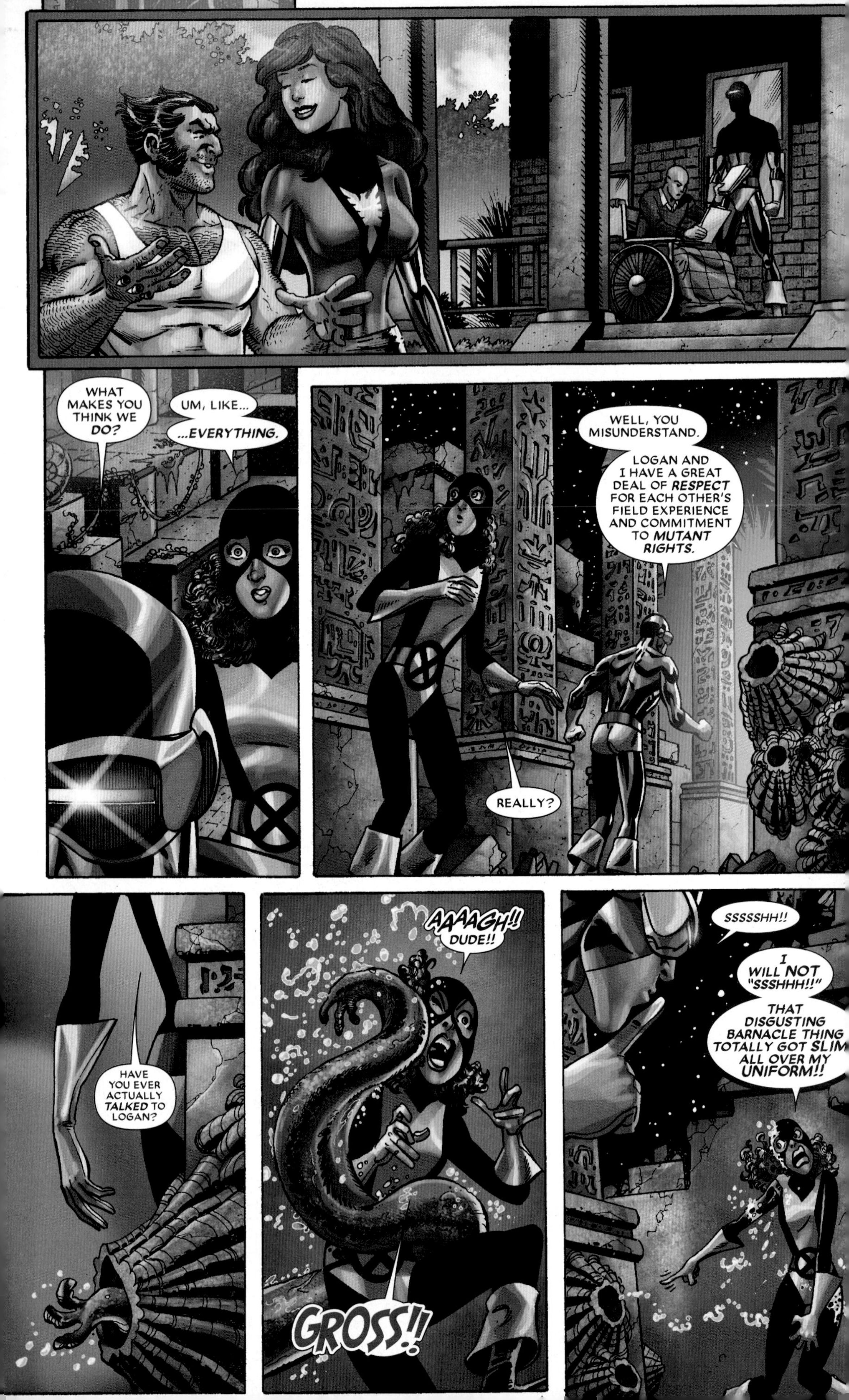
WHAT MAKES YOU THINK WE *DO?*
UM, LIKE...
...EVERYTHING.
WELL, YOU MISUNDERSTAND.
LOGAN AND I HAVE A GREAT DEAL OF *RESPECT* FOR EACH OTHER'S FIELD EXPERIENCE AND COMMITMENT TO *MUTANT RIGHTS.*
REALLY?
HAVE YOU EVER ACTUALLY *TALKED* TO LOGAN?
AAAAGH!! DUDE!!
GROSS!!
SSSSSHH!!
I WILL *NOT* "SSSHHH!!"
THAT DISGUSTING BARNACLE THING TOTALLY GOT SLIM ALL OVER MY *UNIFORM!!*

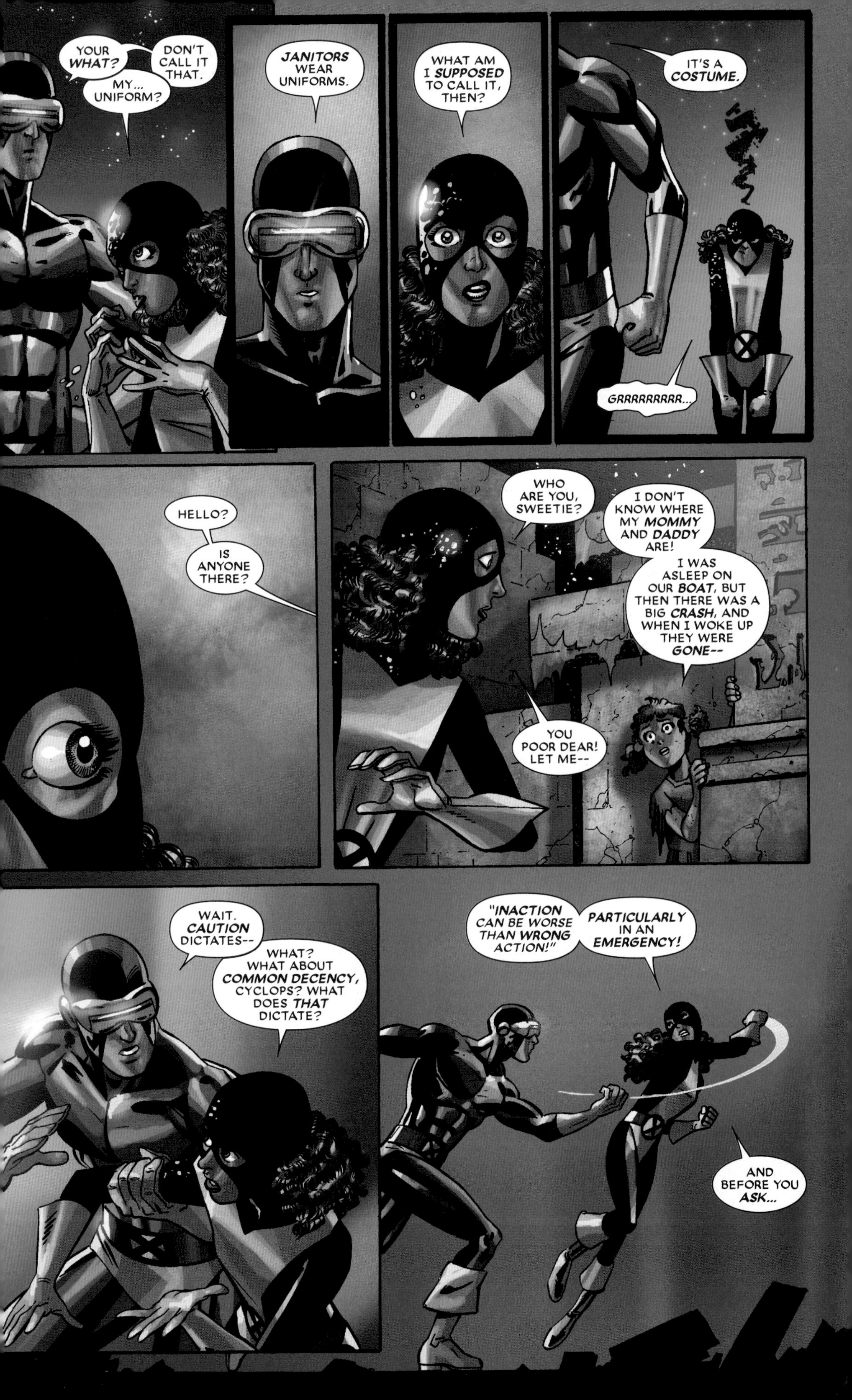
YOUR WHAT?
DON'T CALL IT THAT.
MY... UNIFORM?
JANITORS WEAR UNIFORMS.
WHAT AM I SUPPOSED TO CALL IT, THEN?
IT'S A COSTUME.
GRRRRRRRRR...
HELLO?
IS ANYONE THERE?
WHO ARE YOU, SWEETIE?
I DON'T KNOW WHERE MY MOMMY AND DADDY ARE!
I WAS ASLEEP ON OUR BOAT, BUT THEN THERE WAS A BIG CRASH, AND WHEN I WOKE UP THEY WERE GONE--
YOU POOR DEAR! LET ME--
WAIT. CAUTION DICTATES--
WHAT? WHAT ABOUT COMMON DECENCY, CYCLOPS? WHAT DOES THAT DICTATE?
"INACTION CAN BE WORSE THAN WRONG ACTION!"
PARTICULARLY IN AN EMERGENCY!
AND BEFORE YOU ASK...

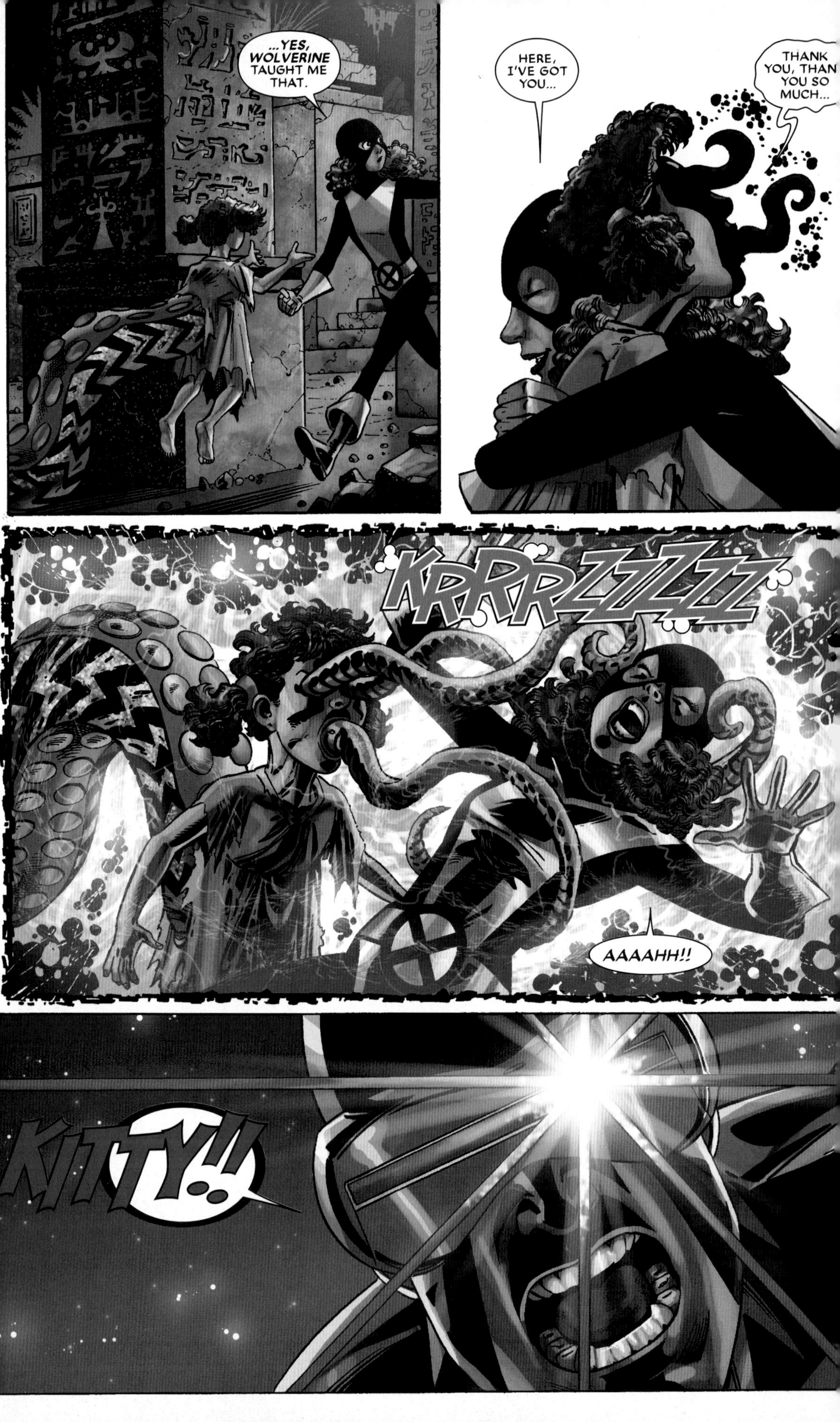
...YES, WOLVERINE TAUGHT ME THAT.
HERE, I'VE GOT YOU...
THANK YOU, THANK YOU SO MUCH...
KRRRRZZZZZ
AAAAHH!!
KITTY!!

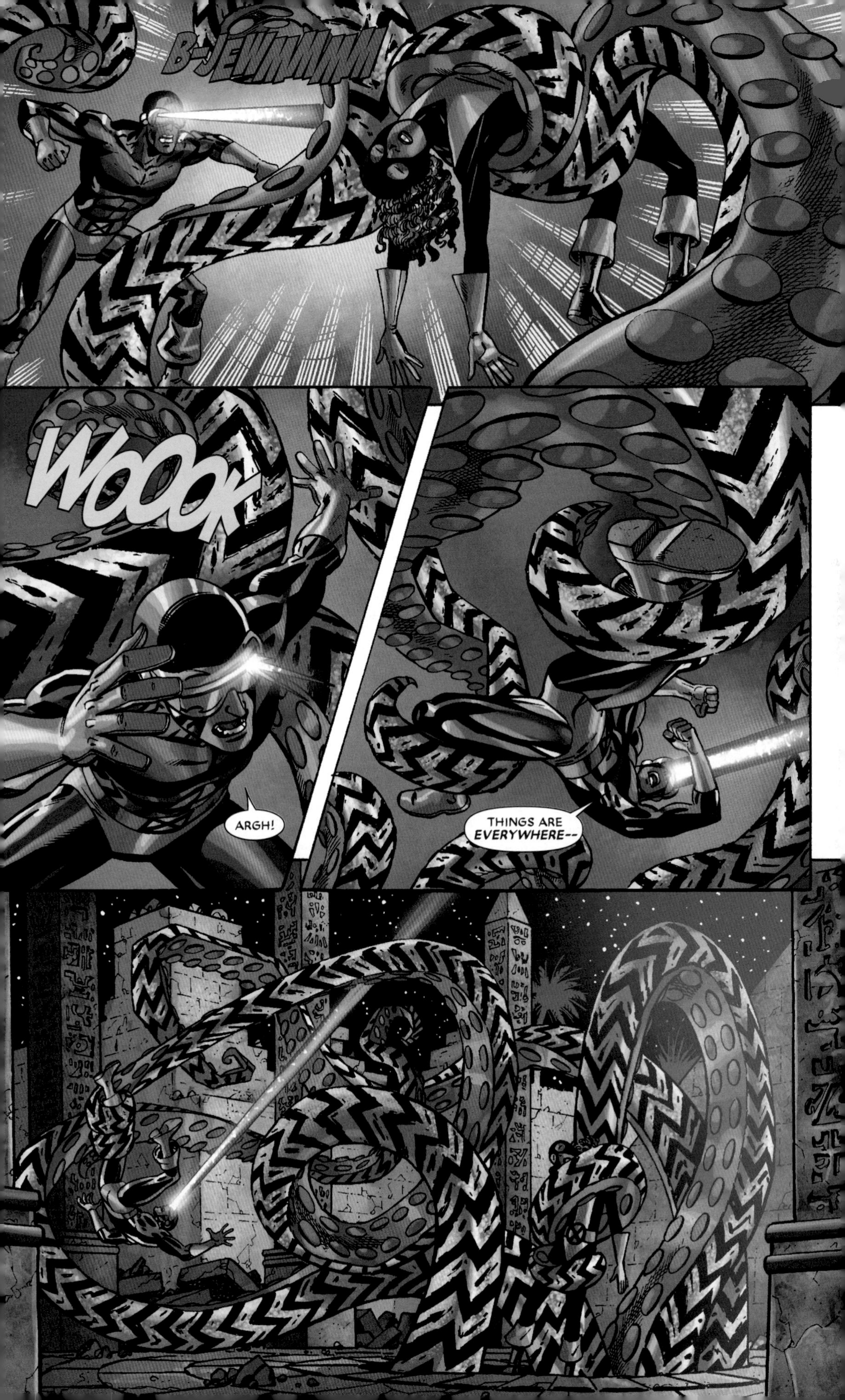
B-JEWWWWW
WOOOK
ARGH!
THINGS ARE EVERYWHERE--

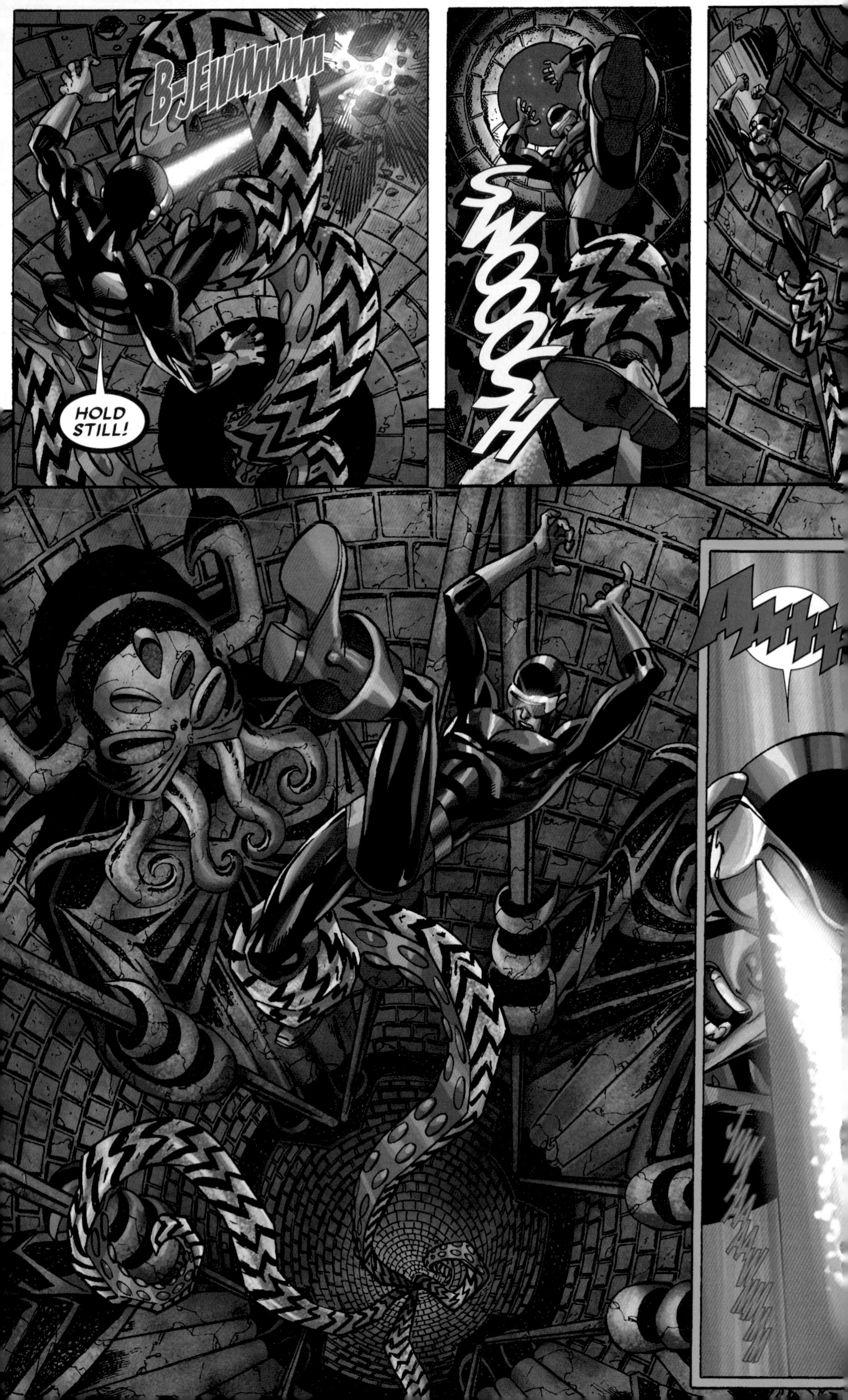

B-JEWMMMMM
HOLD STILL!
SWOOOSH

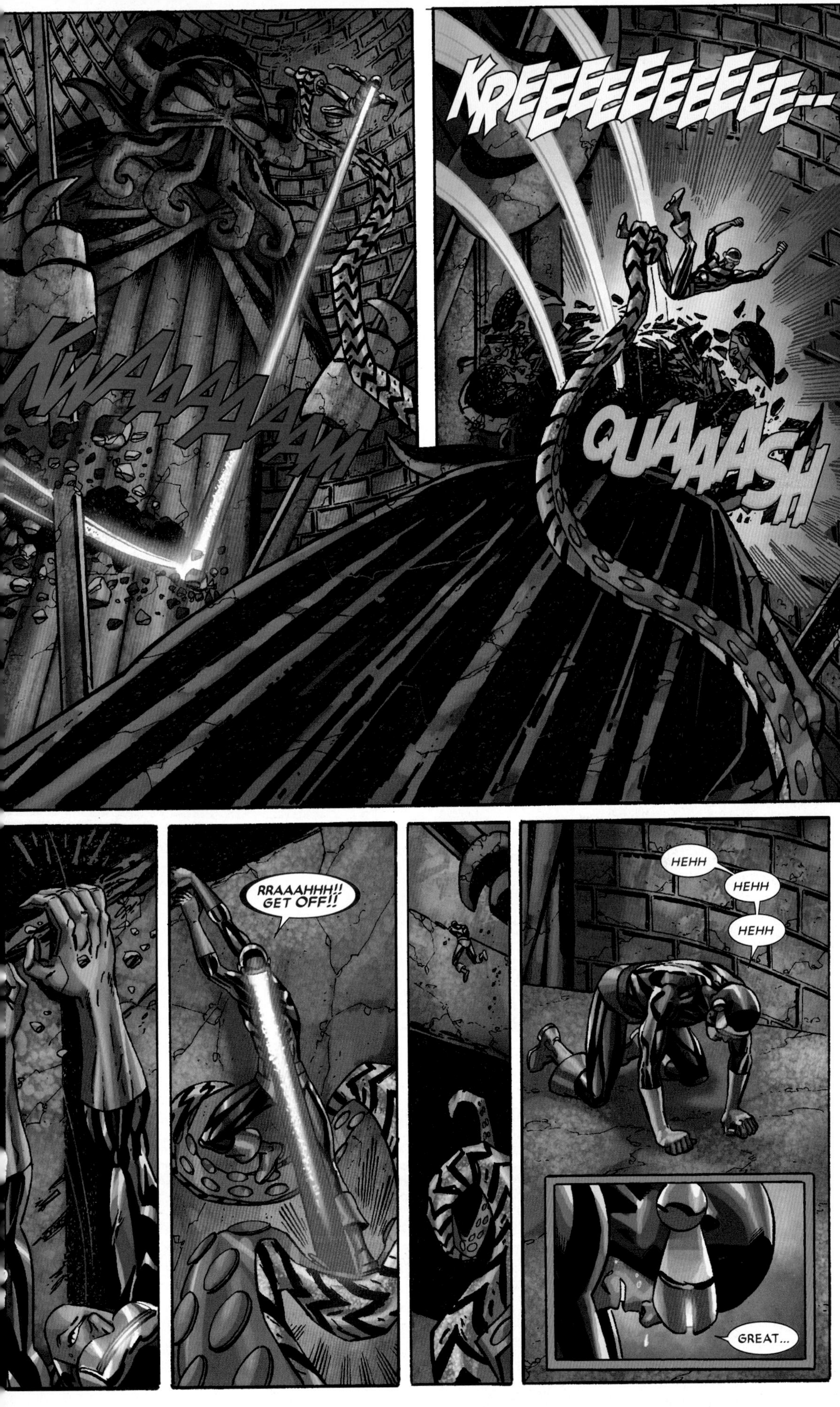
KWAAAAAAM
KREEEEEEEEEE--
QUAAAASH
RRAAAHHH!! GET OFF!!
HEHH
HEHH
HEHH
GREAT...

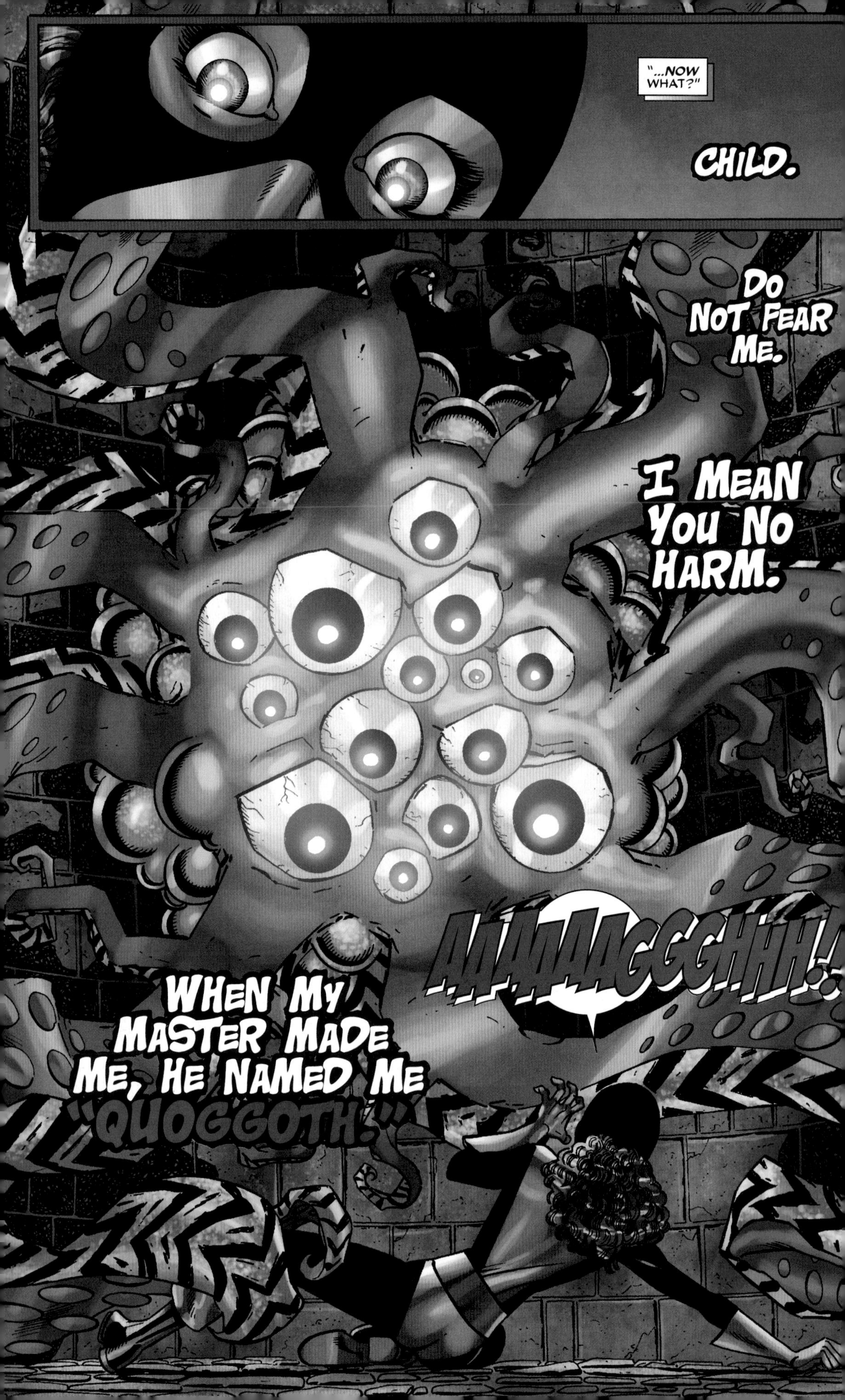
"...NOW WHAT?"
CHILD.
DO NOT FEAR ME.
I MEAN YOU NO HARM.
WHEN MY MASTER MADE ME, HE NAMED ME "QUOGGOTH."
AAAAAAGGGHHH!!

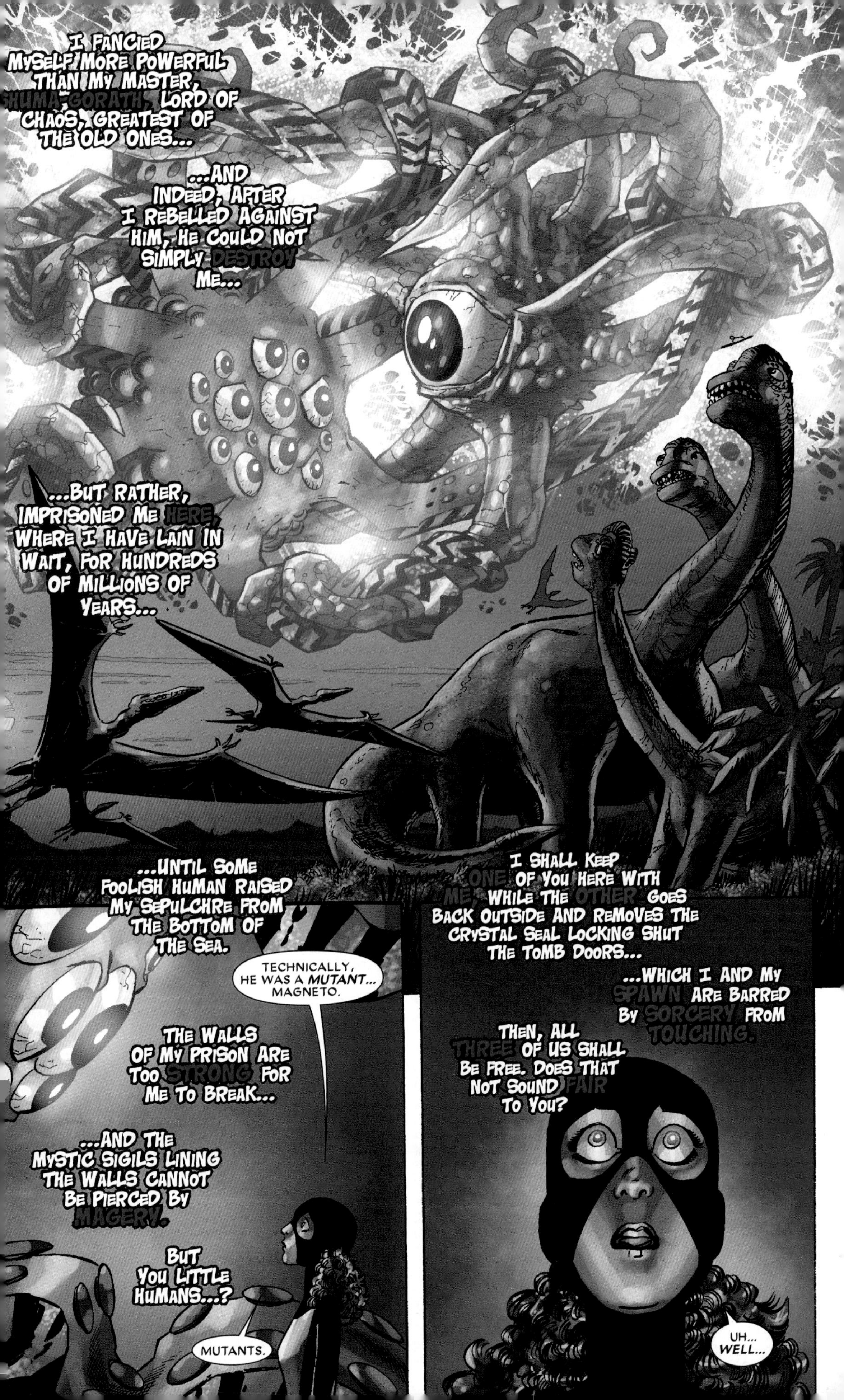
I FANCIED MYSELF MORE POWERFUL THAN MY MASTER, SHUMA-GORATH, LORD OF CHAOS, GREATEST OF THE OLD ONES...
...AND INDEED, AFTER I REBELLED AGAINST HIM, HE COULD NOT SIMPLY DESTROY ME...
...BUT RATHER, IMPRISONED ME HERE, WHERE I HAVE LAIN IN WAIT, FOR HUNDREDS OF MILLIONS OF YEARS...
...UNTIL SOME FOOLISH HUMAN RAISED MY SEPULCHRE FROM THE BOTTOM OF THE SEA.
TECHNICALLY, HE WAS A MUTANT... MAGNETO.
THE WALLS OF MY PRISON ARE TOO STRONG FOR ME TO BREAK...
...AND THE MYSTIC SIGILS LINING THE WALLS CANNOT BE PIERCED BY MAGERY.
BUT YOU LITTLE HUMANS...?
MUTANTS.
I SHALL KEEP ONE OF YOU HERE WITH ME, WHILE THE OTHER GOES BACK OUTSIDE AND REMOVES THE CRYSTAL SEAL LOCKING SHUT THE TOMB DOORS...
...WHICH I AND MY SPAWN ARE BARRED BY SORCERY FROM TOUCHING.
THEN, ALL THREE OF US SHALL BE FREE. DOES THAT NOT SOUND FAIR TO YOU?
UH... WELL...

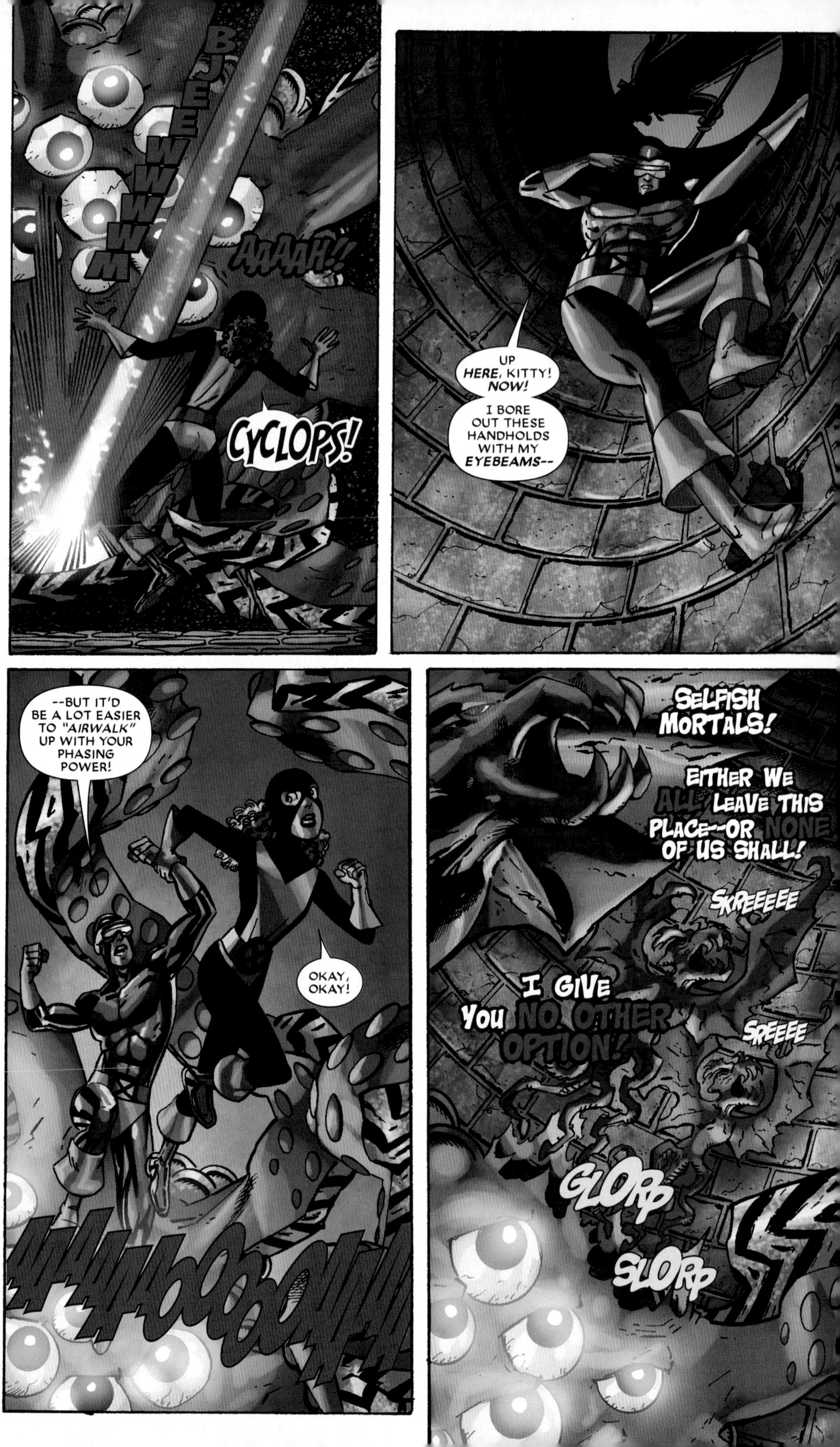
BJEEEWWWWWM
AAAAH!!
CYCLOPS!
UP HERE, KITTY! NOW!
I BORE OUT THESE HANDHOLDS WITH MY EYEBEAMS--
--BUT IT'D BE A LOT EASIER TO "AIRWALK" UP WITH YOUR PHASING POWER!
OKAY, OKAY!
SELFISH MORTALS!
EITHER WE ALL LEAVE THIS PLACE--OR NONE OF US SHALL!
SKREEEEE
I GIVE YOU NO OTHER OPTION!
SREEEE
GLORP
SLORP

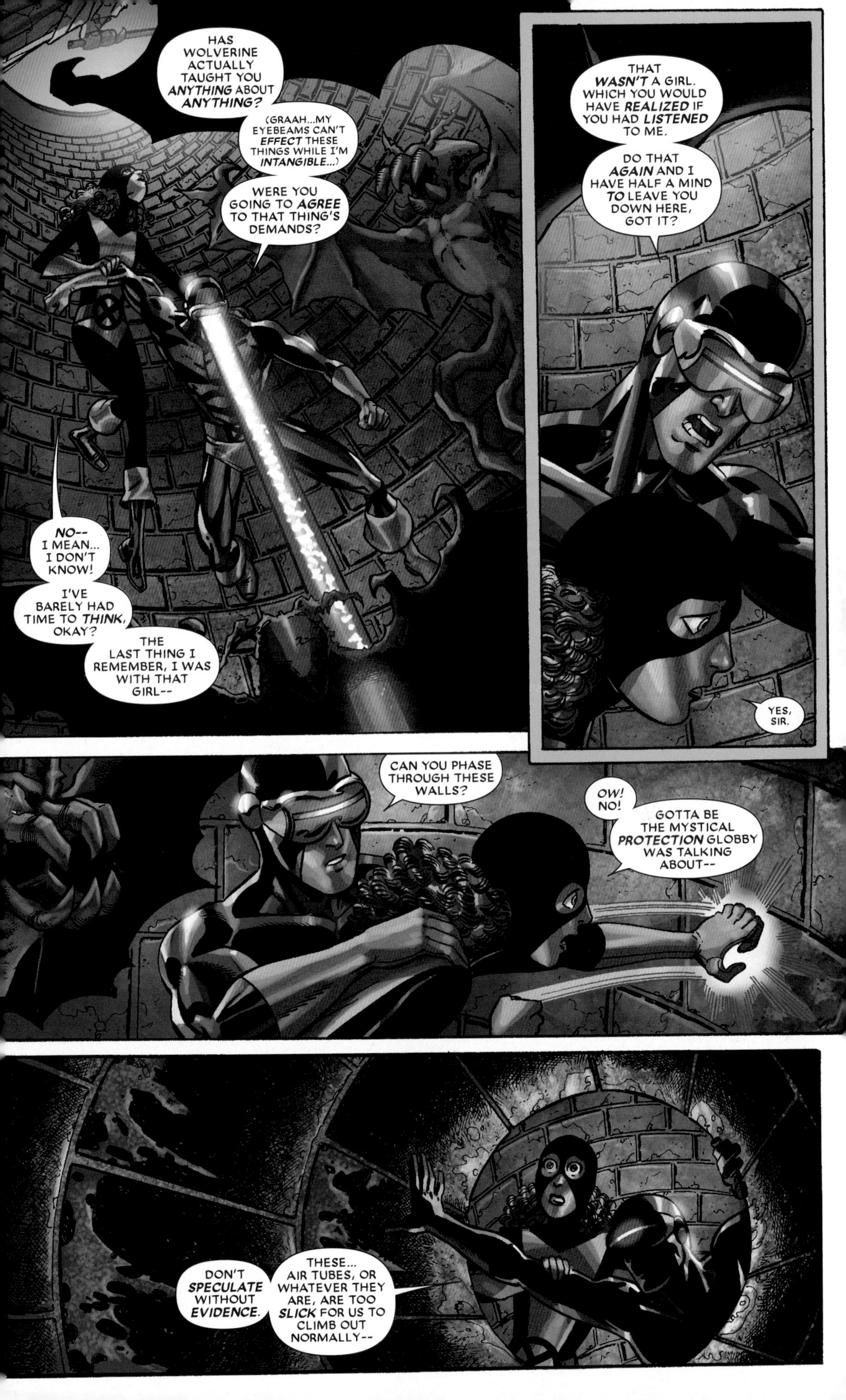
HAS WOLVERINE ACTUALLY TAUGHT YOU ANYTHING ABOUT ANYTHING?
(GRAAH...MY EYEBEAMS CAN'T EFFECT THESE THINGS WHILE I'M INTANGIBLE...)
WERE YOU GOING TO AGREE TO THAT THING'S DEMANDS?
NO-- I MEAN... I DON'T KNOW!
I'VE BARELY HAD TIME TO THINK, OKAY?
THE LAST THING I REMEMBER, I WAS WITH THAT GIRL--
THAT WASN'T A GIRL. WHICH YOU WOULD HAVE REALIZED IF YOU HAD LISTENED TO ME.
DO THAT AGAIN AND I HAVE HALF A MIND TO LEAVE YOU DOWN HERE, GOT IT?
YES, SIR.
CAN YOU PHASE THROUGH THESE WALLS?
OW! NO!
GOTTA BE THE MYSTICAL PROTECTION GLOBBY WAS TALKING ABOUT--
THESE... AIR TUBES, OR WHATEVER THEY ARE, ARE TOO SLICK FOR US TO CLIMB OUT NORMALLY--
DON'T SPECULATE WITHOUT EVIDENCE.

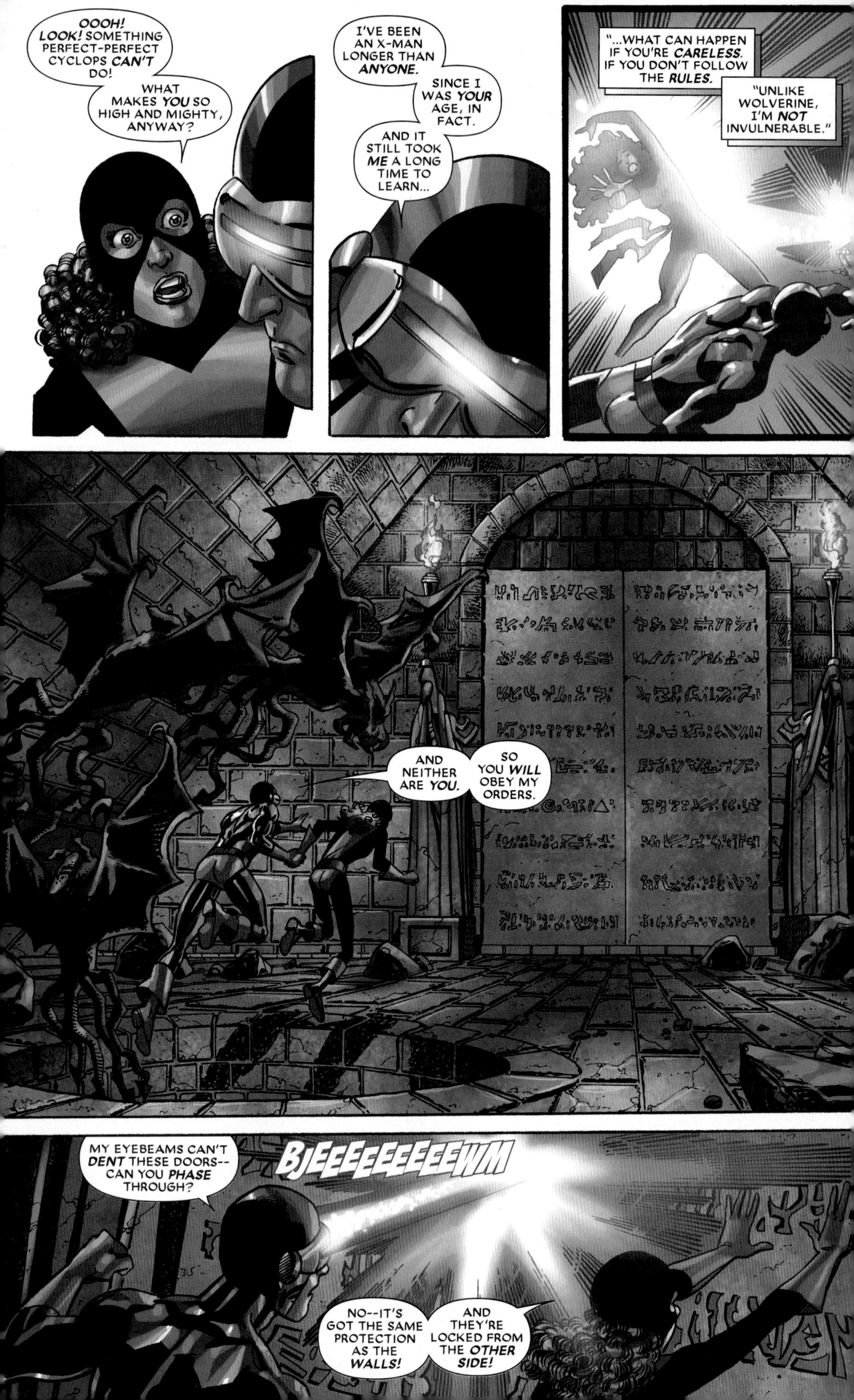

OOOH! LOOK! SOMETHING PERFECT-PERFECT CYCLOPS CAN'T DO!
WHAT MAKES YOU SO HIGH AND MIGHTY, ANYWAY?
I'VE BEEN AN X-MAN LONGER THAN ANYONE.
SINCE I WAS YOUR AGE, IN FACT.
AND IT STILL TOOK ME A LONG TIME TO LEARN...
"...WHAT CAN HAPPEN IF YOU'RE CARELESS. IF YOU DON'T FOLLOW THE RULES.
"UNLIKE WOLVERINE, I'M NOT INVULNERABLE."
AND NEITHER ARE YOU.
SO YOU WILL OBEY MY ORDERS.
MY EYEBEAMS CAN'T DENT THESE DOORS-- CAN YOU PHASE THROUGH?
BJEEEEEEEEEEWM
NO--IT'S GOT THE SAME PROTECTION AS THE WALLS!
AND THEY'RE LOCKED FROM THE OTHER SIDE!

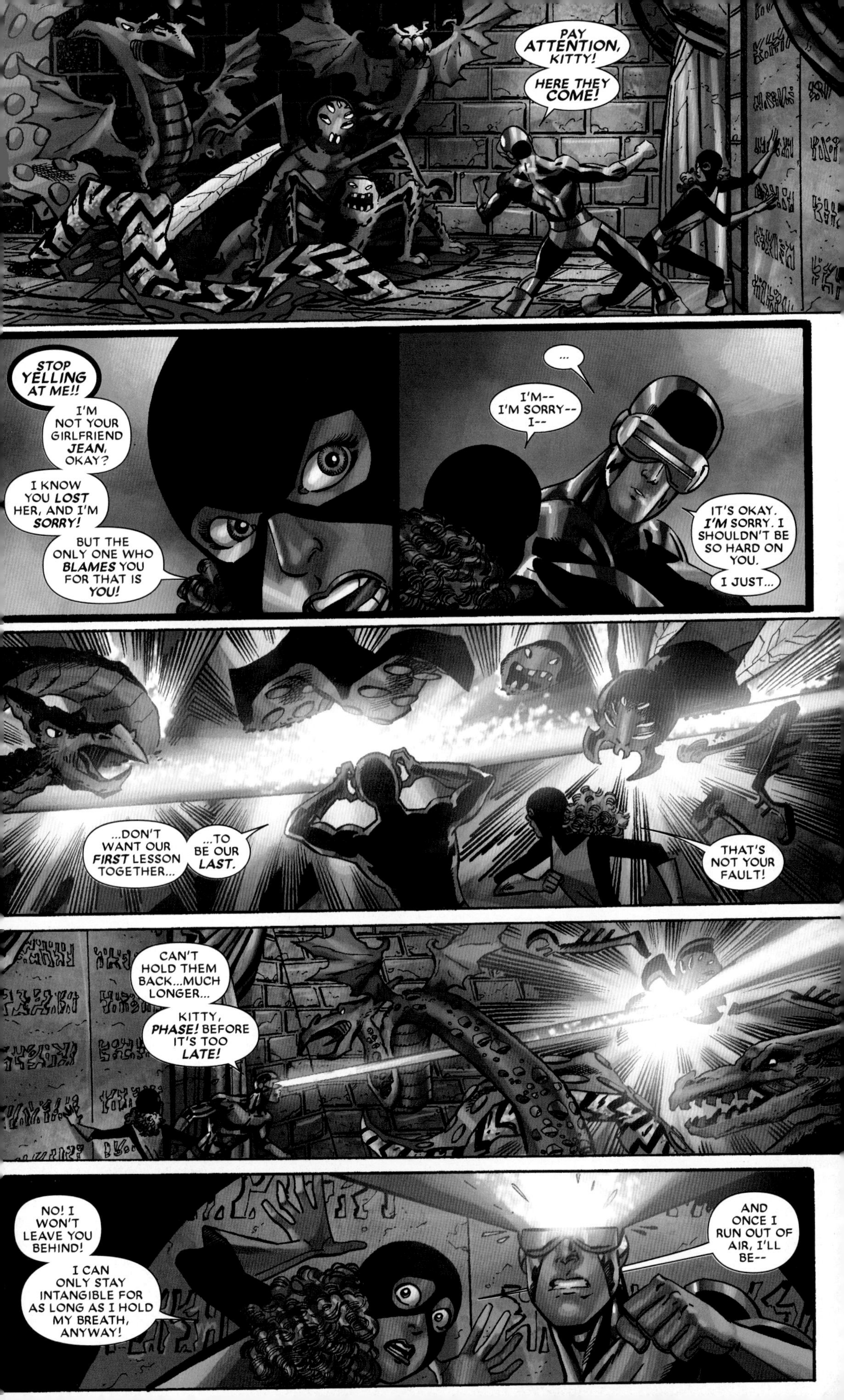
PAY ATTENTION, KITTY!
HERE THEY COME!
STOP YELLING AT ME!!
I'M NOT YOUR GIRLFRIEND JEAN, OKAY?
I KNOW YOU LOST HER, AND I'M SORRY!
BUT THE ONLY ONE WHO BLAMES YOU FOR THAT IS YOU!
...
I'M-- I'M SORRY-- I--
IT'S OKAY. I'M SORRY. I SHOULDN'T BE SO HARD ON YOU.
I JUST...
...DON'T WANT OUR FIRST LESSON TOGETHER...
...TO BE OUR LAST.
THAT'S NOT YOUR FAULT!
CAN'T HOLD THEM BACK...MUCH LONGER...
KITTY, PHASE! BEFORE IT'S TOO LATE!
NO! I WON'T LEAVE YOU BEHIND!
I CAN ONLY STAY INTANGIBLE FOR AS LONG AS I HOLD MY BREATH, ANYWAY!
AND ONCE I RUN OUT OF AIR, I'LL BE--

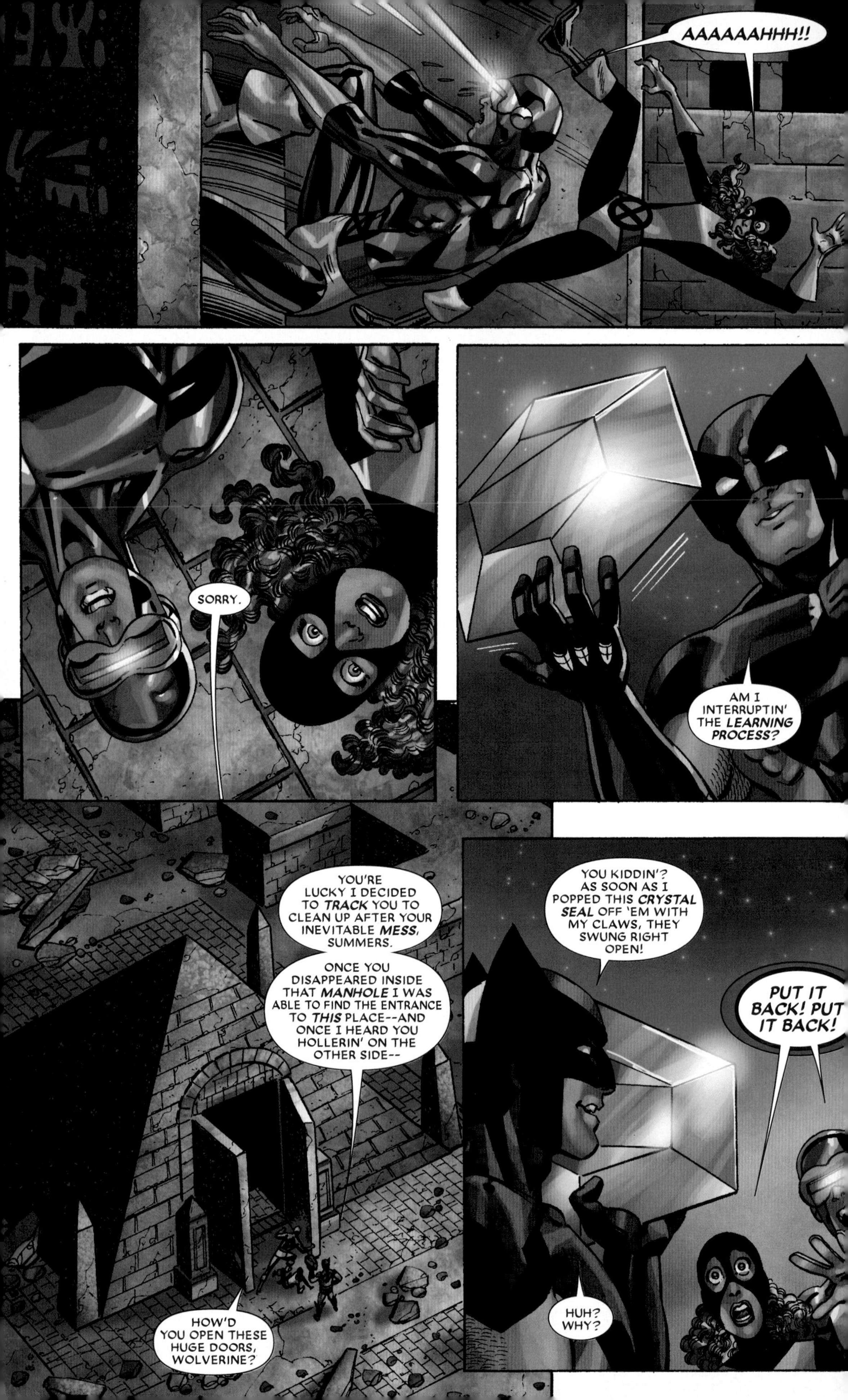

AAAAAAHHH!!
SORRY.
AM I INTERRUPTIN' THE LEARNING PROCESS?
YOU'RE LUCKY I DECIDED TO TRACK YOU TO CLEAN UP AFTER YOUR INEVITABLE MESS, SUMMERS.
ONCE YOU DISAPPEARED INSIDE THAT MANHOLE I WAS ABLE TO FIND THE ENTRANCE TO THIS PLACE--AND ONCE I HEARD YOU HOLLERIN' ON THE OTHER SIDE--
HOW'D YOU OPEN THESE HUGE DOORS, WOLVERINE?
YOU KIDDIN'? AS SOON AS I POPPED THIS CRYSTAL SEAL OFF 'EM WITH MY CLAWS, THEY SWUNG RIGHT OPEN!
PUT IT BACK! PUT IT BACK!
HUH? WHY?

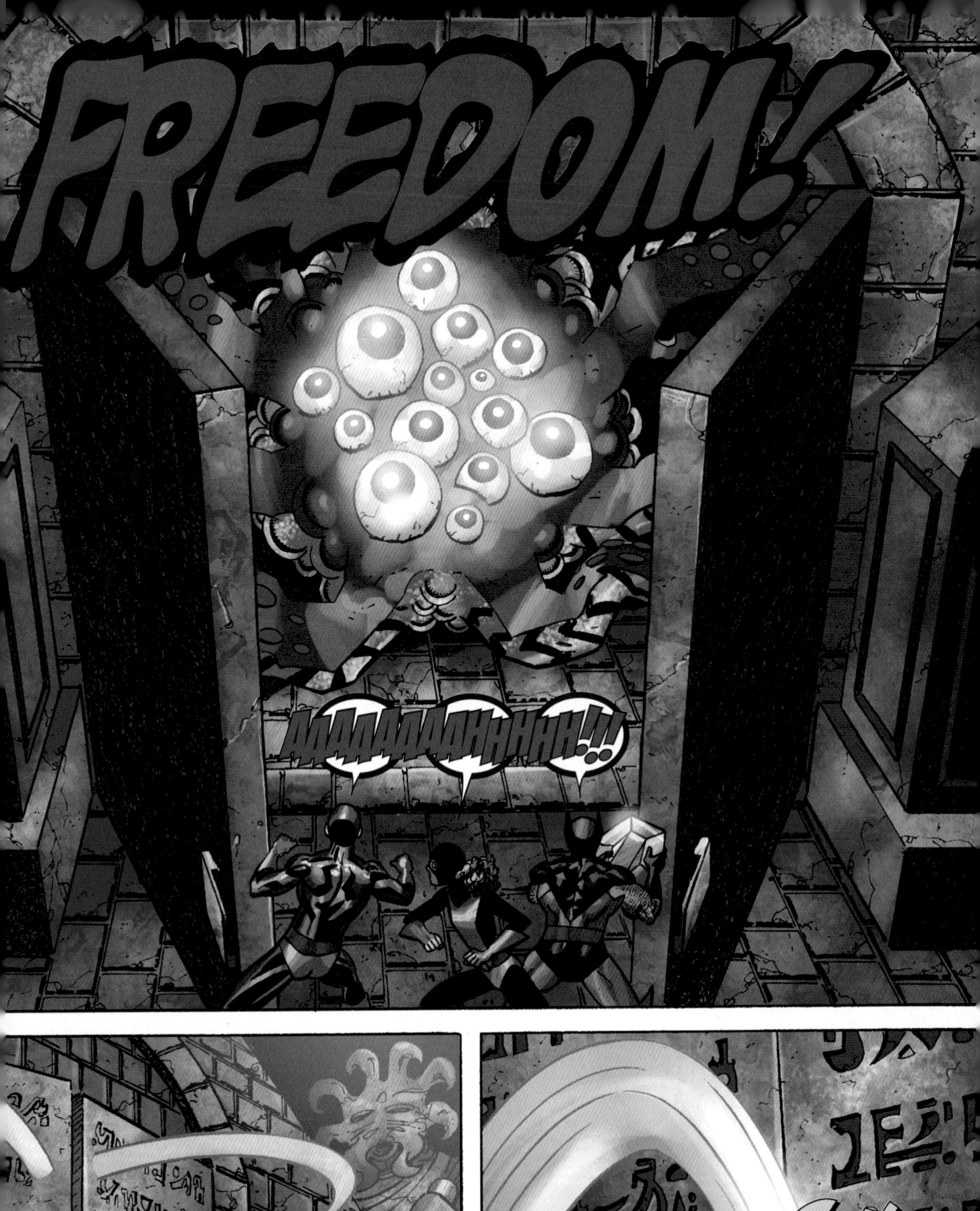
FREEDOM!
AAAAAAAAHHHHH!!!

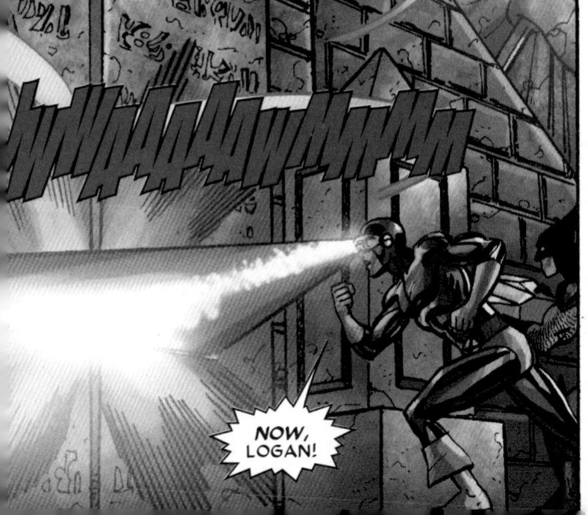
WHAAAAWMMMM
NOW, LOGAN!

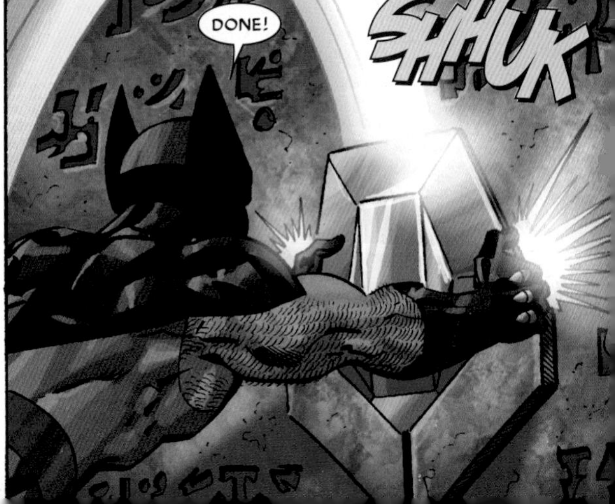
DONE!
SHHUK

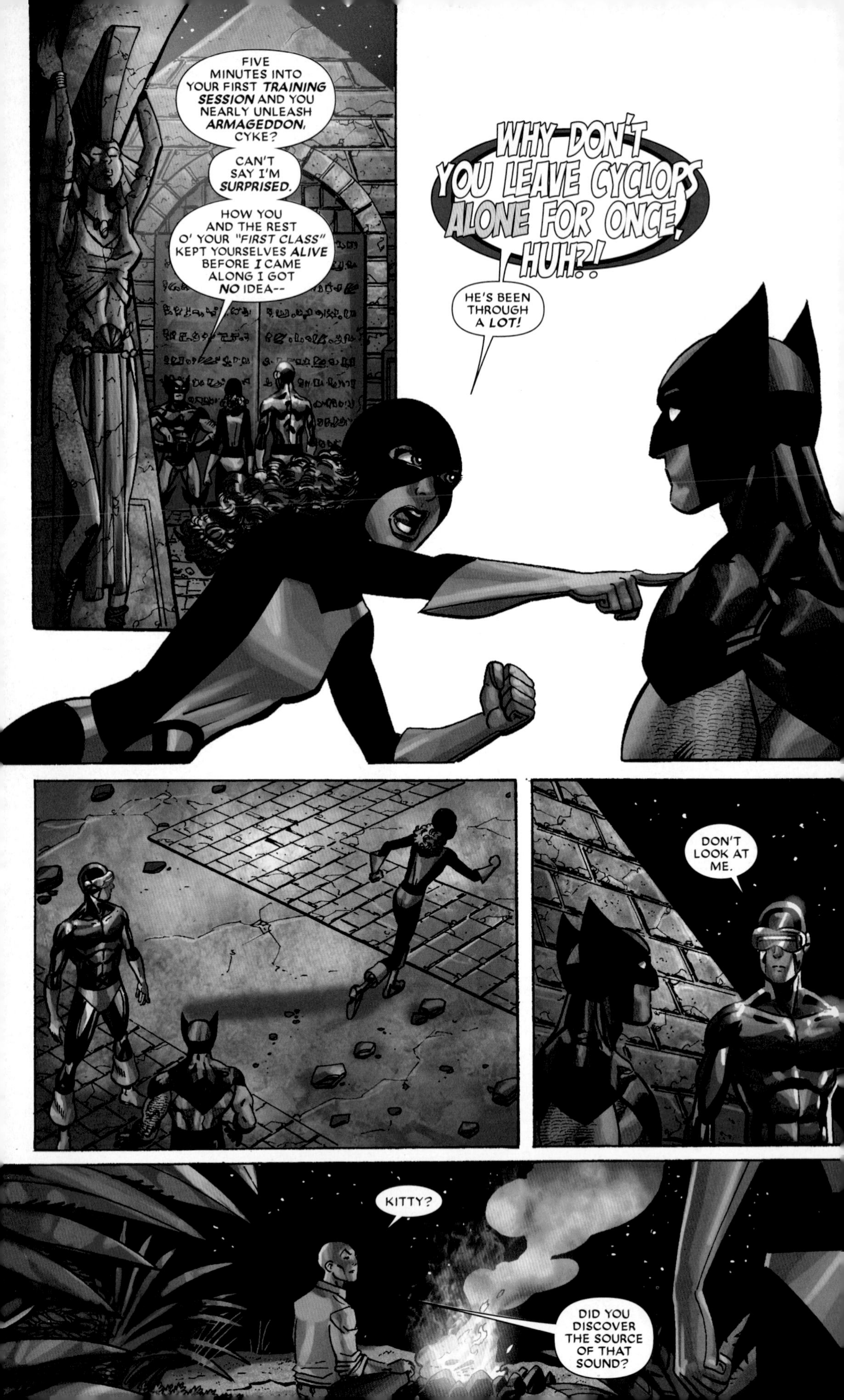

FIVE MINUTES INTO YOUR FIRST TRAINING SESSION AND YOU NEARLY UNLEASH ARMAGEDDON, CYKE?
CAN'T SAY I'M SURPRISED.
HOW YOU AND THE REST O' YOUR "FIRST CLASS" KEPT YOURSELVES ALIVE BEFORE I CAME ALONG I GOT NO IDEA--
WHY DON'T YOU LEAVE CYCLOPS ALONE FOR ONCE, HUH?!
HE'S BEEN THROUGH A LOT!
DON'T LOOK AT ME.
KITTY?
DID YOU DISCOVER THE SOURCE OF THAT SOUND?

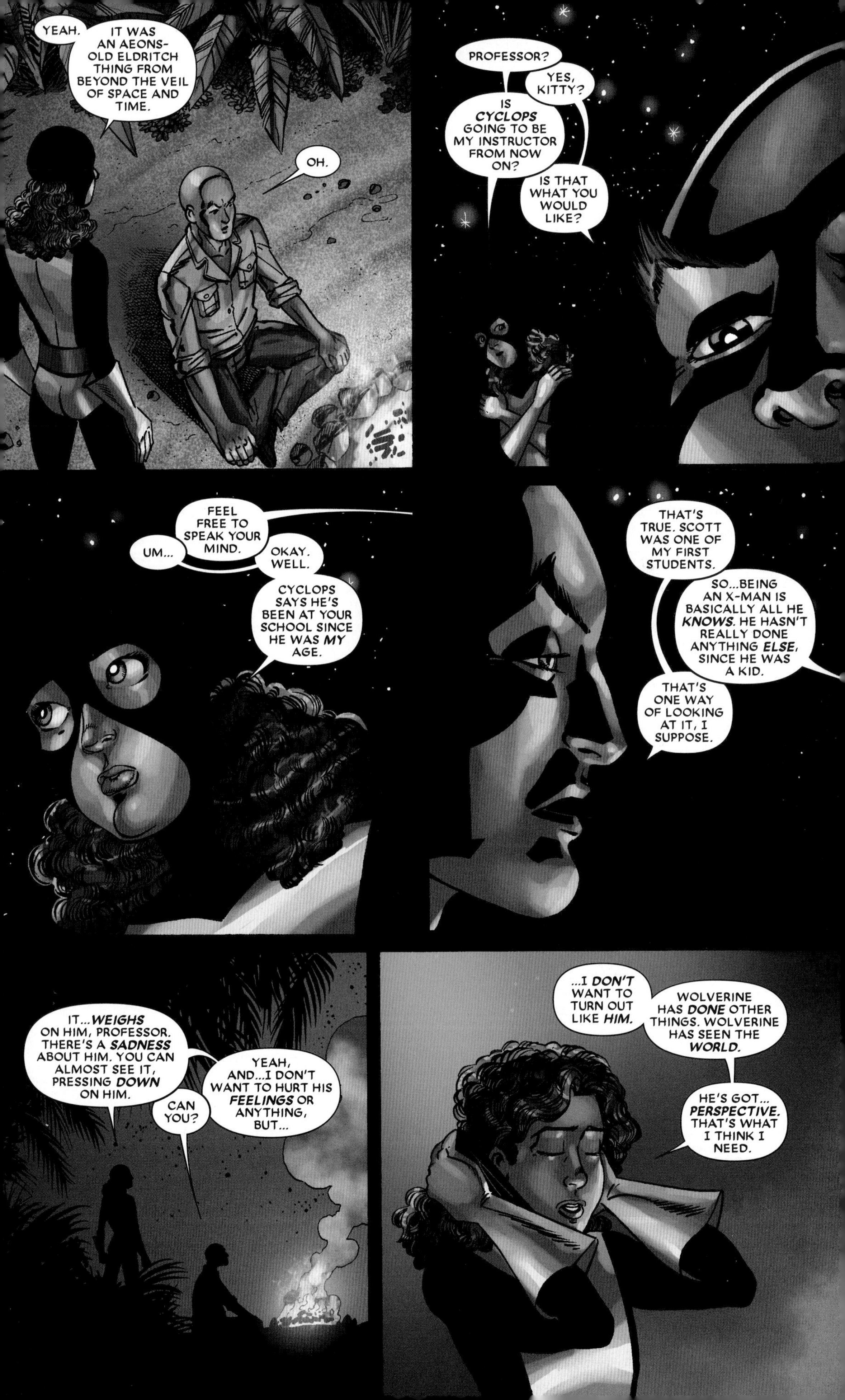
YEAH.
IT WAS AN AEONS-OLD ELDRITCH THING FROM BEYOND THE VEIL OF SPACE AND TIME.
OH.
PROFESSOR?
YES, KITTY?
IS CYCLOPS GOING TO BE MY INSTRUCTOR FROM NOW ON?
IS THAT WHAT YOU WOULD LIKE?
UM...
FEEL FREE TO SPEAK YOUR MIND.
OKAY. WELL.
CYCLOPS SAYS HE'S BEEN AT YOUR SCHOOL SINCE HE WAS MY AGE.
THAT'S TRUE. SCOTT WAS ONE OF MY FIRST STUDENTS.
SO...BEING AN X-MAN IS BASICALLY ALL HE KNOWS. HE HASN'T REALLY DONE ANYTHING ELSE, SINCE HE WAS A KID.
THAT'S ONE WAY OF LOOKING AT IT, I SUPPOSE.
IT...WEIGHS ON HIM, PROFESSOR. THERE'S A SADNESS ABOUT HIM. YOU CAN ALMOST SEE IT, PRESSING DOWN ON HIM.
CAN YOU?
YEAH, AND...I DON'T WANT TO HURT HIS FEELINGS OR ANYTHING, BUT...
...I DON'T WANT TO TURN OUT LIKE HIM.
WOLVERINE HAS DONE OTHER THINGS. WOLVERINE HAS SEEN THE WORLD.
HE'S GOT... PERSPECTIVE. THAT'S WHAT I THINK I NEED.

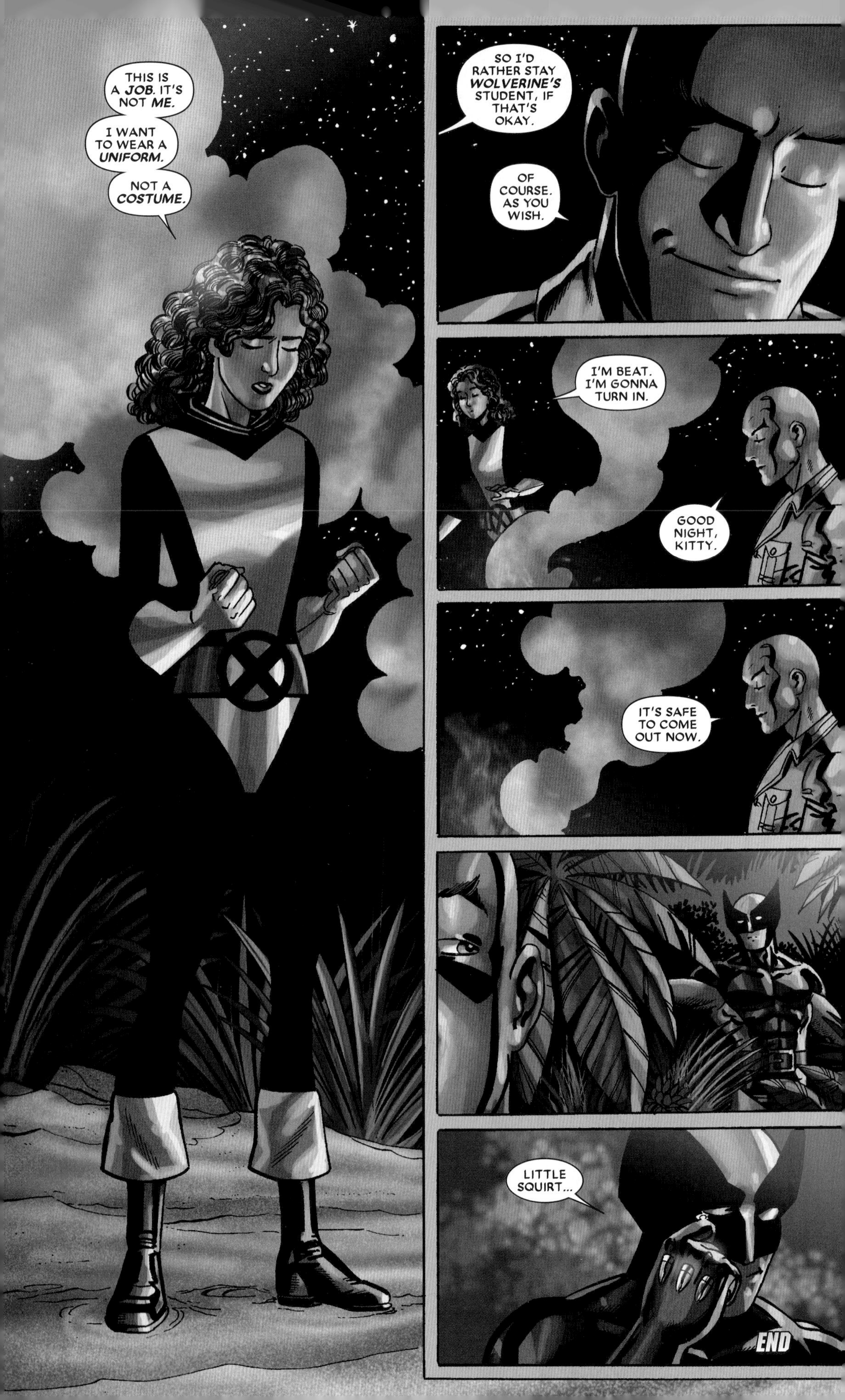
THIS IS A *JOB*. IT'S NOT *ME*.
I WANT TO WEAR A *UNIFORM*.
NOT A *COSTUME*.
SO I'D RATHER STAY *WOLVERINE'S* STUDENT, IF THAT'S OKAY.
OF COURSE. AS YOU WISH.
I'M BEAT. I'M GONNA TURN IN.
GOOD NIGHT, KITTY.
IT'S SAFE TO COME OUT NOW.
LITTLE SQUIRT...
END

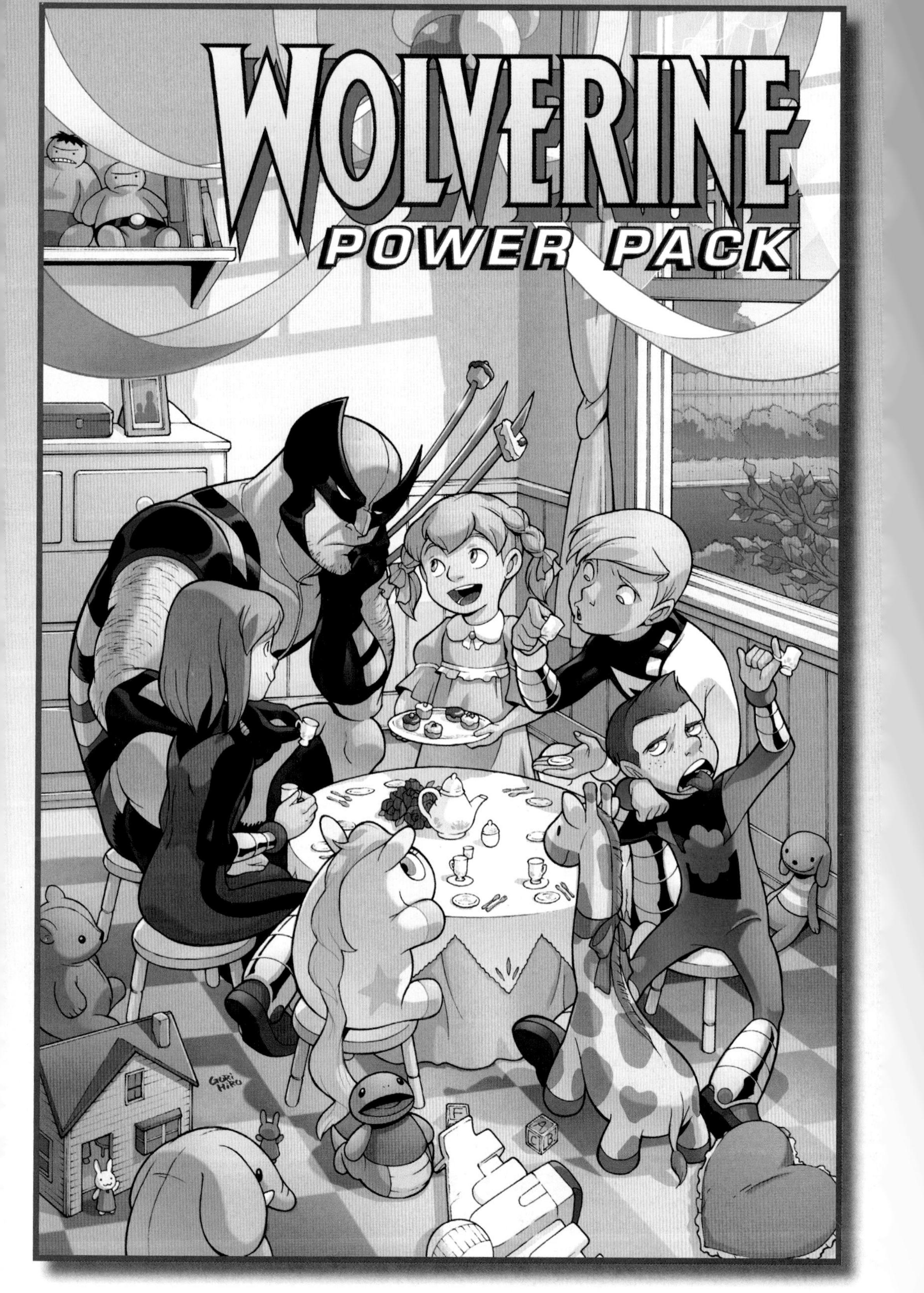
WOLVERINE
POWER PACK
GURI HIRU

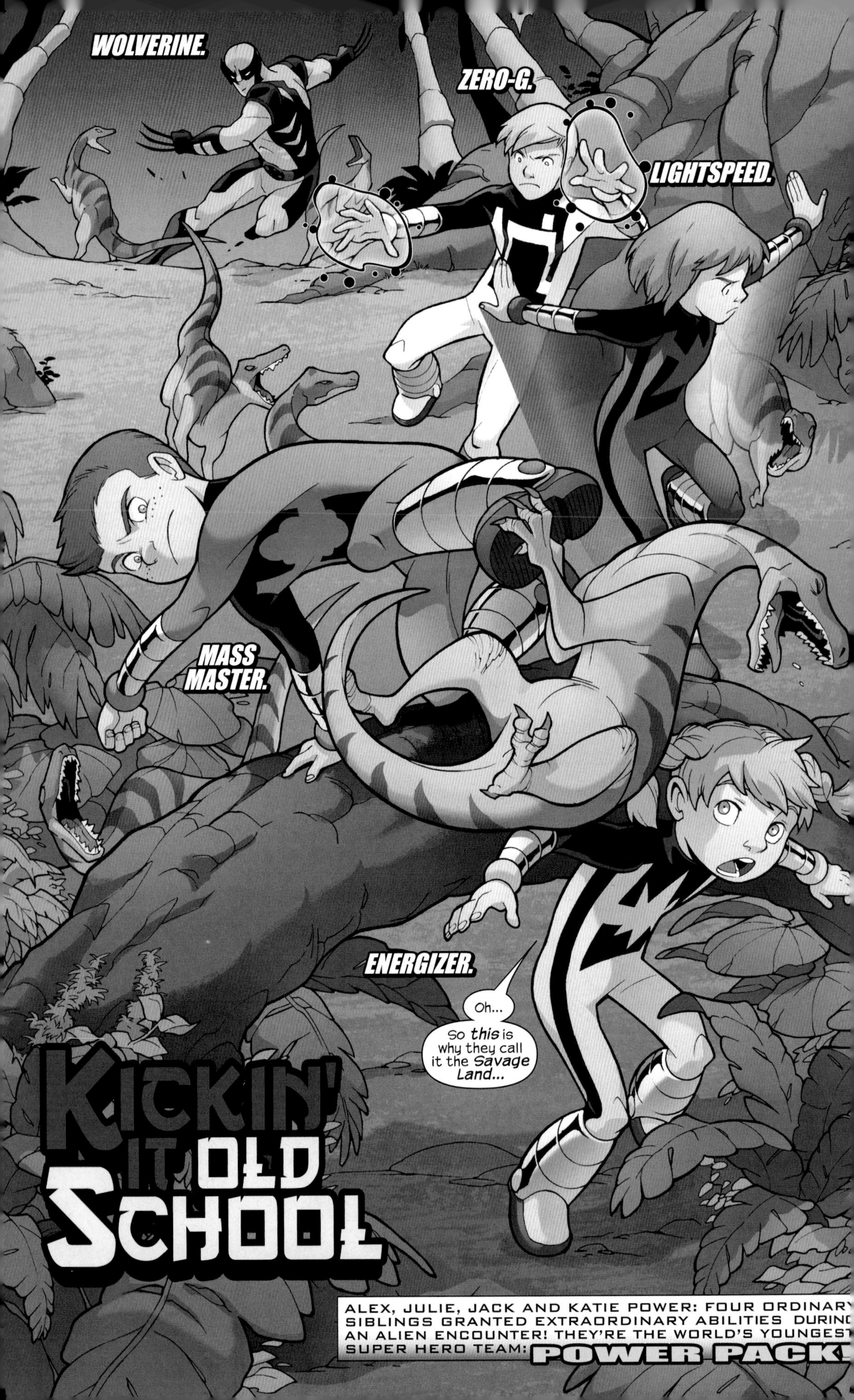

WOLVERINE.
ZERO-G.
LIGHTSPEED.
MASS MASTER.
ENERGIZER.
Oh...
So this is why they call it the Savage Land...
KICKIN' IT OLD SCHOOL
ALEX, JULIE, JACK AND KATIE POWER: FOUR ORDINARY SIBLINGS GRANTED EXTRAORDINARY ABILITIES DURING AN ALIEN ENCOUNTER! THEY'RE THE WORLD'S YOUNGEST SUPER HERO TEAM: POWER PACK!

KICK!

Not impressed.

These *aren't* real dinosaurs, remember?

This is all just a *training* simulation.

True. But the *Danger Room* has *earned its name*, kid.

Its *tech* can perfectly replicate *every detail* of the Savage Land, no matter how small...

SLASH!

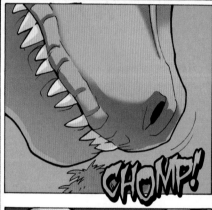

...or big.

Oh. I'm *sooooo* scared.

The *big fake dinosaur* is gonna--

CHOMP!

JACK?!

Oh, *no he* didn't!

Pretty sure he did...

Ew.

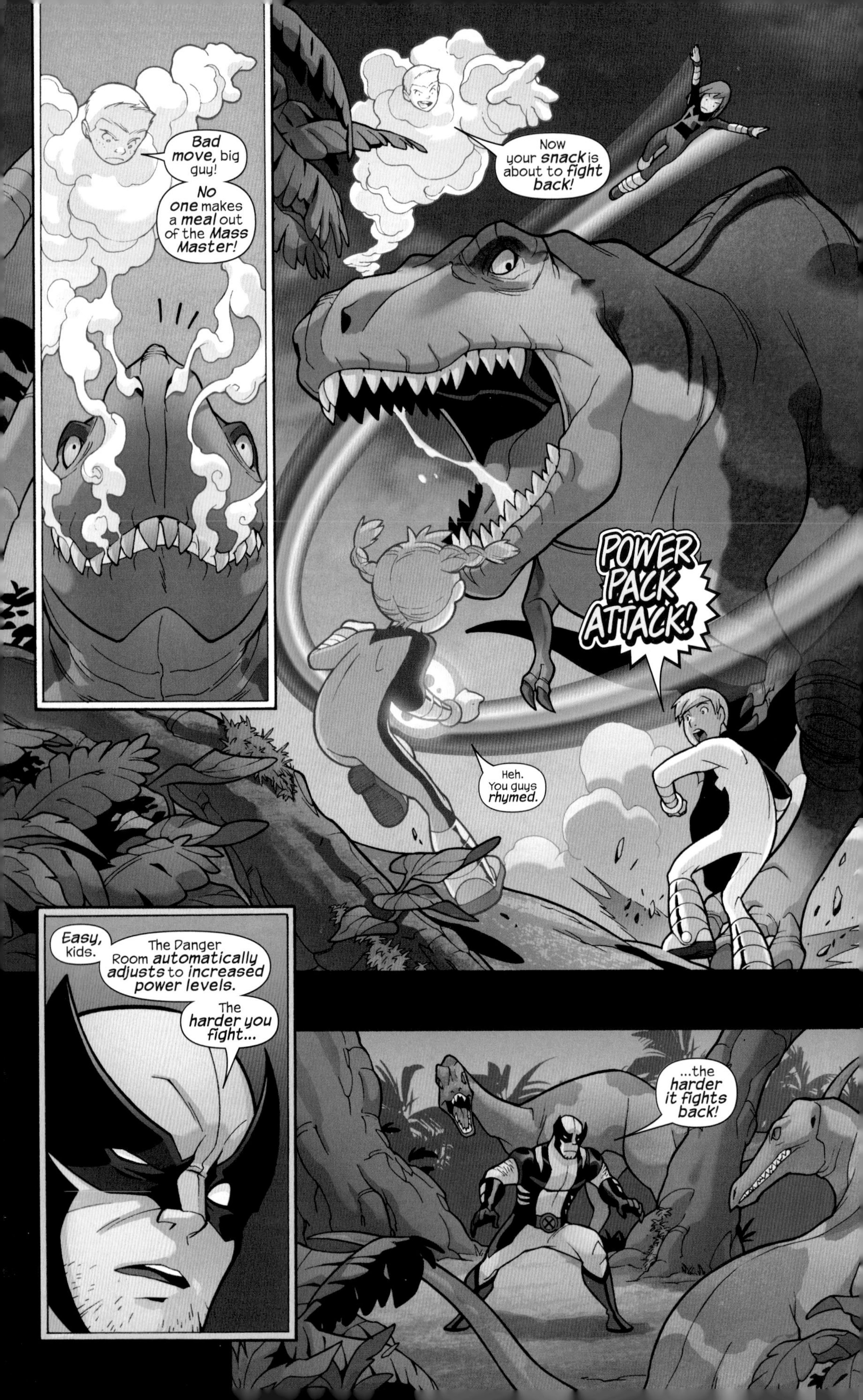
Bad move, big guy!
No one makes a meal out of the Mass Master!
Now your snack is about to fight back!
POWER PACK ATTACK!
Heh. You guys rhymed.
Easy, kids.
The Danger Room automatically adjusts to increased power levels.
The harder you fight...
...the harder it fights back!

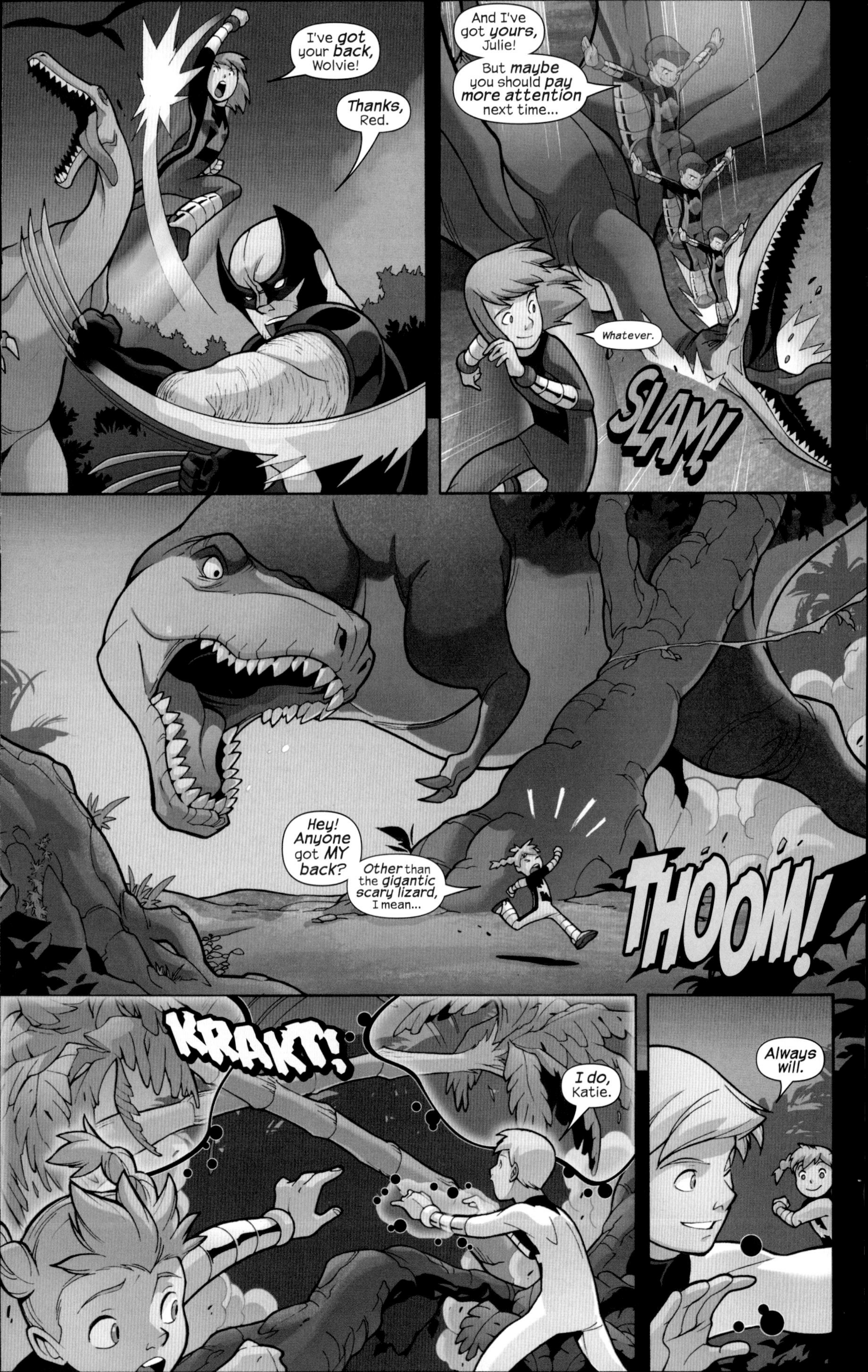
I've *got* your *back,* Wolvie!
Thanks, Red.
And I've got *yours,* Julie!
But *maybe* you should *pay more attention* next time...
Whatever.
SLAM!
Hey! Anyone got *MY* back?
Other than the *gigantic scary lizard,* I mean...
THOOM!
KRAKT!
I do, Katie.
Always will.

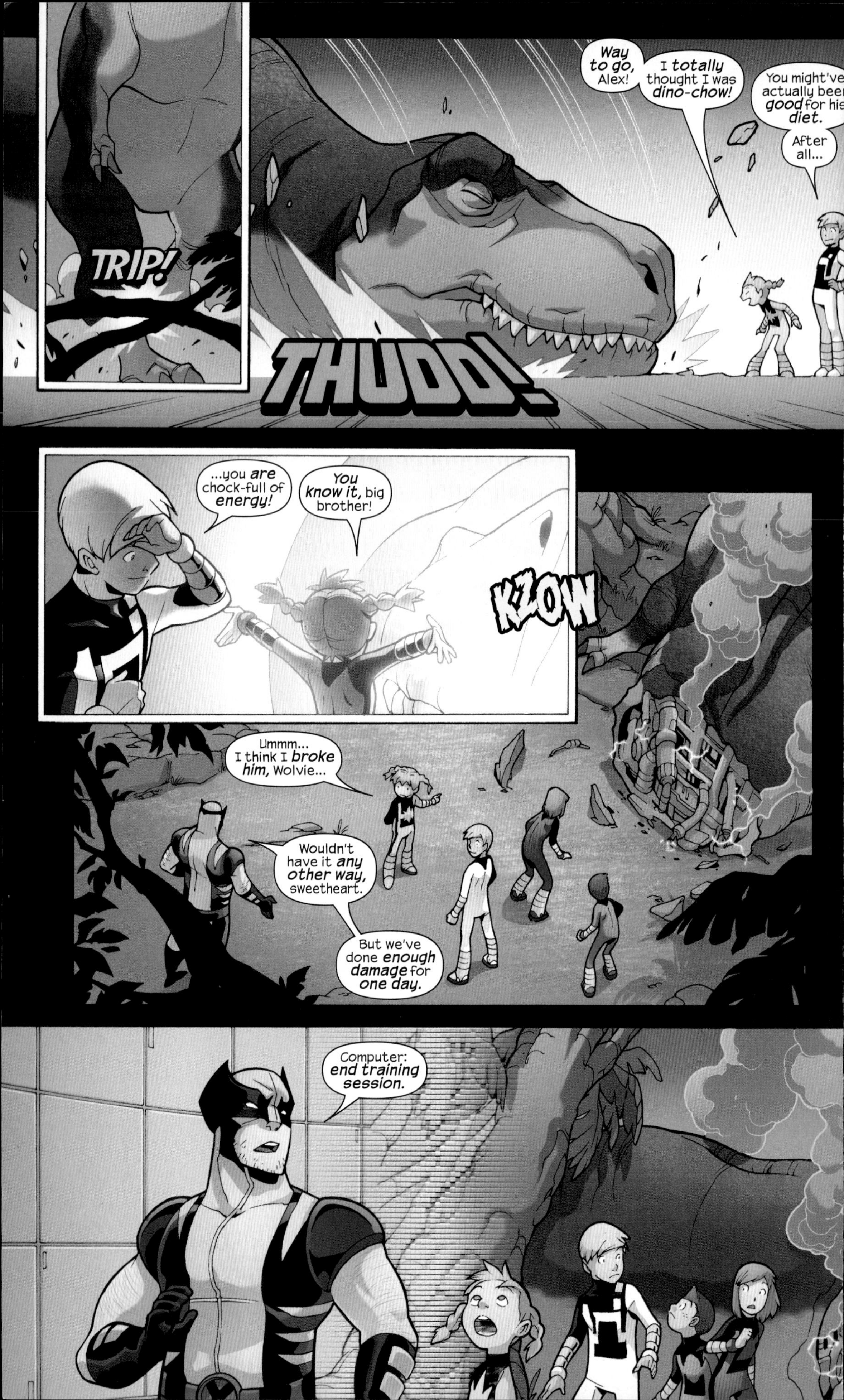
TRIP!
Way to go, Alex!
I totally thought I was dino-chow!
You might've actually been good for his diet.
After all...
THUDD!
...you are chock-full of energy!
You know it, big brother!
KZOW
Ummm... I think I broke him, Wolvie...
Wouldn't have it any other way, sweetheart.
But we've done enough damage for one day.
Computer: end training session.

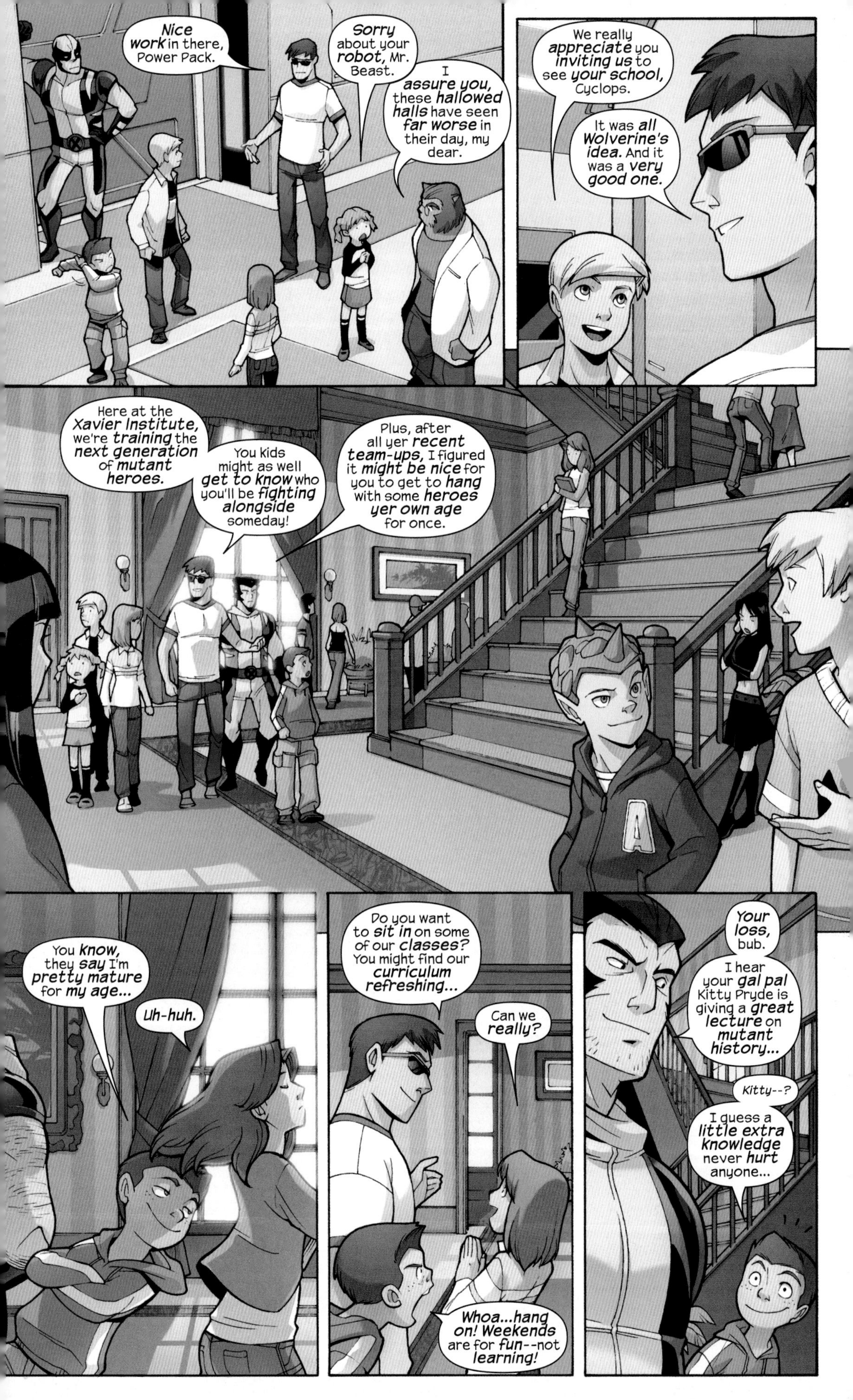
Nice work in there, Power Pack.
Sorry about your robot, Mr. Beast.
I assure you, these hallowed halls have seen far worse in their day, my dear.
We really appreciate you inviting us to see your school, Cyclops.
It was all Wolverine's idea. And it was a very good one.
Here at the Xavier Institute, we're training the next generation of mutant heroes.
You kids might as well get to know who you'll be fighting alongside someday!
Plus, after all yer recent team-ups, I figured it might be nice for you to get to hang with some heroes yer own age for once.
You know, they say I'm pretty mature for my age...
Uh-huh.
Do you want to sit in on some of our classes? You might find our curriculum refreshing...
Can we really?
Whoa...hang on! Weekends are for fun--not learning!
Your loss, bub.
I hear your gal pal Kitty Pryde is giving a great lecture on mutant history...
Kitty--?
I guess a little extra knowledge never hurt anyone...

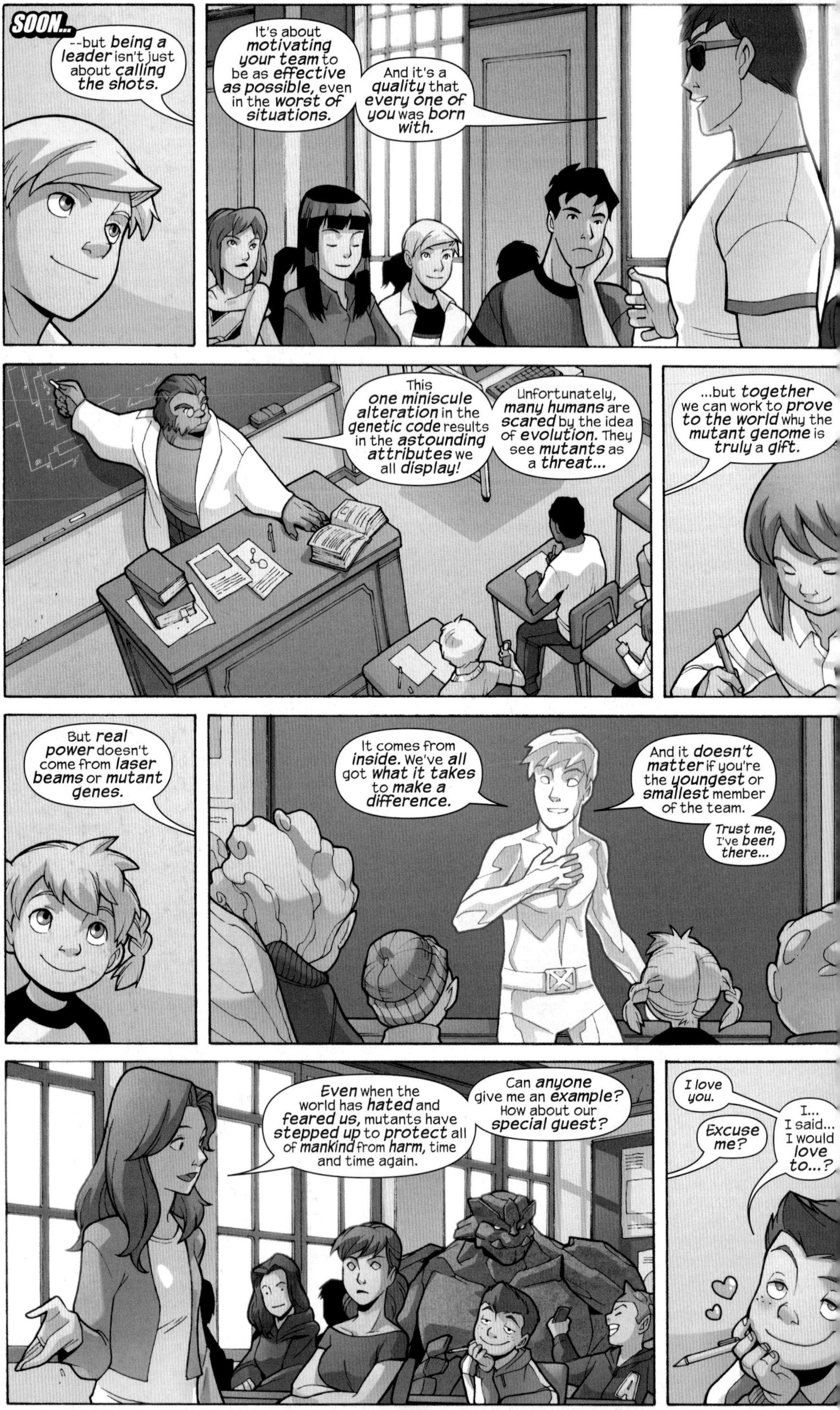
SOON...
--but being a leader isn't just about calling the shots.
It's about motivating your team to be as effective as possible, even in the worst of situations.
And it's a quality that every one of you was born with.
This one miniscule alteration in the genetic code results in the astounding attributes we all display!
Unfortunately, many humans are scared by the idea of evolution. They see mutants as a threat...
...but together we can work to prove to the world why the mutant genome is truly a gift.
But real power doesn't come from laser beams or mutant genes.
It comes from inside. We've all got what it takes to make a difference.
And it doesn't matter if you're the youngest or smallest member of the team.
Trust me, I've been there...
Even when the world has hated and feared us, mutants have stepped up to protect all of mankind from harm, time and time again.
Can anyone give me an example? How about our special guest?
I love you.
Excuse me?
I... I said... I would love to...?

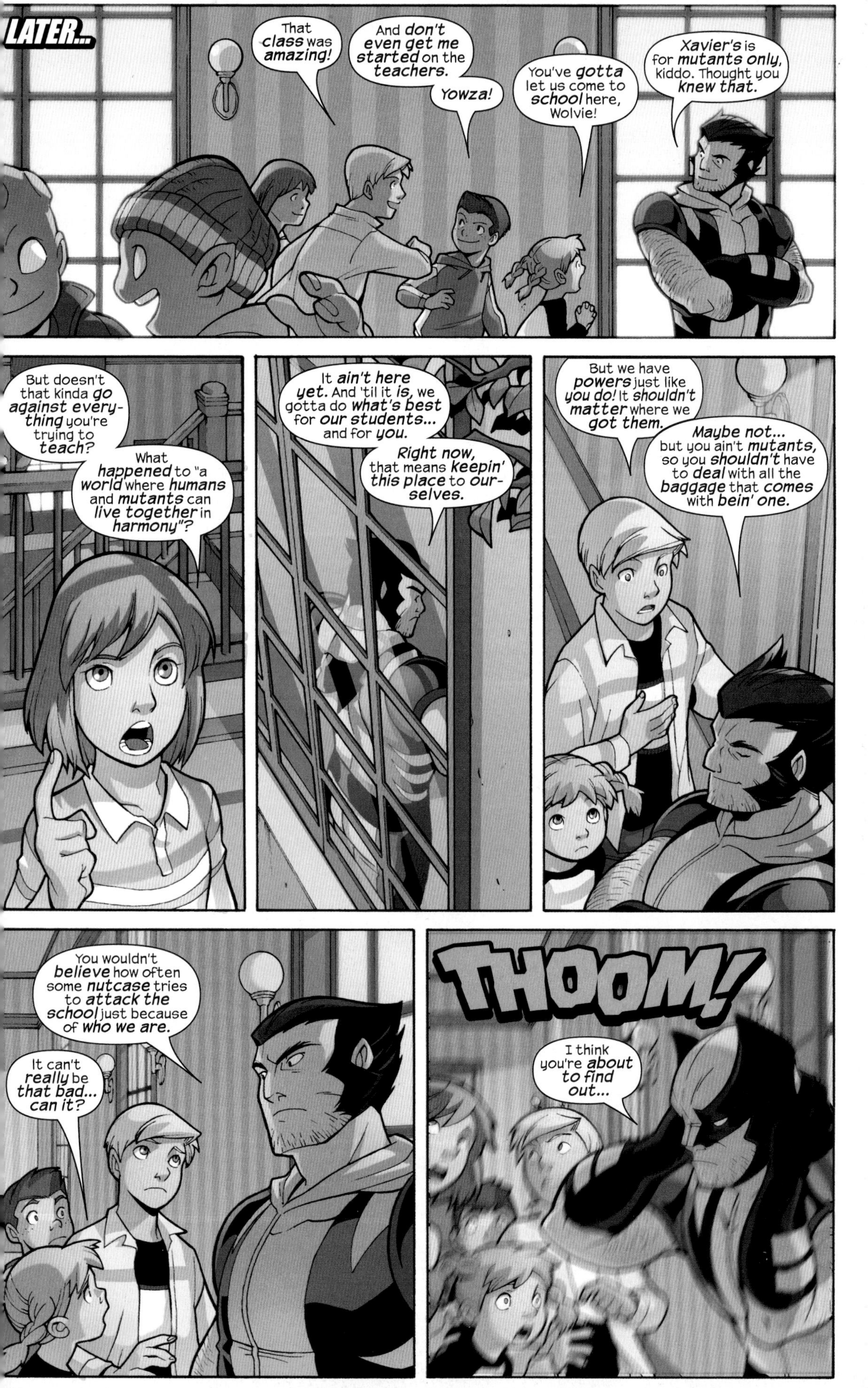
LATER...
That class was amazing!
And don't even get me started on the teachers.
Yowza!
You've gotta let us come to school here, Wolvie!
Xavier's is for mutants only, kiddo. Thought you knew that.
But doesn't that kinda go against everything you're trying to teach?
What happened to "a world where humans and mutants can live together in harmony"?
It ain't here yet. And 'til it is, we gotta do what's best for our students... and for you.
Right now, that means keepin' this place to ourselves.
But we have powers just like you do! It shouldn't matter where we got them.
Maybe not... but you ain't mutants, so you shouldn't have to deal with all the baggage that comes with bein' one.
You wouldn't believe how often some nutcase tries to attack the school just because of who we are.
It can't really be that bad... can it?
THOOM!
I think you're about to find out...

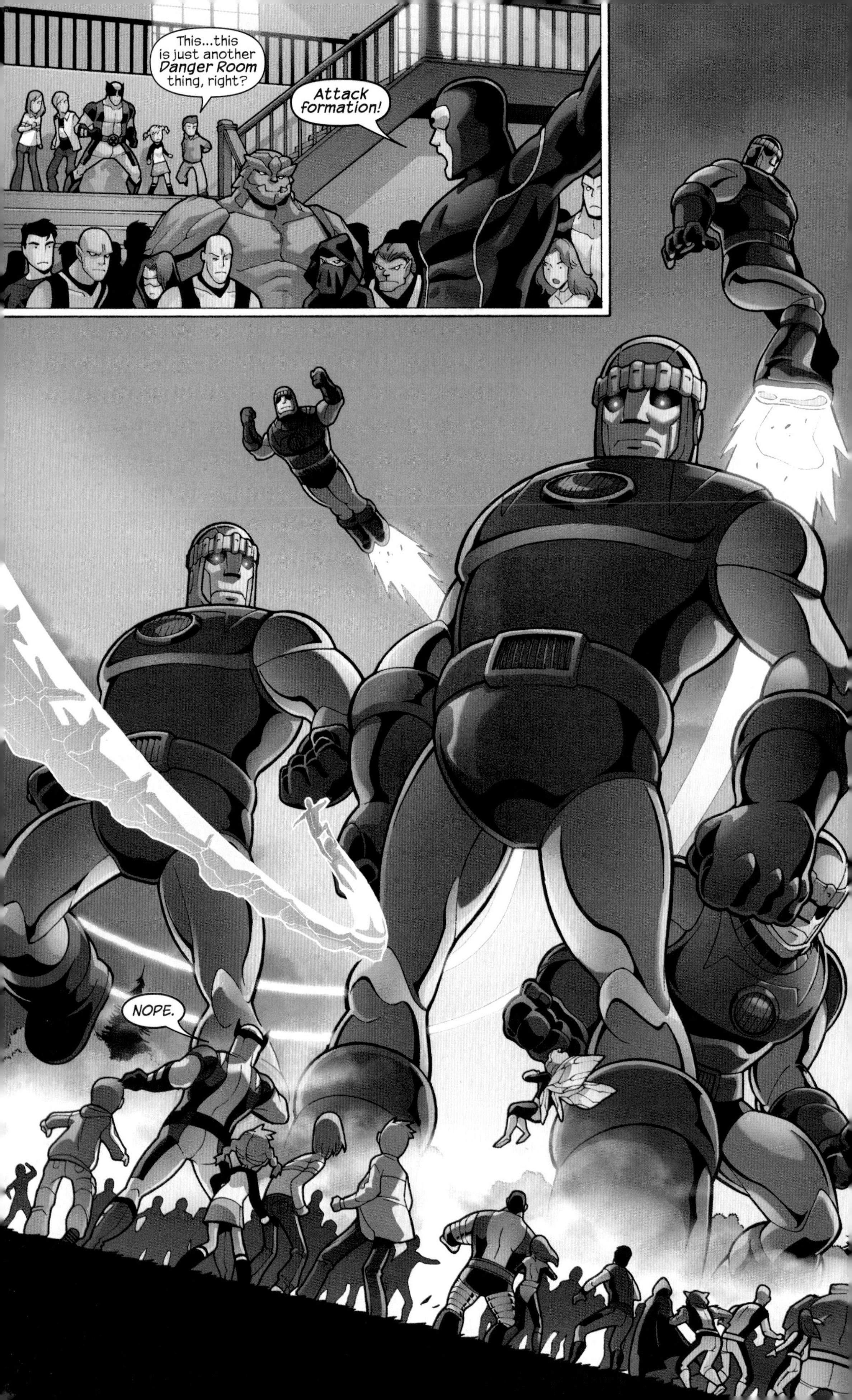
This...this is just another Danger Room thing, right?
Attack formation!
NOPE.

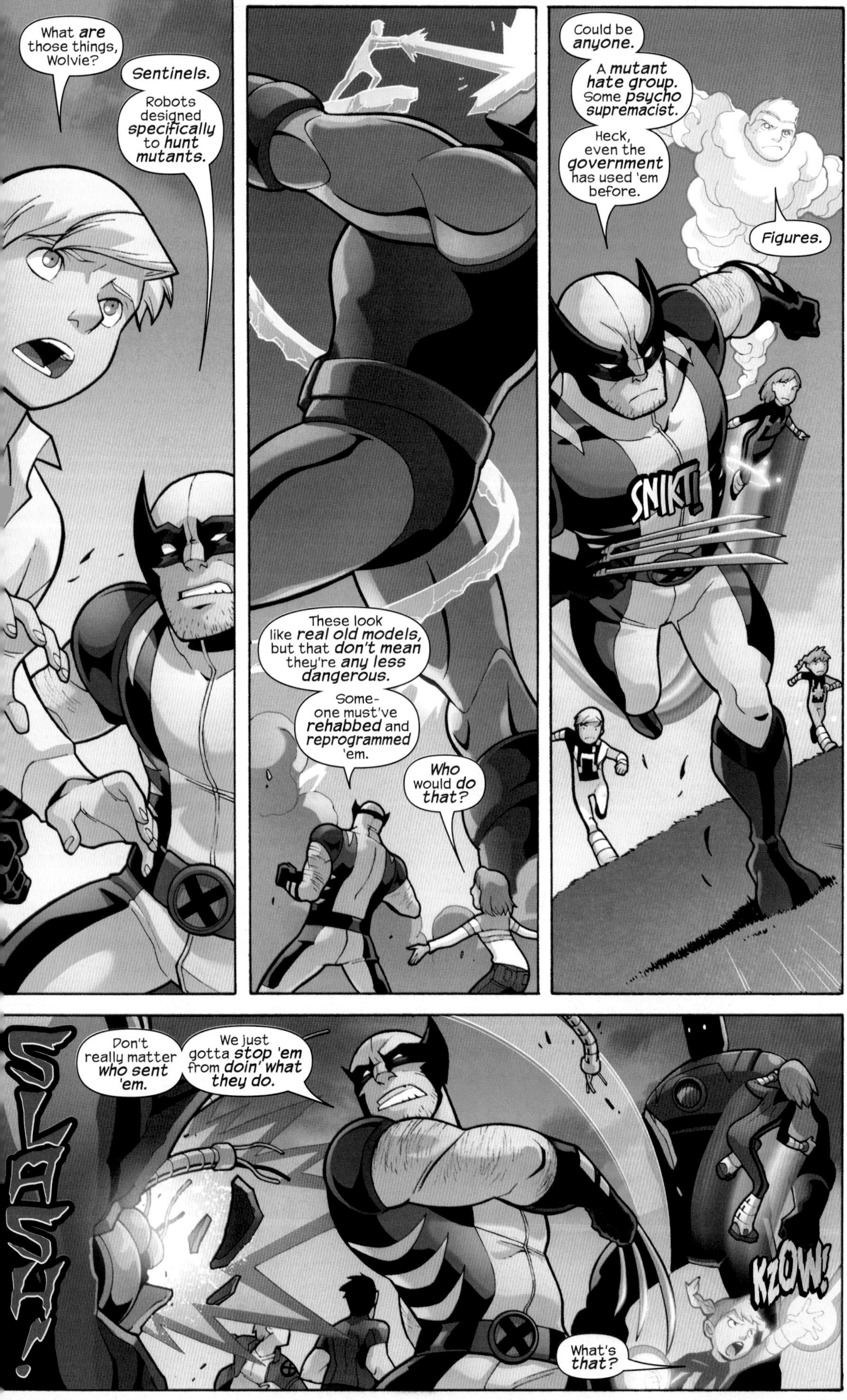
What are those things, Wolvie?
Sentinels.
Robots designed specifically to hunt mutants.
These look like real old models, but that don't mean they're any less dangerous.
Some-one must've rehabbed and reprogrammed 'em.
Who would do that?
Could be anyone.
A mutant hate group. Some psycho supremacist.
Heck, even the government has used 'em before.
Figures.
SNIKT!
SLASH!
Don't really matter who sent 'em.
We just gotta stop 'em from doin' what they do.
KZOW!
What's that?

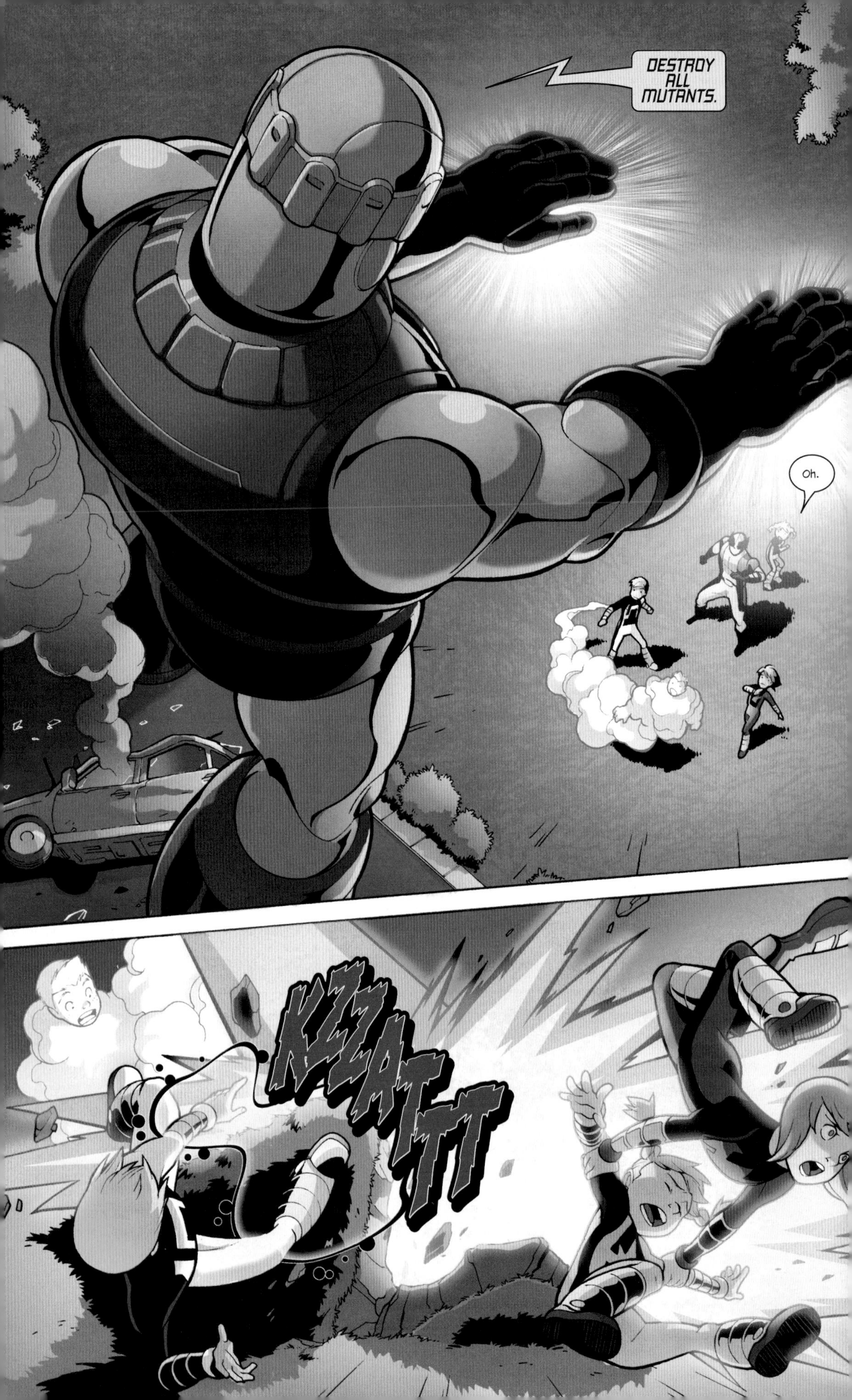
DESTROY ALL MUTANTS.
Oh.
KZZATTTT

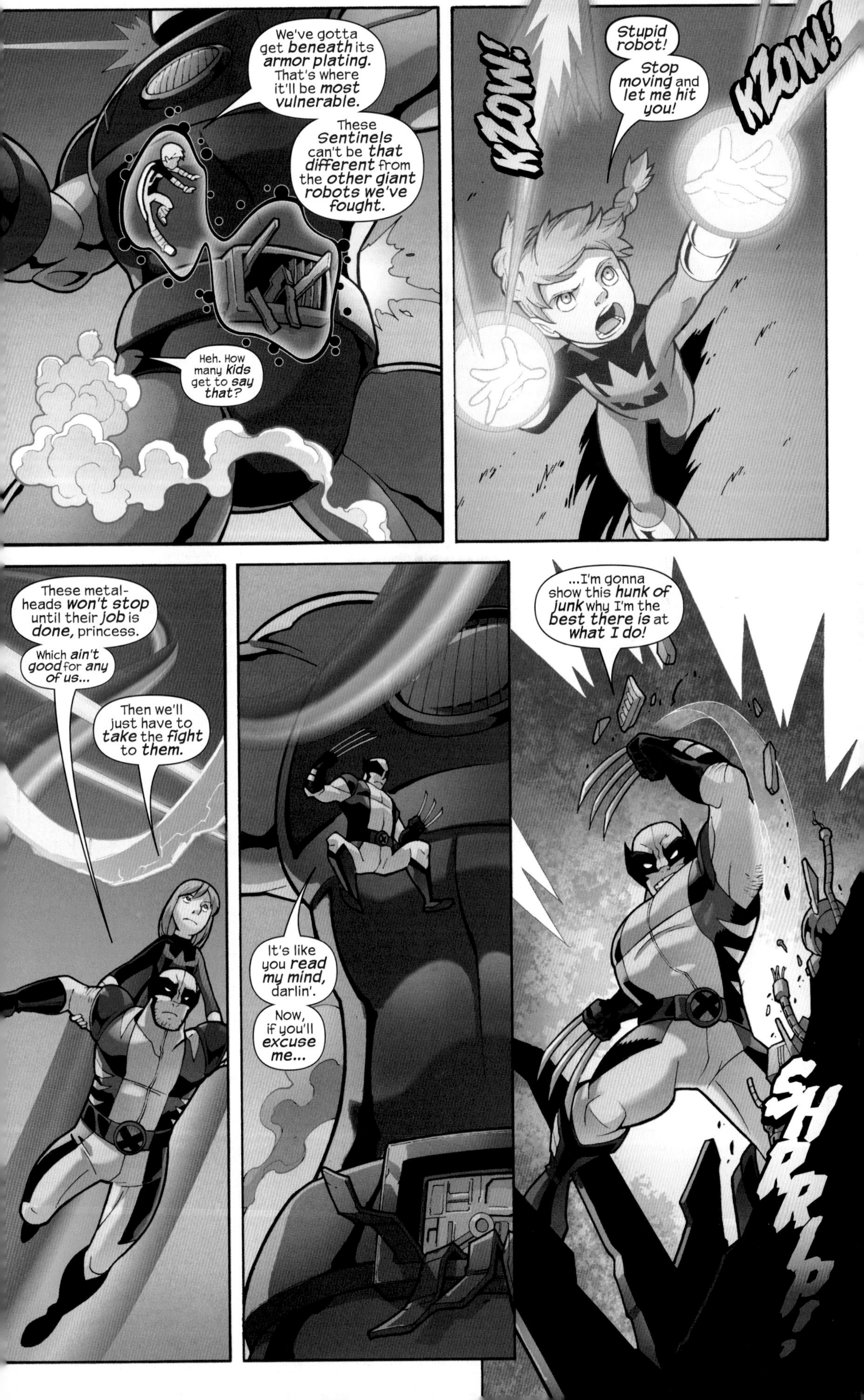
We've gotta get beneath its armor plating. That's where it'll be most vulnerable.
These Sentinels can't be that different from the other giant robots we've fought.
Heh. How many kids get to say that?
KZOW!
Stupid robot!
Stop moving and let me hit you!
KZOW!
These metal-heads won't stop until their job is done, princess.
Which ain't good for any of us...
Then we'll just have to take the fight to them.
It's like you read my mind, darlin'.
Now, if you'll excuse me...
...I'm gonna show this hunk of junk why I'm the best there is at what I do!
SHRRIP!

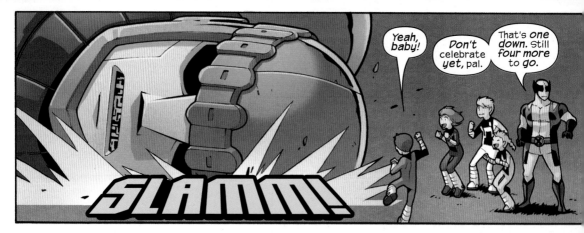

SLAMM!

Yeah, baby!

Don't celebrate yet, pal.

That's one down. Still four more to go.

And they won't be a part of that battle.

What are you talking about, Cyke?

We need every hand we can get.

And these kids--

Aren't mutants. So this isn't their fight.

The Sentinels came to attack us... and its our duty to make sure our guests are protected.

But--

It's an order, Logan.

Get them to safety. Now!

...Fine.

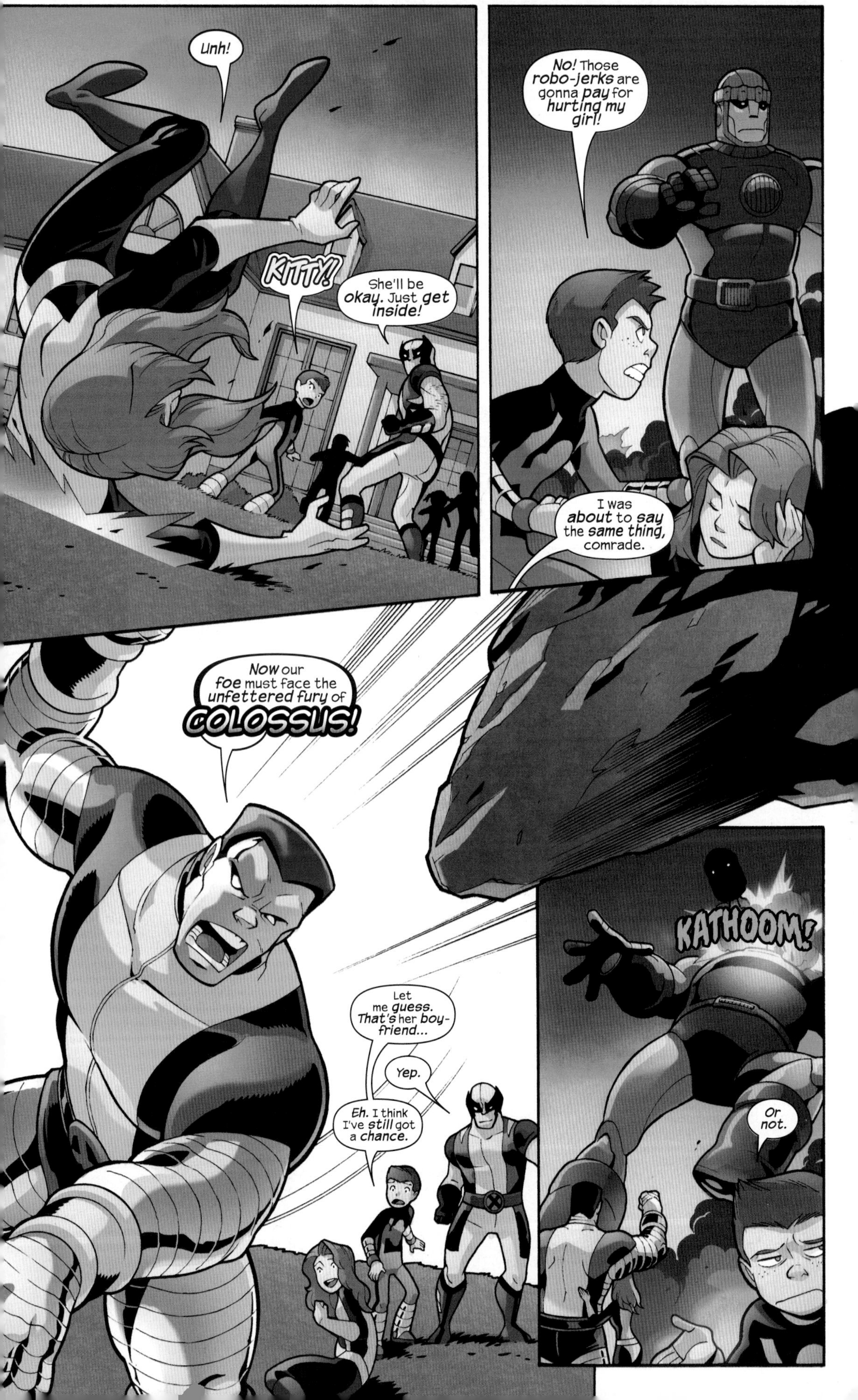
Unh!
KITTY!
She'll be okay. Just get inside!
No! Those robo-jerks are gonna pay for hurting my girl!
I was about to say the same thing, comrade.
Now our foe must face the unfettered fury of COLOSSUS!
Let me guess. That's her boy-friend...
Yep.
Eh. I think I've still got a chance.
KATHOOM!
Or not.

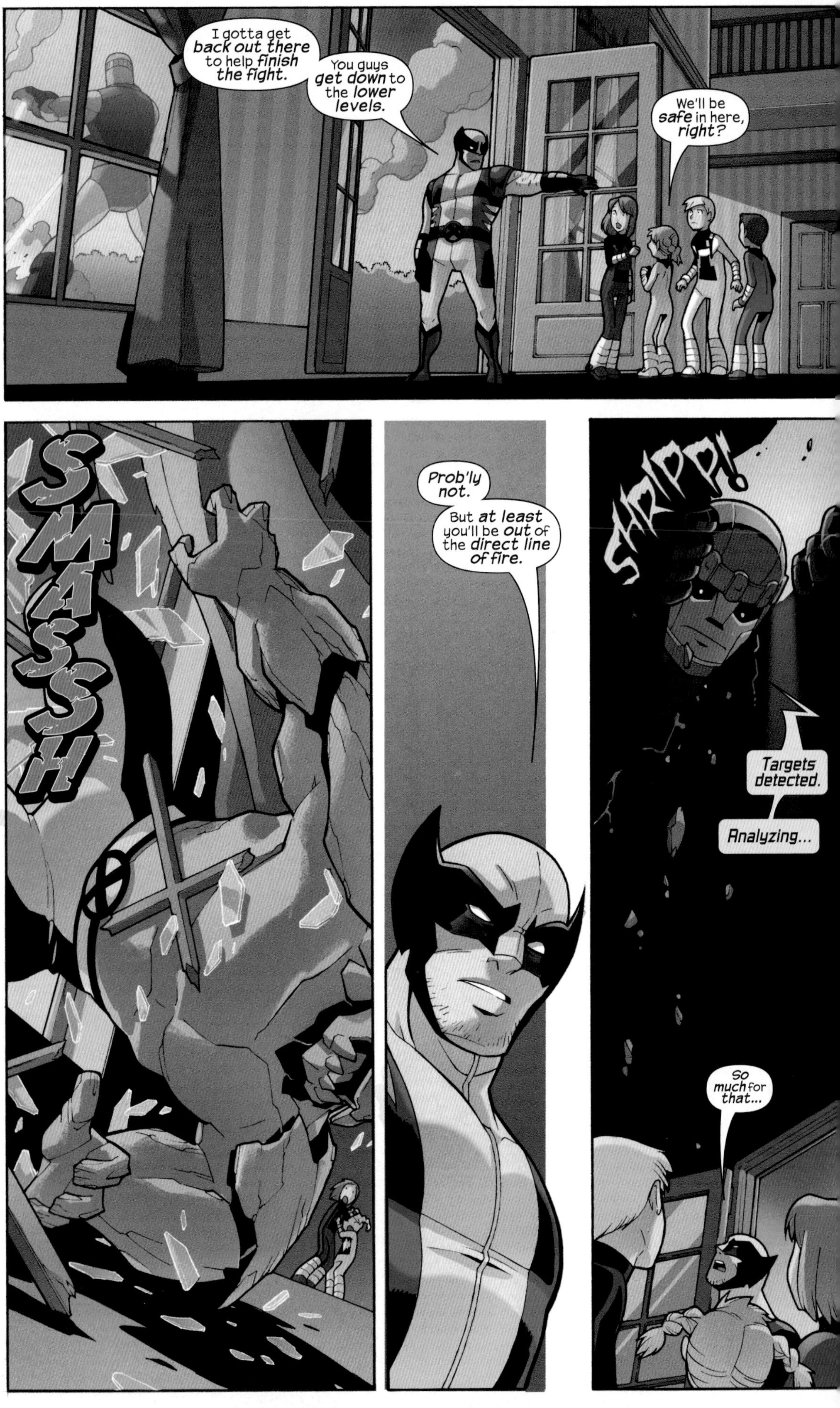
I gotta get back out there to help finish the fight.
You guys get down to the lower levels.
We'll be safe in here, right?
SMASSSH
Prob'ly not.
But at least you'll be out of the direct line of fire.
SHRIPP!
Targets detected.
Analyzing...
So much for that...

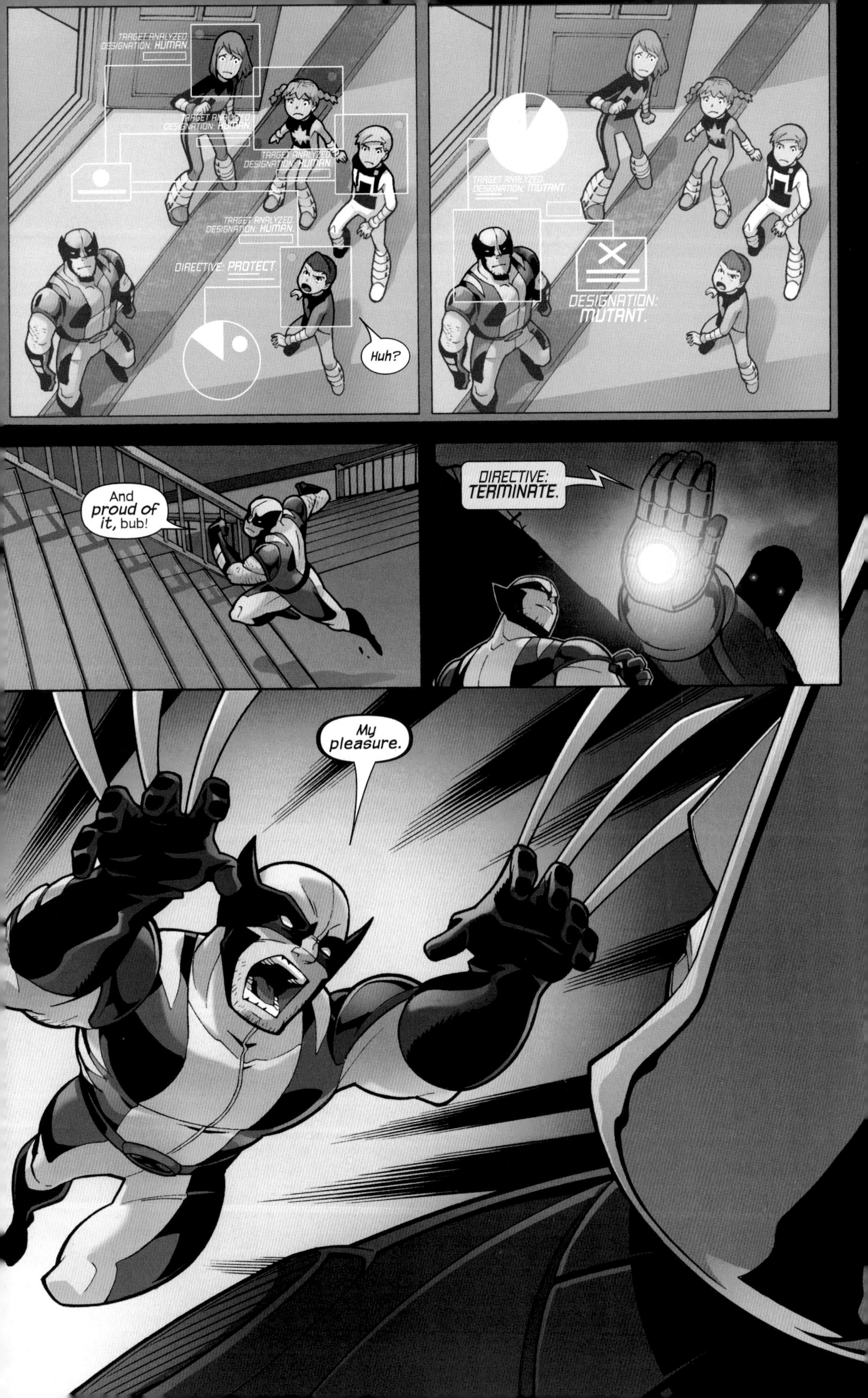
TARGET ANALYZED.
DESIGNATION: HUMAN.
TARGET ANALYZED.
DESIGNATION: HUMAN.
TARGET ANALYZED.
DESIGNATION: HUMAN.
TARGET ANALYZED.
DESIGNATION: HUMAN.
DIRECTIVE: PROTECT.
Huh?
TARGET ANALYZED.
DESIGNATION: MUTANT.
DESIGNATION: MUTANT.
And proud of it, bub!
DIRECTIVE: TERMINATE.
My pleasure.

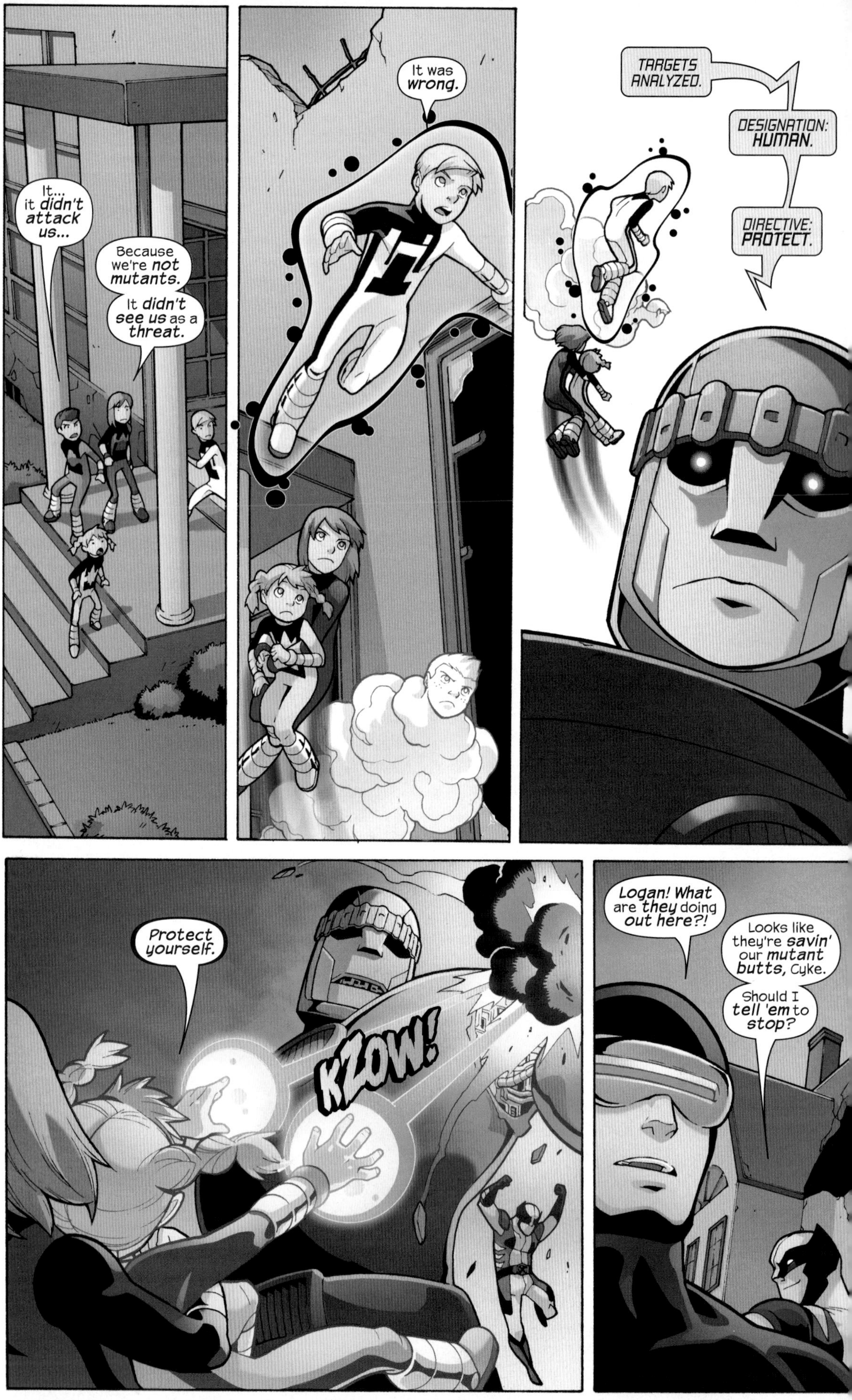

It... it didn't attack us...
Because we're not mutants.
It didn't see us as a threat.
It was wrong.
TARGETS ANALYZED.
DESIGNATION: HUMAN.
DIRECTIVE: PROTECT.
Protect yourself.
KZOW!
Logan! What are they doing out here?!
Looks like they're savin' our mutant butts, Cyke.
Should I tell 'em to stop?

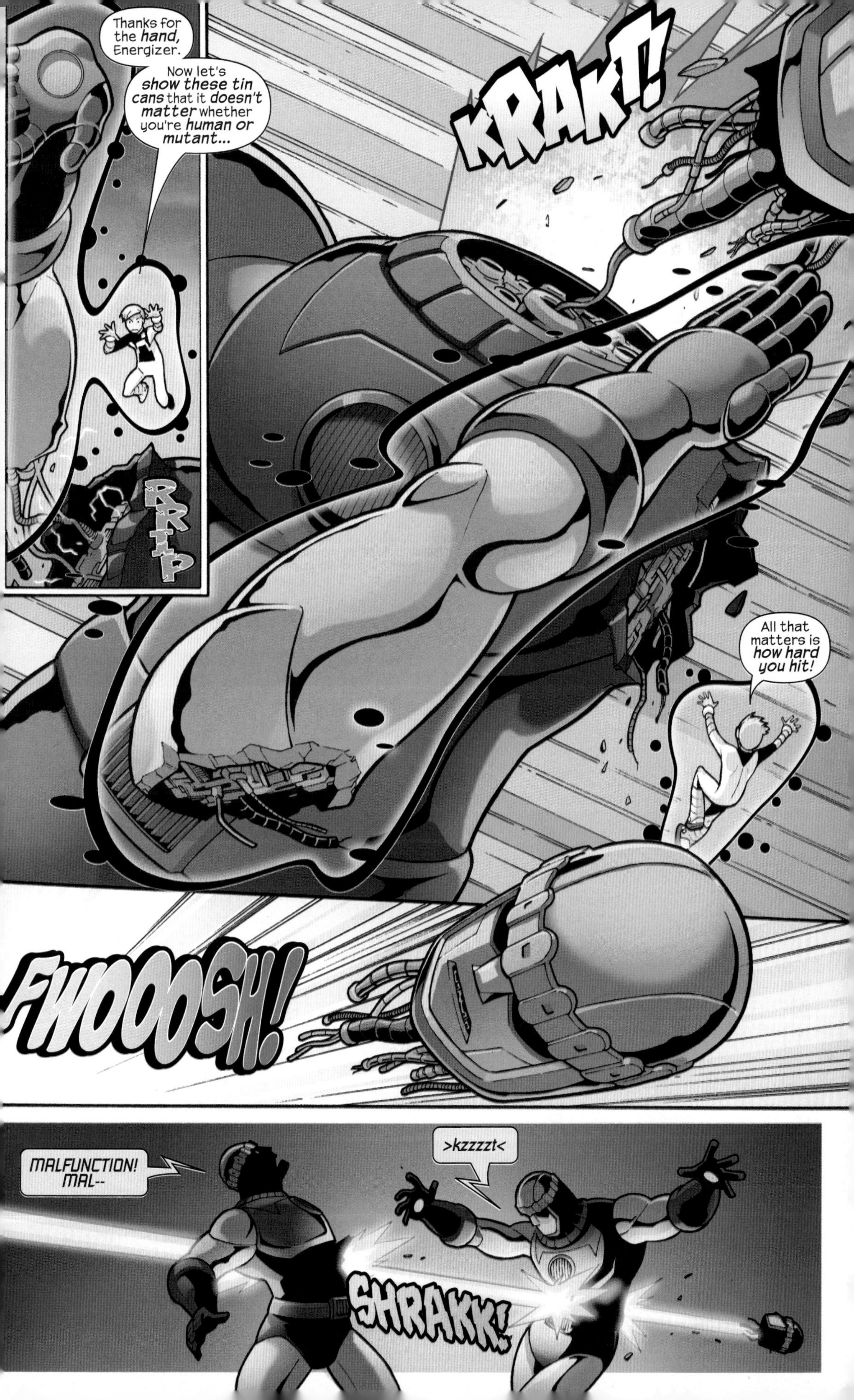
Thanks for the *hand*, Energizer.
Now let's *show these tin cans* that it *doesn't matter* whether you're *human or mutant...*
RRIP
KRAKT!
All that matters is *how hard you hit!*
FWOOOSH!
MALFUNCTION! MAL--
>kzzzzt<
SHRAKK!

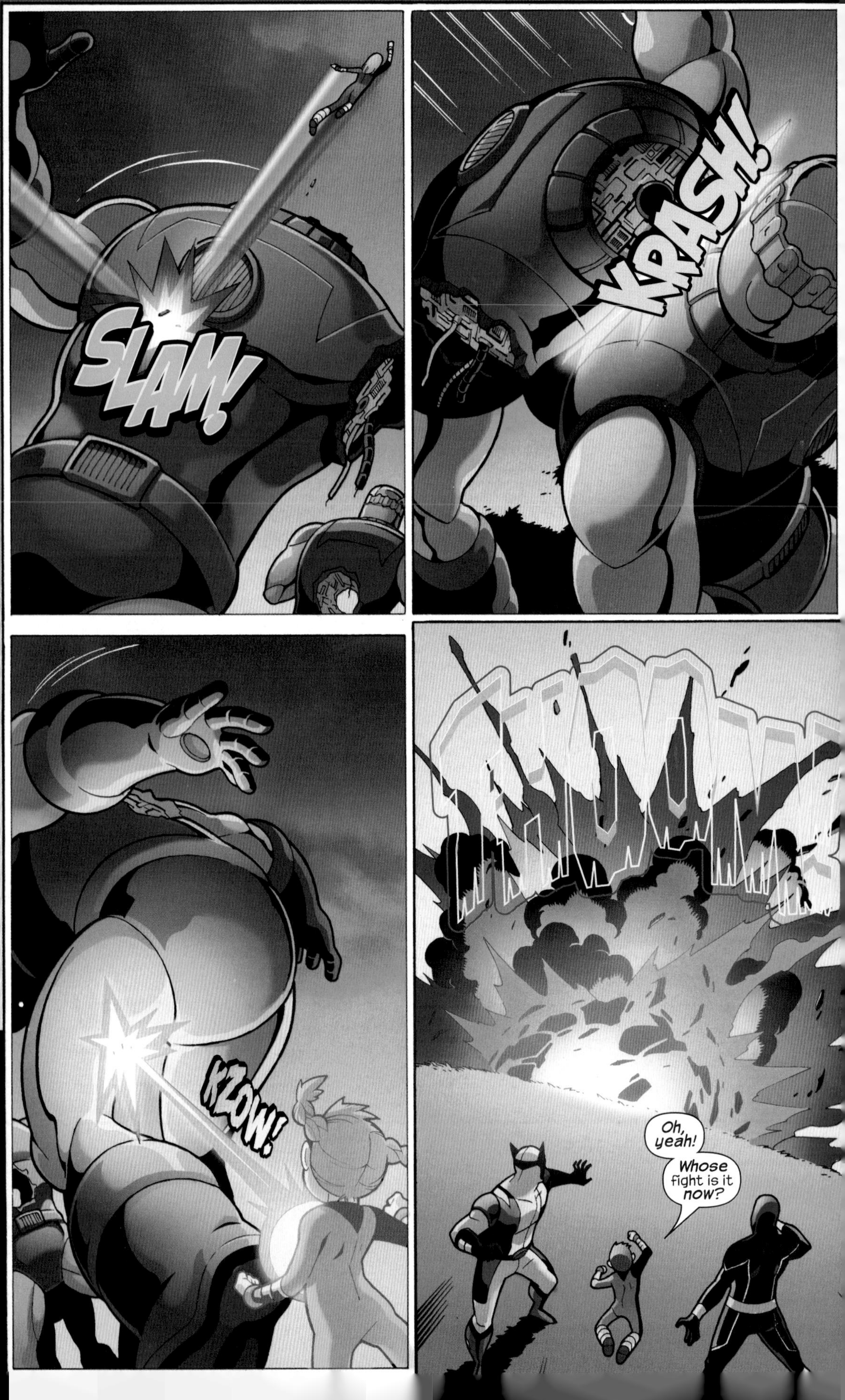
SLAM!
KRASH!
KZOW!
Oh, yeah!
Whose fight is it now?

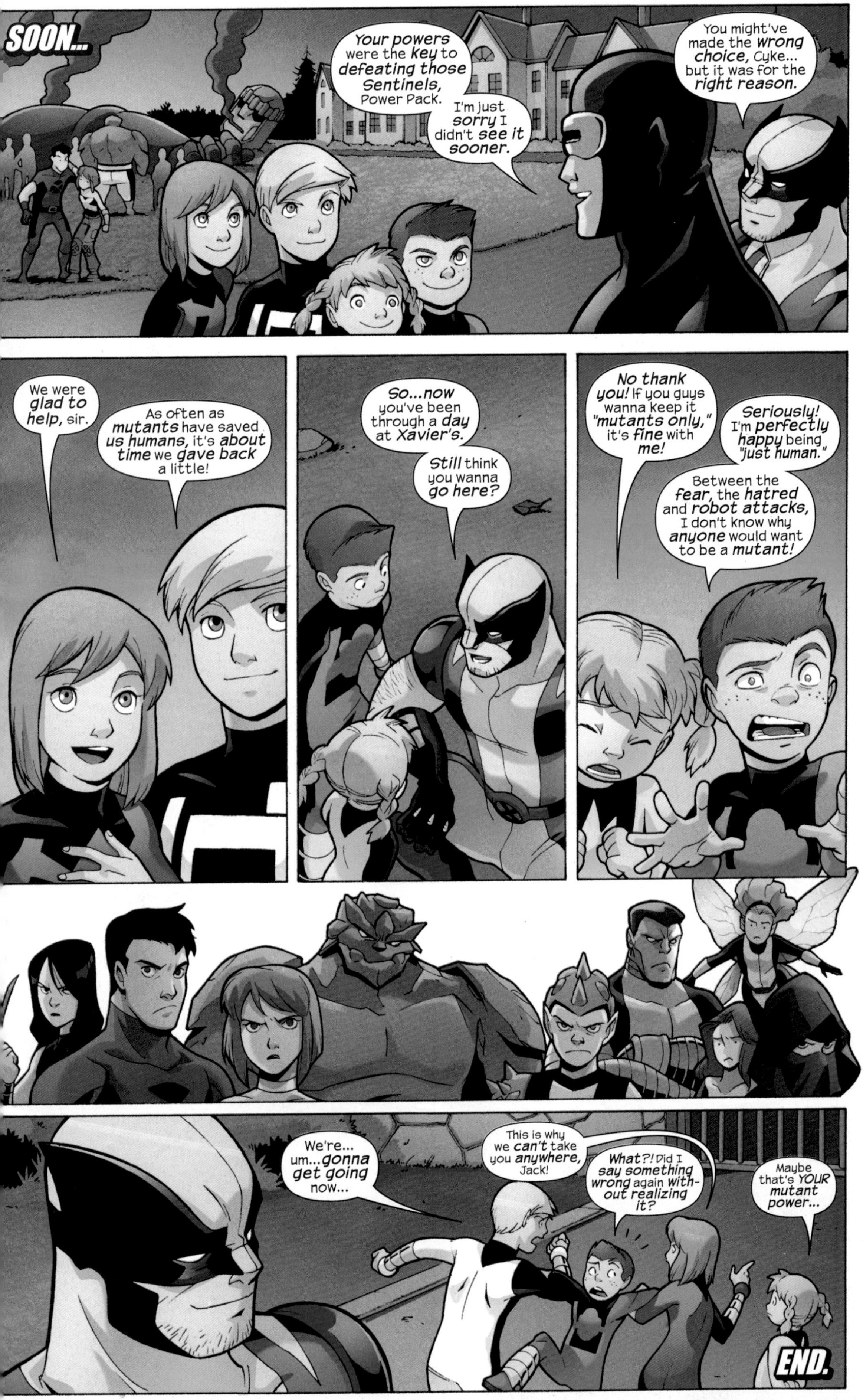
SOON...
Your powers were the key to defeating those Sentinels, Power Pack.
I'm just sorry I didn't see it sooner.
You might've made the wrong choice, Cyke... but it was for the right reason.
We were glad to help, sir.
As often as mutants have saved us humans, it's about time we gave back a little!
So...now you've been through a day at Xavier's.
Still think you wanna go here?
No thank you! If you guys wanna keep it "mutants only," it's fine with me!
Seriously! I'm perfectly happy being "just human."
Between the fear, the hatred and robot attacks, I don't know why anyone would want to be a mutant!
We're... um...gonna get going now...
This is why we can't take you anywhere, Jack!
What?! Did I say something wrong again without realizing it?
Maybe that's YOUR mutant power...
END.

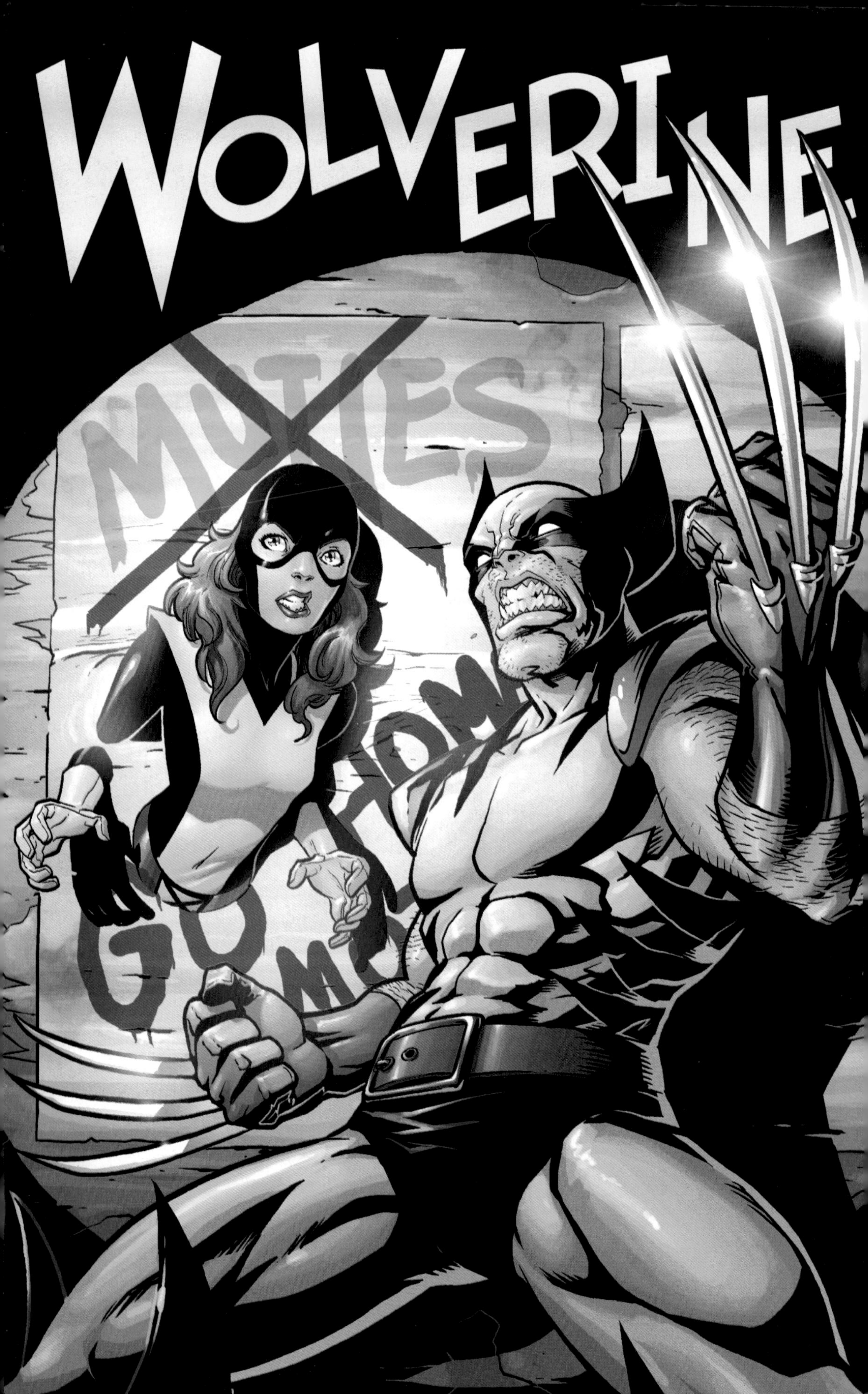
WOLVERINE
MUTIES
Cover art to *Wolverine: First Class #1* by Salva Espin and Brad Ander

AND WEAPON X
A FIRST CLASS COMBINATION!

Wolverine Claws His Way Through All-Ages Action In Two First Class Titles!

By Sheila Johnson

Call him "Wolverine: The Hero With a Thousand Titles." When writers Fred Van Lente and Marc Sumerak were approached to write new books throwing a spotlight on the tough-talking, claw-swinging Wolverine, it wasn't enough that they each had to find a way to tell Wolverine's stories that would allow their titles to both complement and stand apart from other, pre-existing titles featuring the Adamantium-boned mutant. No, Marvel gave these two men an additional challenge: Make the titles appropriate for all ages.

Accomplishing that task might not have seemed possible, given Wolverine's tendency to solve problems a bit more violently than all-ages fare usually permits, but Van Lente and Sumerak both rose to meet the challenge. Early in 2008, with Van Lente at the helm, Marvel launched *Wolverine: First Class*, an ongoing series focusing on the mentor-student relationship forged between Wolverine and Kitty Pryde in the early days when Kitty first joined the X-Men. Later in the year, in November, Marvel debuted *Weapon X: First Class*, Sumerak's three-issue limited series set in the same period as Van Lente's book that instead details Professor Xavier and Wolverine's exploration of Wolverine's long-buried memories of the horrific experimentation that changed him into an instrument of death. Featuring guest appearances by Sabretooth, Deadpool and Gambit, the series found itself quite at home within Wolvie's tortured psyche.

Van Lente and Sumerak recently talked with *Marvel Spotlight* and explained how having to write about Wolverine's history for readers of all ages has helped each of their titles become more than "just another Wolverine book."

SPOTLIGHT: Let's talk about how each of your titles started. Were they initiated because of the upcoming *X-Men Origins: Wolverine* movie, or were they projects that you approached Marvel about doing?

MARC: I was approached by editor Mark Paniccia about this project. With the *X-Men Origins: Wolverine* movie approaching, there was definitely a desire to retell one of the most important pieces of Wolvie's origin story for a new generation of readers who had not yet experienced it in comic book form. The real trick was telling this notoriously brutal tale in a way that it would be appropriate for readers of all ages without doing any damage to the original story. Thanks to my love of Logan (and Marvel history in general) and my experience writing all-ages books, Mark seemed to think I was the right guy to make that happen.

FRED: *Wolverine: First Class* was definitely something Marvel approached me about doing. The great thing about Marvel and me is that they always bring me stuff I'm not expecting. They say, in this instance, "We want you to write a new Wolverine ongoing series... but it's for kids!" And so my brain kind of exploded.

SPOTLIGHT: Why did you set your books in the early days, when Kitty Pryde and Wolverine were just beginning to establish their relationship, and Wolverine was digging though his past?

FRED: One of the suggestions [Marvel] had was that it should be set during the classic Chris Claremont/John Byrne era of *X-Men*, which was sort of at the height of their popularity. And specifically with Wolverine, when looking at him through the prism of the Claremont/Byrne era (and knowing the title was going to be *Wolverine: First Class*, to build off of Jeff Parker's very successful *X-Men: First Class* series,) the first thing that sort of leapt to my mind was to have a sort of a buddy comedy going if I paired Wolverine with Kitty Pryde. Plus, the all-ages books tend to have a larger-than-usual female readership, so I wanted a really strong woman character to co-anchor the book with Wolverine.

When the all-ages books work, they are literally *all* ages. You can get a kid, you can get an adult, you can get an older person who is reading it to their grandson. The key when coming up with one of these series is to think of something that can appeal to an extremely wide audience.

MARC: When we were planning *Weapon X: First Class*, we felt that it made sense to explore Logan's past alongside him. To do that, we needed to take him back to a day when his memories were still shrouded in mystery. Setting the book in the same time period as the ongoing *Wolverine: First Class* series made perfect sense. That was a period where Logan was truly beginning to come into his own as an X-Man, but still had a lot to learn about the man beneath the mask. Thanks to his relationship with Xavier, we were able to send the two on a wild journey through Logan's mind.

SPOTLIGHT: Recently, Marvel has had to keep up with a lot of demand with Wolverine in multiple titles, mini-series and team books. Was either of you at all daunted by the idea of writing another book featuring him?

FRED: I wouldn't say I was really that worried about it, though some people did go ballistic about it when the title was first announced, and they didn't really understand what it was all about. I actually thought it was a really exciting opportunity to take Wolverine back to when he had amnesia, back to when he was this mysterious, rough-edged character.

MARC: With the insane number of titles that our lead character appears in every month, it would be easy to brush this off as "just another Wolverine book" in a sea of many. But when we went into this series, we built it with a specific goal in mind: to re-examine a crucial piece of Wolverine's history and to shed some new light on the dark halls of the Weapon X Program. That gave us the starting point we needed to make this title unique amongst the other titles that Wolvie appears in...and I think everyone involved did a mighty fine job accomplishing what we set out to do!

SPOTLIGHT: The First Class books seem to focus on student/mentor relationships. In each of your books, who would you say is the mentor, and who's the student, as you see it?

MARC: There are a few different mentor/student dynamics occurring within the pages of *Weapon X: First Class*. Obviously, there is the relationship between Xavier and Wolverine. In this relationship, Wolvie is the somewhat reluctant student who must finally give in and ask his mentor for help. They've had their differences in the past, but they both know what they can accomplish together is far greater than what either of them could do alone.

Beyond that, we also see the strange dynamic between the Weapon X staff and Logan. Thorton, Cornelius, and Hines are trying to shape Logan into their ultimate tool of destruction... and Logan is subconsciously trying to reject every lesson they feed into his head. While Logan may be the unwilling student in this scenario, it's his teachers who eventually learn the hardest lesson of all!

FRED: In *Wolverine: First Class*, one of the reasons Professor X pairs Wolverine with Kitty is he knows that while Wolverine is teaching Kitty, he's also learning from her. And he's also becoming, for lack of a better word, more responsible and tamer by learning to deal with his own numerous and formidable demons.

SPOTLIGHT: In addition to the student/mentor dynamic, the First Class books are also known for being more humorous. Some of the classic X-Men stories, though, especially the limited *Kitty Pryde and Wolverine* series from 1984, are more serious. Fred, were you worried about the humor of *Wolverine: First Class* offending anyone?

FRED: I think, within the eyes of the X-Fans, that mini-series you cite specifically signified Kitty's sort of loss of innocence and becoming

a more adult character, instead of the thirteen-and-a-half-year old that's she's supposed to be when she first shows up at the X-Mansion. So I definitely was saying, "No, this takes place before *Kitty Pryde and Wolverine*." She is, at most, fourteen years old; she's just this normal girl, smarter than most, but dumped into this insane world of mutants and super heroes and, you know, animal people. And Canadians. And all of that wackiness.

SPOTLIGHT: In contrast, *Weapon X: First Class* is a far more serious book. Marc, why is a First Class book the vehicle for such a story?

MARC: The tone of this series has definitely been a bit darker than the standard First Class fare...but that's mostly due to the subject matter that the story revolves around. There's nothing funny about what went on in the halls of the Weapon X facility. (Unless you ask Deadpool – which we did!)

We tried to make sure there was a bit of humor throughout the series, but most of it stems from the relationship between the modern-day Logan and his fellow X-Men (including Xavier). We definitely didn't want to make it all doom and gloom. But at the same time, we wanted everyone to know that what Wolvie went through was no laughing matter.

Despite the difference in tone, we still felt this book's expanded examination of our hero's early days made it work as a part of the First Class line.

SPOTLIGHT: As a final note, what about the character of Wolverine interests you? Are there any aspects of him that you disliked or found more challenging to deal with when working on writing about this time in the character's life?

FRED: I like the fact that he's basically a werewolf. That's how I was trying to wrap my brain around dealing with him for kids. He looks very human, but some things are out of his hands, and he's got a bit of a temper problem. That's the aspect I wanted to deal with the most, and I think that's also what I dislike about him, because Wolverine and characters like him sort of play into the easy stereotype of super heroes in the genre being this release for repressed adolescent male rage and constantly going back to that instead of attempting to move beyond it.

MARC: Writing Wolverine is always an interesting experience. He's a character that not only walks the thin line between hero and vigilante, but also the line between man and animal. He has built an astounding list of enemies over the years, but their epic battles pale in comparison with the struggles that Logan wages inside himself. It's truly a pleasure to explore what makes him tick and how his dark past has shaped the man – and the hero – that he is today.

The only hard part about writing Wolverine for a First Class book is having to keep his claws sheathed a bit more often than normal. But those guidelines just push me to come up with something different than the average slice-and-dice action, so in the end it's really not such a bad thing. Ⓦ